FROM POLARIZATION

TO PARADOX

FROM POLARIZATION TO PARADOX

ENTERING THE FIELD OF VALUE

VALUE IS PRIOR TO VALUES, MEANING IS PRIOR TO MEANINGS

. . .

One Mountain, Many Paths: Oral Essays
Volume Thirty-Three

DR. MARC GAFNI

Author: Marc Gafni
Title: From Polarization to Paradox

Identifiers: ISBN 979-8-88834-092-9 (electronic)
ISBN 979-8-88834–091–2 (paperback)
Library of Congress Cataloging-in-Publication Data available

Edited by Elena Maslova-Levin and Talya Bloom

World Philosophy and Religion Press,
St. Johnsbury, VT

in conjunction with

IP Integral Publishers

https://worldphilosophyandreligion.org

JOIN THE REVOLUTION!

CONTENTS

CHAPTER 2   THE SENSUAL AROUSAL OF SENSEMAKING: SEDUCING OURSELVES OUT OF THE DIGITAL TRANCE INTO THE ARMS OF LADY JUSTICE

CHAPTER 5   **TWO EVOLUTIONARY PRACTICES OF HOMO AMOR: LIVE YOUR DREAM AND CONFESS YOUR GREATNESS**

CHAPTER 6   **BASEBALL PRINCIPLES—A HOME RUN INTO THE HEART OF HOMO AMOR**

CHAPTER 7   TO RESPOND TO THE META-CRISIS, WE NEED TO RE-VISION WHO WE ARE

CHAPTER 8   THIS POIGNANT MOMENT OF NEURO-CULTURAL PLASTICITY: A TIME BETWEEN WORLDS AND A TIME BETWEEN STORIES

CHAPTER 9 **HOMO AMOR, THE FULFILMENT OF HOMO SAPIENS, IS RADICALLY PRESENT WITH THE PAST, PRESENT AND FUTURE: JOIN US IN THE HOMO AMOR REVOLUTION**

CHAPTER 13   US ELECTIONS: WHAT DOES IT MEAN TO PARTNER WITH GOD IN THIS MOMENT?

EDITORIAL NOTE ABOUT AUTHORSHIP, EDITING, AND THE RADICAL CONTEXT FOR THIS SERIES

ORAL ESSAYS FROM THE ONE MOUNTAIN, MANY PATHS WEEKLY BROADCAST

This volume is part of the Oral Essays library, a series of lightly edited, compiled transcripts of oral teachings given by Dr. Marc Gafni and the late Barbara Marx Hubbard in their weekly online broadcast, *One Mountain, Many Paths,* which they co-founded in 2017. Originally called an "Evolutionary Church," *One Mountain, Many Paths* became a key venue for the articulation of an inspired and deeply grounded new Story of Value in response to the meta-crisis. Marc and Barbara—together with Zak Stein,[1] Kristina Kincaid, Ken Wilber, Sally Kempton, Lori Galperin, Aubrey Marcus and dozens of other thought-leaders over the years—began to articulate what they call a World Philosophy and World Religion[2] as a context for our diversity.

---

1   Zak, together with Ken Wilber, has been Marc's primary intellectual partner and an initiate lineage holder in CosmoErotic Humanism.

2   This project is grounded in four core organizational frameworks: 1) The Center for World Philosophy and Religion, co-founded by Marc Gafni, Zachary Stein, Sally Kempton, and Ken Wilber, and chaired over the years by John P. Mackey, Barbara Marx Hubbard, Aubrey Marcus, Gabrielle Anwar and Shareef Malnik, Carrie Kish and Adam Bellow, and Kathleen J. Brownback. 2) The Office for the Future, chaired by Stephanie Valcke and Ivan Bossyut. 3) The World Philosophy and Religion Press, founded and chaired by Aubrey Marcus, together with Marc Gafni and Zachary Stein. 4) The Foundation for Conscious Evolution, founded by Barbara Marx Hubbard and currently chaired by Peter Fiekowsky. For a complete list of key leadership, see the Office for the Future website, www.officeforthefuture.com.

Until Barbara's passing in 2019, she and Marc transmitted teachings together as evolutionary partners and "whole mates," weaving together insights and transmissions from their decades of practice, study, teaching, and activism into a synergy of wisdom, a grounded vision for future policy across all sectors of society.

Much of the *dharma* material below comes directly from Marc, so it was originally all in quotation marks—but that looked a little odd. So per his suggestion we removed them, and the reader should consider the paragraphs on the next several pages as one extended quote from him. We are joyfully grateful to Marc for the clarity of his *dharma*, the elegance and "second simplicity" of this language, and the mad, Outrageous Love with which he transmits his teachings.

Barbara and Marc called the mission of *One Mountain* "a Planetary Awakening in Evolutionary Love Through Unique Self Symphonies." We are an evolutionary community with a deeply grounded, radically alive, and "post-tragic" revolutionary spirit. We are activating a new humanity and awakening as a new species: *Homo amor*, the fulfillment of *Homo sapiens*.

One Mountain is committed to articulating a Story of Value that can become the ground for the new society that must be birthed in response to the meta-crisis. We recognize that we are living at a pivotal moment in history. In this "time between stories," the great moral imperative is to tell the new Story of Value. It is ours to do, personally and collectively, with great trembling and ecstatic joy.

FROM DOGMA TO *DHARMA*: ETERNAL AND EVOLVING FIRST PRINCIPLES AND FIRST VALUES

The teachings are grounded in decades of deep study across many wisdom traditions. Over the years, week by week, these teachings were incrementally developed within the framework of the *One Mountain, Many Paths* broadcast. We often refer to these teachings as *dharma*.

This word was originally used in lineage traditions to refer to something like universal law. This is a crucial realization: just as there is universal law in mathematical value, there is also a sense of universal law in ethics and value.

Historically, *dharma* often devolved into unchanging dogma. Evolution was ignored, and the natural process of *dharma* evolution became disconnected from its deep, eternal context. The weakness of the word *dharma* is that too often it did not include the evolving insights of the sciences, it confused local cultural truths with universal truths, and it used words like "eternal," as in "eternal Tao," as opposed to words like "evolution."

Eternal came to mean unchanging, and that kind of thinking often led to overly ethnocentric readings of *dharma*. Local systems would claim their religious and cultural insights as immutable, which stood in the way of the emergence of a genuine world Story of Value that is real, inherent to Cosmos, and backed by the Universe—even as it is also always evolving.

Or, as we often say, "eternal value is evolving value. The eternal Tao is the evolving Tao."

We have shown that, emergent from profound insights in the "interior sciences," eternal does not mean unchanging in time; it means what we call the deeper Field of ErosValue that is beneath culture, geography, and history, which lives beneath all individual and collective values, and beneath time and space itself.

As such, we have gradually transitioned from the term *dharma* to the term *Value*, in the sense of the Field of Value that lives beneath all values. This Field of Value discloses as First Principles and First Values embedded in a Story of Value.

Indeed, as the interior sciences knew and the exterior sciences imply, Reality arises in a Field of ErosValue in which an entire set of mathematical, musical, molecular, moral, and mystical values are the very ground of all being. That Field of Value is eternal—the true ground of the Good, True and Beautiful—even as it is evolving.

But of course, it is equally critical not just to talk about evolving value, but to ground the evolving value in its true nature, the eternal Field of First Principles and First Values, always reaching for ever-more life, ever-more love, ever-more care, ever-more depth, ever-more uniqueness, ever-more intimate communion, and ever-more transformation.

As such, when we refer to the word *dharma*, which still appears in these texts together with the word value, we refer to an evolving *dharma* grounded in an *eternal and evolving* Field of Value. Indeed, eternity and evolution are two faces of the whole, opposites joined at the hip, that characterize the nature of our Cosmos in virtually all of its expressions.

It's in these terms that we ground a robust world philosophy that integrates the validated, leading-edge insights of premodern traditional wisdom, modern wisdom, and more recent postmodern insights, weaving them together into a new whole greater than the sum of its parts.

This new whole is a shared Story of Value rooted in First Principles and First Values that are both eternal and evolving.

These First Principles and First Values of Cosmos are woven together into a new Story of Value as a context for our diversity, a new Universe Story. This new story gives us the best possible responses we have to the mystery, and to the great questions:

- Who am I? Who are we?
- Where am I? Where are we?
- What should I do? What should we do?

It is only through such a shared Universe Story—a narrative of identity and ethos as a context for our blessed diversity—that we can realize how what unites is so much greater than what divides us.

Only a new Story of Value will allow us to both respond to the meta-crisis and participate together in birthing the most true, good, and beautiful world that we already know is possible.

THIS ORAL ESSAYS SERIES IS AN ENTRYWAY TO THE GREAT LIBRARY OF COSMOEROTIC HUMANISM

This Oral Essays series is part of the overarching project of the Great Library at the Center for World Philosophy and Religion, led by Dr. Marc Gafni, together with Dr. Zak Stein. The aim of the Great Library project is to articulate a robust and comprehensive new Story of Value, CosmoErotic Humanism, in the form of dozens of well-researched and extensively footnoted academic works.

Our vision is to provide the philosophical framework that will be vital for navigating humanity through this time of immense crisis and transformation.

To begin your journey into CosmoErotic Humanism, we tenderly refer you to the book *First Principles and First Values*, co-authored by Marc Gafni, Zak Stein, and Ken Wilber, under the name David J. Temple. David J. Temple is a pseudonym created for enabling ongoing collaborative authorship at the Center for World Philosophy and Religion. The two primary authors behind David J. Temple are Marc Gafni and Zak Stein, and for different projects, specific writers will be named as part of the collaboration, such as Ken Wilber and others.

Three other volumes complete this introduction: *A Return to Eros*, by Marc Gafni and Kristina Kincaid; *Your Unique Self*, by Marc Gafni; and *Education in a Time between Worlds*, by Zak Stein.

We hope that the Oral Essays in the present volume, with their informal style of transmission, will serve as an allurement and entryway for you into the more formal books of the Great Library that provide the robust intellectual underpinnings of the new Story of Value.

A NOTE ABOUT THE EDITORS

This Oral Essays collection has been edited by students of the new Story of CosmoErotic Humanism. Each of us has actively participated in *One Mountain, Many Paths*, and most of us have been in deep "Holy of Holies" study with Dr. Marc Gafni for many years.

We have been privileged to find ourselves well-versed in the teachings, and even emerging as lineage-holders of CosmoErotic Humanism.[3]

We view this editing project as a privilege and a deep practice of study and clarification. We experience ourselves as a *mystical editing society*, frequently meeting and conversing together about the content—the depth of knowledge and wisdom offered here—as well as the technical intricacies involved with publishing a beautiful and coherent series of books. In so doing, we function as a "Unique Self Symphony," which itself is a Dharmic

---

3   CosmoErotic Humanism is a world philosophical movement aimed at reconstructing the collapse of value at the core of global culture. Much like Romanticism or Existentialism, CosmoErotic Humanism is not merely a theory but a movement that changes the very mood of Reality. It is an invitation to participate in evolving the source code of consciousness and culture towards a cosmocentric *ethos* for a planetary civilization.

The term CosmoErotic Humanism, initially coined by Dr. Gafni and colleagues, points to a complex, multi-faceted, layered, and nuanced evolutionary set of insights that has evolved over decades of intensive research, teaching, and spiritual practice from deep within a wide range of wisdom traditions (including the Wisdom of Solomon lineage tradition, Bodhisattva Buddhism, and Kashmir Shaivism), as well as multiple disciplines including complexity theory, chaos theory, emergence theory, molecular biology, and the more classical disciplines of the humanities.

The seeds of CosmoErotic Humanism were planted with Dr. Marc Gafni's work on a two-volume, 1,000-page opus called *Radical Kabbalah* (Integral Publishers, 2012). This scholarly work, sourced from deep study within the esoteric lineage texts of the Wisdom of Solomon, points to a non-dual, or acosmic, realization which—unlike the prevailing conceptualization of non-duality—does not efface the human being; rather, it is highly humanistic in its nature. The next step in the evolution of CosmoErotic Humanism was the insight that all of Reality is evolving Eros, which lives in, as, and through the human being.

A failure of Eros leads inexorably to the creation of narratives of "pseudo-eros." CosmoErotic Humanism is a response to the modern mental and social breakdown sourced in the proliferation of multiple forms of pseudo-eros and its broken narratives, such as rivalrous conflict governed by win/lose metrics and the dogmatic denial of intrinsic value in Cosmos, which together generate our current "global intimacy disorder."

term that connotes an omni-considerate collaboration between realized Unique Selves synergizing our unique gifts into a new emergence greater than the sum of the parts. Even as we worked diligently to standardize our editing styles, meeting on a weekly basis to debate the nuances of phrasing, we also operated from within a deep appreciation of the unique style that each editor brought to his or her work. As such, the reader might notice some variation in editing style among the books.

Please note that Dr. Marc Gafni has not reviewed these edited Oral Essays, as he is deeply engaged in writing the formal books of the Great Library. But he has been generous in responding to questions and providing overall guidance in the project. Overall, as Marc's students and students of the *dharma*, we have made it a key project at the Center to publish these pieces of work relatively independently.

OUR UNIQUE ORAL-ESSAY EDITING STYLE PRESERVES THE ENERGY OF THE ORIGINAL TRANSMISSION

Dr. Marc Gafni is a uniquely gifted teacher whose oral transmission is imbued with a quality that has proven transformative for his students. Many of us feel mystically transformed by both the content and the underlying energy of the transmission style. Therefore, as we like to say, *trust the magic ways the dharma comes through your unique understanding!*

As Marc's empowered students, colleagues, and beloved friends, we have a deep knowing that these teachings are vital for the survival and thriving of humanity as we know it, and we recognize the importance of publishing his teachings in a written format that will be accessible by future generations. At the same time, we sought to preserve the Eros of the original oral transmission with all of its nuance, power, and depth. Our intention in the editing process, to the greatest extent possible, has been to keep these spoken artifacts intact in order to maintain the flow of the original transmission. We have therefore chosen not to engage in intensive formal editing, as we found that doing so resulted in the loss of the energetic transmission that is so key to fully receiving the *dharma*.

After experimenting with many ways to present these texts, we developed a specific way of laying out the text on the page. Marc, in collaboration with Zak Stein and Russian intellectual/artist Elena Maslova-Levin—and ultimately all of the editors, through many conversations—developed a unique, artistic presentation of the text, using bolding, italics, bullet points, and other stylistic features which together serve to accentuate the immediacy of the oral transmission.

As part of this editing style, intended to preserve the integrity of the original transmission, we have refrained from removing the frequent recapitulations of key themes. We found that each recapitulation contributes something vital to the rhythm and music beneath the words, like the beating drum of our hearts. These recapitulations not only review previous material but also add important new emphases, perspectives, and elements of the new Story of Value. We ask for your patience as a reader to trust the rhythm of these texts, and we trust you as a reader to have the depth and steadiness to find your way through.

KEY COMPONENTS: LINK TO THE ORIGINAL BROADCAST, EVOLUTIONARY LOVE CODES AND PRAYER

To supplement the written word, each episode includes a QR code linking to the original broadcast on YouTube, as well as occasional links to featured songs and video clips.

Each episode also centers around an "Evolutionary Love Code," formulated by Marc. These codes are part of the ongoing articulation and distillation of the *dharma* as it unfolds and emerges, week by week, over the course of many years, through the mystical process we call Outrageous Love or Evolutionary Love.

Another core component of the *One Mountain, Many Paths* episodes is what Marc and Barbara called "Evolutionary Prayer." Prayer is experienced in *One Mountain* not in the old fundamentalist sense of a "cosmic vending-machine god" who is alienated from Cosmos. Marc refers to this as the "god you do not and should not believe in"—and he often adds, "the god you don't believe in does not exist."

GOD IS THE INFINITE INTIMATE

In fact, in the *dharma* of CosmoErotic Humanism, a new name for God has emerged: the "Infinite Intimate," who appears in first-, second-, and third-person expressions. Marc first shared this name as he heard it whispered in 2023, although earlier intimations and formulations of the name appeared as early as 2010.

In first person, God is infinitely alive and as intimate as our own first-person experience.

In second person, God is the infinitely intimate Personhood of Cosmos that knows our name and holds us—the God about whom we say, *whenever we fall, we fall into Her hands.* This is the God who is our Beloved, Father, Mother, Lover, and Evolutionary Partner.

Finally, in third person, God inheres in all of the First Principles and First Values of Cosmos, and in the laws of science (both interior and exterior) that govern manifest Reality.

Therefore, we have a realization of God as not only the Infinity of Power but also the Infinity of Intimacy.

In *One Mountain, Many Paths*, we are reclaiming prayer at a higher level of consciousness. And we are reclaiming prayer as deep, alive, loving, and intimate conversations with God as the Infinite Intimate who knows our name.

THE INVITATION

We invite you to find your way into this revolution. Each one of our Unique Selves and unique gifts are desperately needed as we co-create this new Story of Value together, as part of the covenant between generations, for the sake of the whole.

Let's *play a larger game* and evolve the very source code of consciousness and culture together.

With mad love,

The Editors

LOVE OR DIE

LOCATING OURSELVES: ARTICULATING THE ESSENTIAL CONTEXT FOR THE ONE MOUNTAIN, MANY PATHS ORAL ESSAYS

SETTING OUR INTENTION

Intention setting is everything.

We're here—as da Vinci was with his cohort in the Renaissance—**to play a larger game, to participate in the evolution of love, which is to tell the new Story of Value rooted in First Principles and First Values.**

- ◆ Our intention is to recognize the critical historical juncture in which we find ourselves.
- ◆ Our intention is to take our seat at the table of history and to say, *we take responsibility for this.*
- ◆ Our intention is to participate as revolutionaries for the sake of the whole.

What we're here to do is revolution; revolution for the sake of the evolution of love.

It's a revolution for the sake of the trillions of unborn lives that will not manifest:

- The unborn loves
- The unborn creativity
- The unborn goodness
- The unborn truth
- The unborn beauty

All of it looks to us.

Not because we're engaged in grandiosity. Not at all!

- We're trembling before She.
- We're trembling with joy at the privilege.
- We're trembling with joy at the responsibility.
- We're trembling with joy at the Possibility of Possibility.
- We have to enact a new story in this moment of time. Because it is only a new story that can change the vector of history.

The most revolutionary act that we can do—the greatest moral imperative of this time—**is to articulate a new story at this time between worlds and this time between stories.**

Story is not made up, as postmodernity suggests. **We all live in inescapable frameworks; our framework is the story we live in.** Right now, Reality lives according to win/lose metrics, a story that is generating existential risk. **We need to change that story.**

When we change that story, when we tell a new story—not a made-up story, but a new Story of Value, rooted in First Principles and First Values—**then it all changes.**

We need to participate in the evolution of the source code of consciousness and culture, which is the evolution of love.

It's the most important, exciting, evolutionary, revolutionary act that we can do to alleviate suffering: to be lovers.

Like Rumi, the great poet of Sufism, we have to be "mad lovers," because it's the only sanity.

To be mad lovers is to see around the corner, to not be so obsessed with the details of the contractions of my life.

Let me see bigger.

Let me take complete care of myself in every possible way, let me completely attend to those in my circle of intimacy and influence, and then—*let me expand my circle.*

That's what we're here for.

- Our intention is to participate in the *LoveForce*, the *LoveIntelligence*, the *LoveBeauty*, the *LoveDesire* that literally animates Cosmos all the way up and all the way down.
- Our intention is to participate in the evolution of love.

   [*In the next few pages we will cover some key concepts which are essential to locating ourselves and setting the context for all the One Mountain, Many Paths Oral Essays. —Eds.*]

OVERVIEW: EROS IS NO LONGER A LUXURY—IT'S LOVE OR DIE

Eros is life.

The failure of Eros destroys life.

Our lack of Eros is poised to destroy the world.

All civilizations have fallen because the stories that they lived in were, in some sense, stories based on rivalrous conflict governed by win/lose metrics. Every civilization was weakened by interior polarization caused by the lack of a shared Story of Value.

We now have a global civilization, but we haven't created a shared Story of Value.

We haven't solved the generator functions that caused all civilizations to fall. Our global civilization has exponential technologies and extraction models depleting the Earth of resources that took billions of years to create, which is going to lead to a civilizational collapse.

Existential risk is risk to our very existence.

The choice is clear: love or die.

It's that simple.

Eros is no longer a luxury. It is an absolute necessity for the survival of the individual and the planet.

In the last half a century, modern psychology has documented an age-old truth: a fully nourished baby who is not held in loving arms will die.

So too, our world, both personal and global—even with all the resources of intelligence and technology at our disposal—will die without being held in love, in the embrace of Eros.

We must embrace a personal path of love and a global politics of love.

Not ordinary love. Not love which is "mere human sentiment," but Eros, or what we sometimes call Outrageous Love, which is the heart of existence itself.

We live in a world of outrageous pain.

The only response is Outrageous Love.

WHAT IS EROS?

Eros is the experience of radical aliveness, moving towards, seeking, desiring ever deeper contact and ever greater wholeness.[4] Eros is the core fabric of Reality's being and the motivational architecture of Reality's becoming.

Eros is what animates the evolutionary impulse itself, from the very inception of Cosmos all the way to our very selves, who awaken to the realization that the evolutionary impulse throbs uniquely in each of us.

The realization of human awakening and transformation that lies at the core of the interior sciences is the invitation—or even the urgent and desperate demand—of a madly loving Cosmos animated by infinities of power and infinities of intimacy.

The demand—the desperate invitation, the plea, the tender and fierce command of Cosmos that lives inside every human being—is to awaken: to awaken to our true nature as unique incarnations of Eros and Ethos that are needed and desperately desired by All-That-Is. Said slightly differently: Reality is Eros. Or: God is Eros.

The failure of Eros destroys life. The collapse of Eros is always the hidden (or not so hidden) root cause for the collapse of ethics.

This is true both personally and collectively. We live in a moment of a worldwide and personal collapse of Eros. Our lack of Eros is poised to destroy

---

4 We define Eros through what we refer to as the Eros equation (one of a series of what we call interior science equations):

Eros = *Radical Aliveness* x *Desiring (Growing + Seeking)* x *Deeper Contact* x *Greater Wholeness* x *Self Actualization/Self Transcendence (Creation [Destruction])*

There are good reasons for the formal language of the interior science equations in these writings, and the reader is invited to explore them on their own, in particular, in our work, David J. Temple, *First Principles and First Values: Forty-Two Propositions on CosmoErotic Humanism, the Meta-Crisis, and the World to Come* (World Philosophy and Religion, 2024).

the world. Humanity is currently experiencing what has come to be known as existential risk, a risk to our very existence, or what I will refer to as the Second Shock of Existence.

EXISTENTIAL RISK: THE SECOND SHOCK OF EXISTENCE

The first shock of existence is the death of the human being—the realization that we will die, which dawns in human consciousness at the beginning of history. We are not talking about the biological fact of death but the *existential* realization of death. Although the interior sciences disclose that death is a portal between two days (there is vast empirical,[5] philosophical,[6] and anthro-ontological evidence[7] for the continuity of consciousness[8]), death is also, in our own direct surface experience, a stark end. And that is obviously not a bug, but a feature in the system.

---

5   We refer to evidence gathered by the most serious of researchers, beginning with Henry and Edith Sedgwick at Cambridge University and William James at Harvard University, and continuing in highly rigorous form for the last 150 years, as recapitulated by Whiteheadian scholar David Ray Griffin in multiple volumes. See also, for example, Dean Radin, *Real Magic: Unlocking Your Natural Psychic Abilities to Create Everyday Miracles* (Potter/TenSpeed/Harmony, 2018), *The Conscious Universe: The Scientific Truth of Psychic Phenomena* (HarperCollins, 2010), and other books. Or see the earlier classic by Frederic William Henry Myers, *Human Personality and Its Survival of Bodily Death* (Longmans, Green, 1907).

6   This requires a cogent analysis of materialism and dualism, and the introduction of the far more cogent third possibility, which we have called "pan-interiority."

7   We discuss Anthro-Ontology in some depth in *First Principles and First Values*, and see also the fuller conversation in David J. Temple, *First Principles and First Values: Towards an Evolving Perennialism: Introducing the Anthro-Ontological Method*—both published by World Philosophy and Religion Press, in conjunction with Integral Publishers. For now, we will simply define it as an "innate and clear interior gnosis directly available to the human being."

8   See Dr. Marc Gafni and Dr. Zachary Stein's essay in preparation, "Beyond Death: Anthro-Ontology, Philosophy, and Empiricism." This essay is slated to appear in the book *Towards a World Religion: Homo Amor Essays*. The essay is also the ground for a larger book by the same authors, *Twelve Portals to Life Beyond Death: Responding to the Second Shock of Existence,* in which we discuss three forms of material: the empirical, the philosophical, and the anthro-ontological, and show how each form discredits the notion of death as the end.

Our first-person experience is that death ends this life. It is not the *totality* of our experience if we go deeper inside, but it is obviously intended to be the central, potent, and painful dimension of every human life. Indeed, as Ernest Becker potently reminded us, the denial of death is at our peril.

All the stories and all the plotlines and all the threads of living end at that moment. Whatever happens beyond, we have an actual experience of ending. **Paradoxically, that ending, the experience of the finality of mortality, is what presses us into life.** From the implicit demand of the first shock of existence, human beings were activated and pressed into creative emergence, and what emerged was all of human culture, both interior and exterior.

The second shock of existence is the realization of the potential death of all humanity. After all the stages of human history—matter, life, and mind in all of their stages of evolutionary unfolding—we have come to this place in the evolution of humanity, in which the gap between our exponentially expanding exterior technologies and our stalled (or even regressing) interior technologies of value has created dire catastrophic and existential risks.

This gap generates extraction models and exponential growth curves, rivalrous conflicts based on win/lose metrics, tragedies of the commons, and multipolar traps, in which everyone has to keep producing to the nth degree, including weaponized exponential threats to our very existence because we are afraid that the other parties are going to do it and not be transparent—hide it from us and then dominate us.

GENERATOR FUNCTIONS FOR EXISTENTIAL RISK

Let's outline clearly the main *generator functions for existential risk.*

Rivalrous conflicts governed by zero-sum, win/lose metrics. Rivalrous conflicts generate extraction models at the core of the economic system and exponential growth curves. Both of these drive and are driven by a contrived system of artificially manufactured desires and needs, delivered into culture by ever more precise forms of micro-targeting to individuals and groups through the ever more immersive environment of the internet.

Next, rivalrous conflicts and exponential growth curves animated by win/lose metrics generate **complicated, fragile world systems** highly vulnerable to myriad forms of collapse. Fragile local systems are made exponentially more fragile on a global level by our inability to meet global challenges with social, legal, political, economic, and ethical infrastructures that remain largely local.

All of this is a direct result of the failure to develop more adequate interior technologies that would be sufficiently compelling to displace "rivalrous conflict governed by win/lose metrics" as the motivational architecture for the human life world.

This failure has led to the conditions that will cause the implosion of systems that are already and quite literally on the brink of collapsing themselves. That's what we mean by the *second shock of existence.*

To recapitulate: the second shock of existence is not the death of the human being, but the potential death of humanity.

It is the *Death Star* moment of our species.

THE DECONSTRUCTION OF INTRINSIC VALUE

We stand in this moment poised between utopia and dystopia, at a time between worlds and a time between stories. We need a new Story of Value, eternal yet evolving, rooted in First Principles and First Values, which would become a universal grammar of value and a context for our diversity.

This is exactly what the Renaissance was. It was a time between worlds and a time between stories. In the Renaissance, we had been recently challenged by the Black Death, a pandemic that swept across Europe. The Black Death destroyed between a third to half of Europe and a huge part of

Asia. People died horrifically, brutally, in the streets. They had no idea how to meet this challenge, and so, in response to the Black Death, da Vinci and Ficino and their cohorts understood that they had to tell a new Story of Value.

That story was the story of modernity. Did they get it right?

- They got part of it right, which birthed, to use Jürgen Habermas' phrase, "the dignities of modernity," such as new ways of gathering information and universal human rights.
- But they also deconstructed the source of Value. They lost the basis for the Good, the True, and the Beautiful.

The basis used to be divine revelation: *God told us.* But this claim was owned by religion, and every religion began to overreach and over-claim. The revelation was thus often mediated through cultural categories and wasn't fully accurate.

Modernity threw out revelation, but was unable to establish a new basis for value.

Value was just assumed to be real. As it says in the founding document of the American Revolution: *We hold these truths to be self-evident*—that is, *we don't really have a basis for value; we just take it as a given.*

In other words, modernity took out a loan of social capital from the traditional world. The source of value was never worked out.

And then, gradually, value began to collapse.

- The Universe Story began to collapse.
- The belief that the Good, the True, and the Beautiful are real began to collapse.
- The belief that Love is real began to collapse.

As Bertrand Russell is reported to have said, "I cannot see how to refute the arguments for the subjectivity of ethical values, but I find myself incapable of believing that all that is wrong with wanton cruelty is that I do not like it."

What do you do if you grew up in a world in which value is not real? A world without a source of value, without a Universe Story, without a story of human identity, without a story of desire, without a narrative of power?

In the words of W.B. Yeats, *the center does not hold.*

- You have a collapse at the very center of society, because you no longer have Eros.
- You no longer have a Reality in which value is real, and so you have this lingering sense of emptiness.
- You have a complete collapse at the very center.
- We become *the hollow men and the stuffed men,* gesture without form.

And that's the source of our current existential risk.

THE DEEPER ROOT CAUSE OF THE META-CRISIS: A GLOBAL INTIMACY DISORDER

Above, I have outlined the major generator functions of existential risk. But there is a deeper cause for the existential risk that lurks underneath the rivalrous conflict governed by win/lose metrics and the fragile systems they engender.

And we cannot take the Death Star down without discerning and addressing this. We have already alluded to this root cause above, but at this point we need to make it more explicit so that, from this context, the adequate root response will become clear.

Modernity threw out the revelation, but was unable to establish a new basis for value.

This ostensibly surprising statement can be understood in a few simple steps:

1. All of the catastrophic and existential risk challenges we face are global: from climate change to artificial intelligence, pandemics, systems collapse, and exponential arms races.
2. Every global challenge self-evidently requires a global solution.
3. Global solutions can only be implemented with global co-ordination.
4. Global co-ordination is impossible without global coherence.
5. Global coherence is only possible if there is a global resonance between the parts.
6. Global resonance is only possible if we have global intimacy.

ONLY A SHARED STORY OF VALUE CAN GENERATE GLOBAL INTIMACY

Global intimacy—just like intimacy in a couple—is only possible when there is a shared story.

Not just a shared history, but a shared Story of Value.

- It is only a shared global story that can generate a new emergent quality of intimacy: global intimacy.
- A shared Story of Value must be rooted in shared ordinating values, or what we have called evolving First Values and First Principles.
- Intimacy requires a shared grammar of value as a matrix for a shared Story of Value.

The global intimacy disorder is the root cause for existential risk. The global intimacy disorder underlies the core generator functions for existential risk.

The global intimacy disorder is rooted in the failure to experience ourselves in a field of shared intrinsic value. This failure derives from the deconstruction of value.

Indeed, it is wholly accurate to say that **the root cause of the two generator functions of existential risk is the failed story of intrinsic value, or what we might also call the breakdown of Eros.**

1. The first generator function is **the success story**. Our modern success story is rivalrous conflict governed by win/lose metrics, which violates all the terms of the Intimacy Equation: there is no shared identity and no mutuality of recognition, feeling, value or purpose, and instead of *relative* otherness, there is *alienated* otherness. Such a story generates complicated fragile systems with no allurement or intimacy between the parts, systems which optimize for efficiency (as an expression of win/lose metrics) and not for resiliency and life.

2. The second generator function is **the deconstruction of intrinsic value** itself. The deconstruction of value is the sense that human value does not participate in the intrinsic value of the Real, for the Real is dogmatically declared to have no intrinsic value. Thus, there is no shared identity between the interior of the human being and Reality. There is no common participation in a field of shared intrinsic value. Instead of being intimate with value, we are alienated from value. And only intrinsic value can arouse will: political, moral, and social will.

To sum up, without a shared grammar of value there is no global intimacy, and therefore no global coherence, and no global coordination in response to catastrophic and existential risk, which means, put simply, there will be, quite literally, no future.

HEALING THE GLOBAL INTIMACY DISORDER
REQUIRES THE EVOLUTION OF INTIMACY

But we are not hopeless. On the contrary, we are filled with great hope. Hope is a memory of the future. That memory of the future *is* the direct hit that takes down the Death Star, the culture of death. **The direct hit must be**—as it has always been in history—**the emergence of a new stage of evolution.**

Crisis is an evolutionary driver, and every crisis is, at its core, a crisis of intimacy: from the oxygen crisis of the single cells dying which generated multicellular life at the dawn of existence, to the existential risk in this very moment.[9]

The direct hit is therefore structurally self-evident: the evolution of intimacy itself.

What is intimacy, as a structure of Cosmos all the way down and all the way up the evolutionary chain? We engage this inquiry in depth in other writings, but for now we will simply adduce what we have called the "Intimacy Equation":

Intimacy = shared identity in the context of [relative] otherness x mutuality of recognition x mutuality of pathos x mutuality of value x mutuality of purpose

Intimacy is about the capacity of parts to generate a *shared identity* while retaining their otherness, or distinct identity. This requires multiple mutualities, including recognition, pathos (or feeling), value, and purpose. The parts must recognize and feel each other, even as they share value and purpose. But all of this must lead to intimate union—and not pathological

---

9 We demonstrate this principle in some depth in the multi-volume series, *The Universe: A Love Story* (forthcoming) (https://worldphilosophyandreligion.org/early-ontologies), *The Intimate Universe: Global Intimacy Disorder as Cause for Global Action Paralysis* (forthcoming), and in other writings of CosmoErotic Humanism.

fusion, where the distinct identity of the parts disappears—like subatomic particles that successfully become an atom, or two people who successfully become a couple.

THE DECONSTRUCTION OF VALUE IS THE DECONSTRUCTION OF INTIMACY

We have identified the global intimacy disorder as the root cause of the existential risk. But the underlying ultimate failure of intimacy is the deconstruction of value itself.

The deconstruction of value means that human value does not participate in any sense of intrinsic value of the Real. This is not about individual *values,* but about *the Field of Value* that underlies all of them. **When the human being**—moved, often sincerely or even nobly, by myriad cultural, historical, and psychological confusions—**claims to have stepped out of the Field of Value, then intimacy itself is deconstructed.**

The deconstruction of value is the deconstruction of intimacy.

In the absence of a shared Story of Value, a story that is an authentic expression of Reality's Eros, a story rooted in *pseudo-Eros* takes center stage and becomes the generator function for existential risk. Our modern pseudo-Eros story is *rivalrous conflict governed by win/lose metrics.* Such a story catalyzes in its wake the second generator function of existential risk: *complicated fragile systems with no allurement or intimacy between the parts.* It is in that sense that we have argued that the first generator function for existential risk is the success story.

- The failure of intimacy is precisely the impotent experience that there is no shared identity between the interior of the human being and Reality. **There is no shared identity in the sense of any kind of common participation in a field of shared intrinsic value.**
- **But only a shared Story of Value can arouse the global will**

required to engage catastrophic and existential risk. For it is only global political, moral, and social will—and we can even say *erotic* will—that can generate the most Good, True and Beautiful world that we have always known is possible.

THE EVOLUTION OF LOVE IS THE TELLING OF A NEW STORY

Coupled with the Intimacy Equation is the scientifically grounded realization, in both the exterior and interior sciences, that Reality is a progressive deepening of intimacies, or, said slightly differently:

Reality is Evolution. Evolution is the evolution of intimacy.

♦ The evolution of intimacy requires—both personally and collectively—a deeper, more accurate discernment of the nature of our universe, ourselves, and our beloveds.
♦ This new discernment generates a new global Story of Value.
♦ The new global Story of Value generates an emergent, heretofore unseen global intimacy and heals the global intimacy disorder.

The new Story of Value is the direct hit that takes down the Death Star and replaces it with the hope that invokes the memory of our best future.

Global intimacy facilitates global coherence, which facilitates global coordination, which activates the possibility of our creative and effectively coordinated global responses to the global meta-crisis in its entirety and its specific expressions.

To solve Bertrand Russell's challenge—the apparent argument for the subjectivity of ethical values—**we have to reground value theory in eternal yet evolving First Principles and First Values, and articulate a new Story of Value.**

This is what we call CosmoErotic Humanism.

CosmoErotic Humanism—together with other emergent strands—**needs to become the ground of a world religion as a context for our diversity**. We need religion, even as we need science, to articulate a shared global grammar of value.

As we said at the beginning, our choice is simple: love or die.

- To love means to participate in the evolution of love, which is the evolution of the human Story of Value.
- To love means to evolve and activate a new cultural enlightenment—rooted in a new narrative of identity, a new narrative of value, a new narrative of intimate communion, a new narrative of desire, a new narrative of power—all of which will birth new narratives of economics and politics.
- The evolution of love is the telling of a new story.

The new story that must be told is a love story, for in fact that is the deepest truth of Reality, rooted in the best exterior and interior sciences, that we have at this moment in time:

- Reality is not merely a fact. Reality is a story.
- Reality is not an ordinary story. Reality is a love story.
- Reality is not an ordinary love story. Reality is an Outrageous Love Story.

Story doesn't mean it's *made-up*.

It means doing the hard work of integrating the validated insights of the traditional world, the modern world, and the postmodern world.

This is the intention at the heart of telling the new story of CosmoErotic Humanism.

ABOUT THIS VOLUME

WE LIVE IN A WORLD OF OUTRAGEOUS PAIN

We live in a world of outrageous pain.

Postmodernity—with its correct critique of pre-modernity's often fundamentalist and dogmatic stories about value—has deconstructed value and said it is not real.

This all began in modernity, with David Hume and others as not the only but the major motif of modernity. Modernity took out a hidden loan of social capital from premodernity (the traditional period). The loan was the declared reality of value. It did not need to be discussed. The sources of value—which were no longer recognized to be revelation as it was in the premodern period—did not need to be established. Instead, value was taken to be self-evident. This is what CosmoErotic Humanism calls common sense sacred axioms of value.

Post modernity called in the hidden loan that modernity took from the traditional period and overtly declared value to be utterly without source and ground. As such, in the post-modern zeitgeist, we no longer perceive ourselves and others as being in a shared Field of Value. At the same time, regressive religious fundamentalism is on the rise all through the world. Outrageous pain is caused when we fail to recognize that we are all in a shared Field of Value.

In the absence of a shared Field of Value, individual values are decontextualized from the Field of Value. Decontextualized value then turns into either pseudo value or anti value.

Pseudo value imitates value in distorted form. Anti value stands against the value[1].

Evil is often originally sourced in a value that is decontextualized from the whole and turned into an absolute.

Any value or goal, taken by itself and transformed into an absolute becomes first extremist, then absurd, then grotesque and then potentially evil.

Take for example security, life, choice, aliveness, sexing, competition, fulfillment, justice, revenge, egalitarian, sameness or oneness or union, distinction, uniqueness, transformation, intimacy. Each of these are first principles and first values of Cosmos. When an individual value does not live in creative tension with other values in the field of value and together with those other values create a new whole, the result is virtually always, in one way or another, outrageous pain.

Outrageous pain happens when we take one value and reject other values; we take one experience and reject other experiences; we take one insight and reject other insights — and then we build an idolatrous worldview based on that one value or experience or insight. Idolatry is the deification of one value in alienation or even disassociation from the larger Field of Value.

The chosen value becomes not only our idolatrous commitment but the core of our identity, thus, no relationship with any other value is truly possible. No synergy, no dialectical emergence, no holding of the perspective of another value is possible. Compromise becomes not only impossible but ugly. The very notion of compromise becomes both heretical and—from the perspective of the aesthetics of value—ugly.

Conversation then naturally becomes impossible. Conversation becomes pseudo conversation because genuine exchange is not possible.

---

[1] We discuss these more deeply in the writings of Cosmc Erotic Humanism. See for example, David J. Temple, First Principles and First Values: Forty-two Propositions on CosmoErotic Humanism (2024).and David J. Temple, Value is Real (forthcoming).

The result is polarization and outrageous pain.

The core realization of CosmoErotic Humanism is that Reality is Eros Value at its very core. Eros Value itself can be fairly described as consciousness and relationship. When we say Value or Eros Value is fundamental, we mean that consciousness and relationship are the fundamental properties of Cosmos out of which all and everything and everyone emerges. Values themselves therefore, just like the rest of Cosmos, must live in their natural state of relationship. To artificially alienated values from each other is to destroy the structure of Reality. Hence there is an inherent need and desire for all values to live together in the larger Field of Value—which activates the sensuality of their dialectical dance towards ever greater wholeness (which itself is ever deeper and wider Eros Value).

To create a new world, we must realize that the Garden of Eden is not monistic paradise, but pluralistic paradox, rooted in a shared Field of Value, in which we never forget that what unites us—the Field of Inherent Value—is always so much greater than that which divides us. The prior wholeness of value is the ground for all future synergies in which new wholeness emerges.

In this book, we look at multiple contexts of this dynamic of value-idolatry and polarization which generate outrageous pain. Some of these contexts include the Supreme Court Roe Vs Wade conversation around abortion, as well as conversations around immigration, federal elections, name defamation on Twitter feeds and more.

Our intention is to articulate new frameworks for conversation (the Field of Value) that allows us to move from the outrageous pain of polarization to the Eros of paradox. The result is the evolutionary emergence of new wholeness. This new wholeness arises from the dialectical dance of value, which is always eternal and always evolving within the Field of Value.

We alluded above to the broader theme of outrageous love and outrageous pain. The relationship between these two experiences, as well as outrageous beauty, and the relationship between each of them, is part of the core value structure and plotline of Cosmos.

Of particular note in this writing is that **Outrageous Beauty is created from the Outrageous Love, the Eros, between values**. It is a dialectical dance between distinct values, driven by a yearning for ever deeper and wider value, that has the capacity to generate a larger whole, a new quality of wholeness. This itself creates a new quality of outrageous beauty.

The new synergy, generating the new beauty, is a direct result of the Eros Value desire that arises in response to outrageous pain.

Some dimensions of this dance of relationship are addressed in this volume.

THE ONLY RESPONSE TO OUTRAGEOUS PAIN IS OUTRAGEOUS LOVE

The only response to outrageous pain is Outrageous Love.

In response to outrageous pain the moral imperative of today is to tell an Outrageous Love story.

> Reality is not a fact; Reality is a story.
>
> Reality is not an ordinary story; Reality is a love story.
>
> Reality is not an ordinary love story; Reality is an Outrageous Love story.
>
> Reality is an Outrageous Love Story, rooted in First Principles and First Values.

When we locate ourselves within a shared Field of Value and a shared grammar of value, we understand that what unites us is so much greater than what divides us.

WE LIVE IN A WORLD OF OUTRAGEOUS BEAUTY

We live in a world of Outrageous Beauty. Beauty is not superficial. Beauty is a core value of Cosmos. Beauty is the ability to contain oppositions 1. It's the symmetry that is created when diverse threads come together and a new wholeness is manifest.

In the interior sciences of Hebrew wisdom, the Zohar describes the ten luminations of the Divine. The sixth of these luminations is called *Tiferet*. *Tiferet* means Beauty and it also means wholeness. Wholeness is when diverse values which oppose each other synergize in a stunning symmetry that generates a whole greater than the sum of any of the parts. **Beauty holds seemingly contradictory values together in paradox.**

The New Story of Value is a Story of Outrageous Beauty

When we locate ourselves in a shared Field of Value, which is the Field of Beauty, then contradiction becomes not polarization but paradox.

The line of self and the line of value run in parallel to each other. Indeed, at their core they are identical. Self. Value.

We recognize each other in the Field of Value: *We are part of the same True Self. We are part of the same True Value.* From within that Field of True Self and that Field of True Value, which is the Field of Beauty, we can hold contradictory values together in paradox. We recognize that individual values are part of a larger wholeness.

1. At each of the levels of the Five Selves, we have a different relationship to distinct values and to the larger Field of Value.

2. At the level of separate self, we perceive separate values as being alienated from each other.

3. At the level of True Self, we have the realization of the Field of Value as One Eros Value.

4. At the level of Unique Self, we perceive distinct values as being in-dividuated expressions of the larger Field of One Eros Value

5. At the level of Evolutionary Unique Self, we have a realization of the catalytic, evolutionary quality of each distinct value, both on the other values in the One Field of Value as well as on the One Field of Value itself.

6. At the level of Unique Self Symphony, there is a new wholeness of musical and moral value that emerges from the synergy between each unique instrument of value, between each unique value.

In order to evolve the source code of consciousness and culture, in order to move beyond polarization, we must tell a new Story of Value which is a story of Outrageous Beauty that weaves together the leading insights of Eros Value from across space and time in a new synergy, a new beauty, a new wholeness.

Volume 33

These oral essays are edited talks delivered by Marc Gafni between September 2020 and November 2024.

CHAPTER ONE

HEROES ARE THE EARLY ADOPTERS OF HOMO AMOR: A FOREVER COMMITMENT TO COSMOS

Episode 204 — September 6, 2020

WHO WE ARE IS WHERE WE PLACE OUR ATTENTION

We set intention by placing attention.

Let's fall in. Let's fall on each other, as it were, but fall on each other in the sense of falling into each other's hearts, into each other's arms, into each other's open fields of activist, revolutionary presence. **And we set our intention not by adding information but by invoking the depths of Reality as we know it, and we place our attention.**

I want to share something about how we set intention by placing attention, because it's so big and it's so powerful. Let's get audacious here. Let's get fierce here.

Who you are, who we are, is where we place our attention.

You can be, in life, in the "missing tile syndrome": we can be inside together, and we can be in all of the glory, all of

1

the wonder, all of the urgency, all of the delight, the deep Outrageous Love and First Values and First Principles that we're articulating, and then we get stuck because *there's a tile that's out of place*—one tile is out of place.

Then we lose our focus.

All of our energy gets drawn into a vortex of a missing tile.

We pour our Eros into being right about whatever our issue is.

We lose ourselves.

Oh my God, then our open heart—and the children all over the world that we want to hold hands with, and the old people that we want to hold hands with, and the pandemic that we want to potentiate into new possibility, and the promises that need to be kept and the shimmering joy that's the inside of Cosmos—all of it disappears.

Here's my promise to you, our promise to each other. **The way you/we step into this revolution, the way we take our seat at this table is the way we take our seat at *every* table.**

THE WORLD NEEDS OUR HOLY AUDACITY: IT'S TIME FOR A NEW STORY

This is an invitation to me and an invitation to you. This is our life right now. Our life is not next week, and our life does not happen the week after.

Our life is right now at this moment when the world madly needs us. The world needs our audacity.

I want just to feel that for a moment: *the world needs our holy audacity*. The world desperately needs us to be here in this da Vinci moment, in this time between worlds, in this time between stories, to articulate new First Values out of which we can construct a new story. It's time for a new Story of Value.

At the leading edges of philosophy today—where I know most people don't read; there's a few of us weirdos, in the world who are writing and reading at that crazy edge—**there's what they call the ontological turn.**

The ontological turn, meaning, *there's a realization growing from different quarters about the importance of looking at Reality itself.*

And we're central in that ontological turn. I think that we're one of the most important voices in the world. And I want to say that audaciously. I don't know of a place in the world that's articulating a more coherent and critical Story based on First Values.

So we're central in this, and we're privileged to be in it, and we're responsible to it.

But **it's part of a larger movement**—this ontological turn—**which is this realization that the deconstructions of postmodernity went too far.** It's not just that we're present to the movement, to the ontological turn. **I think we're at the center. We're the beating heartthrob.**

And we're rippling out into this movement; we're moving this in Reality.

- People like Alfred North Whitehead and Charles Sander Peirce were part of it at the beginning.
- My evolutionary beloved partner and whole mate, Barbara Marx Hubbard, was a deep partner in it.
- My dear friend Ken Wilber is part of this conversation in a real way.

But it's a critical conversation.

IT'S A WILD COSMOEROTIC UNIVERSE, ALL THE WAY UP AND ALL THE WAY DOWN

We have to revision the Cosmos. The Cosmos is much wilder, more wondrous, more magical, and more Real than we thought it was. We abandoned the Cosmos and we reduced the Cosmos to a particular story: *We are material beings that are over when we die and all the other stuff is just kind of fringe stuff. We're the only intelligent beings in the Cosmos.*

The only way we can talk to each other is through very limited physical ways.

We dethroned the notion of an infused, creative divinity in Cosmos: *we're by ourselves, a lonely speck in the world.*

Who was the greatest proponent of this view? He did it beautifully—he was just dead wrong. It was Carl Sagan. Carl was a wonderful man. Carl is the best exemplification of the attempt at dignity within the position I just articulated: *It's a Cosmos that's ultimately empty.*

We're an irrelevant speck of dust in this universe of 100 billion galaxies. The notion that we would ascribe any sort of ultimate meaning to what we're doing is absurd, an act of hubris that we need to move beyond.

Of course, Sagan is moving directly out of existentialism, but **that movement**—that infuses Landmark and the Forum: *meaning is not real, it's just what you create*—**No, that's not true.**

Meaning is Real. We can talk to each other across Cosmos.

I have a friend, a young man in Belgium. I won't say his name. He's 12 years old. I'm talking to him every couple of weeks these days. *I can feel him across the world when he's having a good week.* Why can I feel him, with no communication? Because *there are invisible lines of connection everywhere.* It's a wild, CosmoErotic Universe—all the way up and all the way down.

Articulating this new story, and knowing our place in this new story actually begins to refashion the world.

CNN: "OUR SUCCESS STORY IS MORE IMPORTANT THAN THE LARGER GOOD"

I want to give you just one example. Why is Donald Trump the president of the United States? I'm not going to take issue on conservative or liberal issues. I happen to be a traditional neoconservative on a number of issues and an ultraliberal on other issues, and anyone who tells you they're a conservative or a liberal on one side or the other has stopped thinking. You have to look at each position carefully and integrate a larger and more interesting position, not just parrot old positions. Knowing how to gather information is a different conversation.

However, I think tragically today **I think we can all pretty much agree across the spectrum that Donald Trump is a tragic figure.**

But the breakdown of America didn't begin with him. Our real issues don't begin with him. We're looking for someone to blame. It's kind of like Osama bin Laden: *we have someone to kill.* No, that's not true.

The structural issues, the second shock of existence—catastrophic risk, existential risk—**all of that has nothing to do with Donald Trump. But Donald Trump is an expression of a broken system.** He shouldn't be president in terms of leadership, integrity, ethos, values.

How did Trump become president? It didn't happen because "bad people" voted for him. It didn't happen because, *the Russians meddled with the election.* That's not why it happened. It happened because the liberal media was in the red—and Barack Obama himself pointed to this obliquely at the last White House dinner.

The liberal media—CNN, for example—covered Donald Trump insanely.

The liberal media, in general, the print and the electronic media, was in the red— and Donald Trump generated ratings.

5

CNN covered him incessantly, because he actually took CNN from being a loser to a winner. They were in debt, they were about to break, and he took them from being in the red to being in the black. **CNN made a decision: The win/lose metrics of *our* success story is more important than the larger good.**

I want everybody to get that. It's not just that CNN made that decision. The liberal media, up and down the system of the media—and, again, I'm a huge liberal on so many issues—made a decision based on win/lose metrics, and as Obama pointed to, actually elected Donald Trump president.

WE HAVE A BROKEN SYSTEM OF WIN/LOSE METRICS ROOTED IN SEPARATE SELF AND MATERIALIST ASSUMPTION OF COSMOS

It's such a big deal. You've got to get it. In other words, the way our system works—and Barbara and I have talked about this together for the last ten-twenty years—the win/lose system, every department is win/lose. "You have to be a success." To be a success means *you win, and someone else loses*. It's evaluated by metrics.

The metrics are status, financial gain, and commodification. And everyone is playing in that system in one way or the other, whether it's spiritual teachers who are commodifying Spirit and selling it, whether it's corporations, whether it's individuals, or whether it's liberal NGOs.

It's not a conservative/liberal issue. That's a huge mistake. That's the polarization of Reality. It's not about that. There are fabulous conservatives in America, such as George Will and Charles Krauthammer. There are fabulous, gorgeous conservative thinkers all across America, and there are fabulous liberal thinkers. That's not the issue. **The issue is *it's a broken system*.** The system is based on win/lose metrics, all the way up and all the way down, rooted in a separate self and a materialist, dogmatic, implicit assumption of the Cosmos.

Now, what Trump does is he exemplifies to an absurd, grotesque sense this notion of winner/loser. He'll even say: *Veterans of the war—those guys are losers. Why did they fight?* But you've got to understand: *Trump is an expression of the deeper structure of the system itself.* That's what he is.

The system generated Trump, not a couple of crazy villains in Russia who obviously did some bad stuff, and not a bunch of crazy, bad rednecks in America, the "bad people"—or Hillary Clinton's terrible phrase, the "basket of deplorables." That's another us-them phrase.

What happened is a broken system, not a conspiracy theory but a broken system. A broken story elected Donald Trump as an expression of all that's broken in the story.

Do we need to replace Donald Trump as president? Yes, we do. Am I making sure to register to vote for Joe Biden? Yes, of course I am, because that's obviously necessary. But that's not going to get us home, friends. The only thing that's going to get us home is going to articulate a new story of a Cosmos that lives in us—a story where I begin to know, begin to feel in my body:

> The CosmoErotic Universe is alive in me in person.

> Evolution lives in me in person.

> The deepest heart's desire of the Infinity of Power and Intimacy that generated the Big Bang is alive in me.

WHAT DOES REALITY WANT FROM ME IN THE NEXT MOMENT?

What does Reality need from me in the very next moment?

What is the deepest heart's desire of all Cosmos uniquely configured as me?

In my unique configuration of intimacy, desire, and consciousness, what does Reality need as me?

How am I standing for goodness, truth, justice, and beauty?

How am I alive as the Eros of the Cosmos flowing through me, completely and madly committed to creating a better world, everywhere I can, in my unique circle of intimacy and influence? This revolution that's our revolution, how do I make it mine? How do I step up?

How do I say, "Oh my God, this is our gospel, this is the new gospel"? The new gospel is us. Gospel is the good news, and the good news is the new story. How do I step into that story, and become a teller of that story?

How is my voice imprinted in the noosphere?

That's what the whole thing is about. Everything else is a detail. Everything else doesn't matter. We're between utopia and dystopia. We started in 2016. We started together, a whole bunch of us, a Unique Self Symphony. We're a We-Space. We did this because we want to blow the world open.

But, oh my God, this is ours to do. We have a seat at the table. It's our table. Reality needs us. **If we can get that, we can drop into it deeper:**

- We can articulate new and deeper first principles.
- We can tell this Story.
- We can gather the resources.
- We can begin to feed the hungry.
- We can begin to enact a new vision of Reality.

We're going to be the difference; we're going to be the Archimedean lever that changes the world. That's what we're here for. We're here for that level of revolution.

WE LIVE IN A MAGICAL COSMOS

Remember, it's a much stranger Cosmos than we think. **We know that "things" are not Reality. Reality is fields and relationships.** That's what

Reality is. Let's just get the weird Cosmos we live in. When I say weird, I mean it in the most beautiful way. It's a magical Cosmos, empirically.

In science, when something breaks the rules of classical materialist science we call it an anomaly: *it doesn't fit into the rules. We're not sure what to do with it and we usually ignore it.*

But if you get all the information available in Reality today, for real—as I have had the delight, the honor, the privilege to spend my last forty years studying across the sciences, across the traditions, across the interior and exterior domains of study—if you look across the board:

There's only one anomaly in the Universe and that's materialist science.

Materialist science, of course, has an important truth. It's one way of looking at the world, one way of enacting, one critical perspective on Reality—but it's a total anomaly if you actually think that's the world.

I'll give you the simplest example that everybody here knows. We have so much data in the world today that shows when a person is infused with love, a mother who can barely lift a sack of potatoes picks up a piano off of her child. How does that happen? If the laws of physics were the only thing operating in the world, and the laws of physics were materialist principles, how could it be that a woman who physically does not have much strength and power can pick up a piano off of her baby to save her baby's life? It happens all the time.

We call those people heroes. But we call them heroes because they're holding a deeper truth of Reality.

HEROES ARE EARLY ADOPTERS OF HOMO AMOR

Every society has heroes, because heroes are the early adopters of *Homo amor*. *Homo amor* is the New Human and the New Humanity. That's

9

where Reality is going. *Homo amor* means, literally, that just like matter became life and life became self-reflective mind which is the first three Big Bangs, then self-reflective mind, the human being, sought its own triumph.

Just like matter triumphs in life and life triumphs in mind (the physiosphere: matter; the biosphere: life; the noosphere: the world of thinking, information, the self-reflective mind, the three levels of reality, the narrative arc of Cosmos), so then self-reflective mind triumphs in *Homo amor*, in the New Human and the New Humanity. That's where we're going.

Heroes are early adopters of *Homo amor*. **A hero always is suffused by love.**

Now, sometimes it's love of country. Sometimes it's love of a country that's unjust, so you can actually have heroes whose love is misplaced: they love their fascist country, and they do feats of heroism in battle. So, we need to evolve love; love needs to be deepened and evolved. The evolution of love is the trajectory of Cosmos.

But a hero is always animated by love. **And the hero accesses power that's not available in our ordinary lives.**

That's the nature of Reality. When that becomes democratized, when we all become heroes, everything will change.

I become a hero by living my unique life, by giving my unique gift, by accessing my unique superpower.

There's not one of us who doesn't have literal and direct access to superpowers.

EVERY MOMENT IS A NEW INVITATION TO THE EVOLUTION OF INTIMACY

These are first principles of value that we've talked about before, and that we'll be talking about again this year, but that's the Universe Story.

10

I remember when Barbara called me for the first time and said, "Oh my God, I just read this thing you wrote saying that evolution is the evolution of intimacy. It was the missing piece for me. We've got to bring this into the world." So we started talking and we spent the last five years of her life trying to land these ideas in the world. I am wildly excited that we're going to start publishing some of the great new steps in the new story. We would talk about this every day. Every day Barbara would call me, sometimes two, three, four times a day. "So, let's talk again. What does it mean that evolution is the evolution of intimacy?"

We get to be excited anew every second. Because it's actually a new moment. It's not just psychologically a new moment, that's not the truth; it's not just a mere psychological thing. **In terms of the way the structure of physics operates**—virtual particles popping in and out of existence in every second, the quantum foam, the quantum vacuum—**Reality is literally rebirthing itself every moment.**

We're literally in a new moment, a new presence of time. And time in the original Hebrew is *zeman,* or "invitation." **There's literally a new invitation now that never existed before.** And then I can say *hineini. Hineini* means *here I am.* **I hear Reality calling me and I say:** *here I am.*

It's not about success. It's not about win/lose metrics.

How do I sing my love song in Reality? How do I respond to Reality's urgent invitation that I access my deepest heart's desire, which is to live the unique love song, the unique songline of my life, to give my gift, and be that quality of Evolutionary Love that only I can be?

PRAYER AS PROTEST: HALLELUJAH

We've spoken previously about prayer as protest. What is prayer as protest? What does that mean? Shouldn't I be thanking the Infinity of Power? No, but I'm protesting.

God in me protests against God.

You get the paradox in that? You can't get Cohen's holy and broken *Hallelujah* unless you get the protest in it. We love Leonard Cohen. Leonard Cohen is awesome. Leonard Cohen emerges from a tradition of protest. Leonard Cohen's *Hallelujah* is about King David.

> *I heard there was a secret chord that David played and it pleased the Lord, and you don't really care for music, do you?*

What do those words mean? Do you feel the irony in that? Do you feel the protest in that? Do you feel Leonard Cohen somehow cajoling, teasing, and protesting?

> *Now, I've heard there was a secret chord that David played and it pleased the Lord.*

Then he says to God,

> *But you don't really care for music, do you?*
> *It goes like this, the fourth, the fifth,*
> *the minor fall and the major lift,*
> *the baffled king composing hallelujah.*

This is not an old song of premodern medieval faith.

> *Your faith was strong, but you needed proof.*
> *You saw her bathing on the roof.*
> *Her beauty and the moonlight overthrew you.*
> *She tied you to a kitchen chair.*
> *She broke your throne and she cut your hair,*
> *And from your lips she drew the hallelujah.*

This is the story of David and Bathsheba and being overcome by desire and not being able to access the dignity of desire. It's an amazing story.

There's this story in the Talmud, in the mystical text, where David says to God: *God, I'm going to make you a bet.* It's on page 97a in the Talmud. This is what Leonard Cohen is basing his song on.

God says: *David, you want to make a bet with me? What kind of bet do you want to make?*

David says: *God, test me. I can handle anything.*

God says: *Are you sure?*

David says: *I've got this covered, God.*

Imagine that Bill Cosby voice when Bill Cosby hadn't had such a horrific and tragic dimension of his life and we could access Bill Cosby easily. So imagine that Bill Cosby voice. *Hey, David, don't make that bet. That's not a good idea.*

David says to God: *I'm making the bet. Test me. I can handle anything.*

The very next day, David is on the roof.

> *Your faith was strong, but you needed proof.*
> *You saw her bathing on the roof.*

He sees Bathsheba bathing on the roof. And she's married to one of his generals who's named Uriah. David goes through a complex set of political machinations to claim his desire for Bathsheba.

But it's not holy desire—it's wicked desire.

It's not David at his best.

It's not the dignity of desire.

It's not the gorgeousness of desire.

Desire gets a bad name here. Then David realizes it's a broken story. So David fails.

Then God says to David: *David, look what happened. You failed.*

13

And David says: *Of course I failed, God, because, God, you said I would fail and I said I would succeed, so I thought it would be disrespectful to succeed, because I would be disobeying you.*

The mystical text says: In that moment, *David protests God through laughter*.

What a strange story. Meaning: *why do we fall, why do we break sometimes, why is desire so complicated, and why is it all so hard sometimes?*

So we protest. David laughs—and there's a protest in his laughter.

Then he says to God,

> *You say I took the name in vain.*
> *I don't even know the name,*
> *but if I did, well, really, what's it to you?*

Then Leonard Cohen really gets it, as David.

> *There's a blaze of light in every word.*
> *It doesn't matter which you heard.*
> *The holy or the broken hallelujah.*

Do you get that this is a protest song? It's a protest song which says,

> *Even though it all went wrong,*
> *I'll stand before the Lord of Song*
> *With nothing on my tongue but Hallelujah.*

Can you feel that?

> *I did my best, it wasn't much.*
> *I couldn't feel, so I tried to touch.*
> *I've told the truth,*
> *I didn't come to fool you.*

Can you feel what's happening here? It's the realization that *it's not easy*, that sometimes *it's a hopeless place.*

> *Baby, I've been here before.*
> *I know this room,*
> *I've walked this floor.*
> *I used to live alone*
> *Before I knew you.*
> *I've seen your flag on the marble arch.*
> *Love is not a victory march.*
> *It's a cold and it's a broken Hallelujah.*

Just feel that. **Feel the desire for desire itself and for the beautiful purity of desire.**

This is my favorite part of the song.

> *There was a time when you let me know*
> *What's really going on below*
> *But now you never show it to me, do you?*
> *Remember when I moved in you,*
> *The holy dove was moving, too,*
> *And every breath we drew was Hallelujah.*

It's a protest that says: *I've got to re-find that time, I've got to find my way back to Eden.* Then, God, sometimes I'm so angry at You I'm not even willing to talk about You clearly, and I'm going to say:

> *Maybe there's a God above,*
> *But all I've ever learned from love*
> *Was how to shoot at someone who outdrew you.*
> *It's not a cry you heard at night.*
> *It's not somebody who's seen the light,*
> This song is not about premodern faith.

It's a cold and it's a broken Hallelujah.

Can you feel that, everybody? *Hallelujah!* Does everyone get that? It's *Hallelujah.*

Hallelujah means pure, pristine praise, and when it's all good: it's gorgeous, it's numinous, it's sweetness and light. And Hallelujah also means brokenness and drunken intoxication.

Love is not a victory march.
It's a cold and it's a broken Hallelujah.

It's a protest. But here's the thing. Prayer as protest means:

I'm in relationship. I haven't left; I'm in the story.

We're together in the story.

I'm not leaving.

I'm going to be with you, God, forever.

I'm going to hold Your hand.

IN RELATIONSHIP TO GOD: I'M STAYING FOREVER

I want to ask you, if you're willing, to make a promise with me? I'm going to make a promise to you. Let's see if we can promise each other. Can we look each other in the eyes and say: *I'm staying forever. Until the world becomes what the world needs to be, I'm staying.*

Love's not a victory march.

It's not about: *Did I like that insight or like that insight?* We're going to do the deepest *dharma* and the deepest First Principles and the deepest First Values. We're going to blow it away together.

But that's just the expression of it. It goes deeper than that:

There's a blaze of light in every word.

16

It doesn't matter which you heard,
The holy or the broken hallelujah.

We can be here together, and we can confess our greatness, and we can confess our vulnerability, and we can love each other madly.

We're going to love it open all the way, no matter what.

We're going to close. And we're going to open again. We're going to reach deeper.

We're going to know that sometimes we come closer, and sometimes we step back. But we never look away.

That's what it means to be in relationship to God. That's what it means to know that God needs our prayer, just like we need God's need of our prayer.

We pray to God, and God prays to us. Prayer creates God. And God is way beyond prayer. God is a figment of our imagination. And our imagination is a figment of God. It's all so Real.

- Spirit is real.
- Intimacy is real.
- Consciousness is real. It didn't emerge from mere material senseless matter. It birthed everything.

So, let's go to Leonard Cohen, and let's pray together like we've never prayed before. I am so, so honored to be with you. We're so honored to be with each other. Leonard Cohen, the holy and the broken *Hallelujah*, inside all the way.

CHAPTER TWO

THE SENSUAL AROUSAL OF SENSEMAKING: SEDUCING OURSELVES OUT OF THE DIGITAL TRANCE INTO THE ARMS OF LADY JUSTICE

Episode 293 — May 22, 2022

WE ARE HERE TO FIND A NEW WAY OF BEING HUMAN

What a joy to be together in this moment, poised between dystopia and utopia, when **we have the power to create a more beautiful world in which every child has food, and every human being *knows*:**

I am needed by All-That-Is.

I am not a bug of the system; I'm a feature.

My life is filled with intrinsic, irreducible, and irreplaceable value.

No one else that ever was, is, or will be, can nourish Cosmos with the value that I can provide.

We can articulate a new narrative of identity, a vision of the new human and the new humanity.

We can download that narrative, we can evidence that narrative, we can ground that narrative in a Great Library—a new Renaissance.

The Great Library—this new Renaissance—is the core of what we are up to at the Center for Integral Wisdom, and our sister think tank, the *Foundation for Conscious Evolution*, which is part of our broader umbrella that we call *The Office for the Future* (this name was actually originally coined by my beloved Barbara Marx Hubbard, a co-founder of our weekly broadcast, One Mountain, Many Paths).

We understand that we need to be those people in the world today who are not going to look away.

We are not here for entertainment—although it's gorgeous to be together.

We are not here to feel good—although it feels so good to be together.

We are here to feel to be omni-considerate for the sake of the whole.

We are here to feel the goodness of the whole.

We are here to find a new way of being human.

That's what being a human being means.

Being a human being means I participate in the evolution of culture and consciousness, and I find new and ever deeper ways of being human— particularly when I hit a moment of crisis, when the old way of being human is not working.

A NEW STORY OF VALUE IS THE MINOR FLUCTUATION POINT THAT JUMPS THE SYSTEM TO A HIGHER LEVEL OF ORDER

We are at this moment of *the inflection point*—what my dear friend, Ervin Laszlo, calls the **chaos point**.

In 1972, Ervin wrote the authoritative cultural book on *Systems Theory*. One of the principles is: **When a system is far from equilibrium, and**

everything is in chaos, there is the possibility of a minor fluctuation point that can jump the entire system to a new higher order of being, to a higher coherence.

A couple of years ago I was in Tuscany, and we spent about 10 days, Ervin and I, and we talked about this deeply: *What is this inflection point, what is this chaos point?*

Ervin spent an enormous amount of time analyzing the crisis itself, and I spent more time focusing on the response. What I said to Ervin, after listening to his beautiful unpacking of the chaos point is that **our work here at the Center for Integral Wisdom is to actually *be* that minor fluctuation point.**

"Minor fluctuation point" doesn't mean that it is *minor*—it means that that particular fluctuation point is what jumps the system to a higher order.

In systems theory, when the system is far from equilibrium, and chaos reigns, it doesn't mean that we are gone. It doesn't mean all is going to fall apart. It means that **something can move the whole system to cohere anew**—a new allurement between the parts that actually *jumps* the entire system.

It is a beautiful image, and it's accurate.

What we have understood, so many of us, in the last decade of day-and-night work, is that **this minor fluctuation point that jumps the entire system is a new Story of Value, rooted in First Values and First Principles.**

What moves culture, what changes the trajectory of the future, what organizes Reality, is story.

This is why we go to movies—to be entranced by a story. A story takes us in, and we follow it's thread.

We understand our lives in terms of storylines. Because story (or *narrative*) is not a social construction of Reality. **Narrative itself is a *First Principle and First Value* of Cosmos.**

Here's a simple way to say it—I'll say it in the terms of the great traditions: **God loves stories.** That's how great traditions say it (I am translating this particular sentence from Aramaic). *Story* is a First Principle and First Value of culture itself. To evolve the story is to evolve consciousness and culture.

WE HAVE TO OVERTHROW THE OLD STORY OF WHAT IT MEANS TO BE HUMAN

I am madly delighted and excited to be with you, because this is the headquarters of the revolution. That's what we are here for.

We are the headquarters of the revolution. It means we are committed to overthrow the order of society, which is based on rivalrous conflict governed by win/lose metrics—which is the old story. **We have to overthrow the old story**, because if we don't overthrow the old story, then that story is going to lead to the inexorable conclusion that emerges from the vectors of its plotlines.

We did a big *Success* summit a bunch of years ago, to articulate what this broken success story looked like. I sat with my dear friend, John Mackey, who's the Founder of Whole Foods and an earlier Chair of our think tank.

We articulated together this vision of Success 1.0, which is **premodern success**: straight obedience to your local God.

The next stage, **modern success**, means:

- Rivalrous conflict based on win/lose metrics: where *I win, you lose.*
- I've got to stand out to achieve, meaning I've got to be able to *commodify* my worth and get paid for it in a particular way.
- Some kind of personal achievement, a personal success story.

22

Of course, each of these has some validity, but **when this "success story" becomes the overriding plotline of Cosmos, what does it lead to?**

It leads to **existential risk.**

It leads to a win/lose metrics, which creates an **extraction model of massive consumption.** We extract from the earth in a few decades what took billions of years for the Earth to create.

We need to keep filling ourselves up with *pseudo-eros*, because we are disconnected from the true Eros of Cosmos.

Our success story means we don't have real Eros, so we place someone else outside the circle to give ourselves an illusion that we are inside the circle. To be in Eros is to be inside the circle, but we are not inside the circle because value has collapsed.

We've lost access to First Values and First Principles. We don't know what we stand for, so we have to cover it up with *pseudo-eros*, which means: consumption, consumption, consumption, more success, more success, more success.

We create exponential growth curves and fractional reserve banking (meaning only a fraction of bank deposits are backed by cash on hand and available for withdrawal).

And this creates not *complex* systems (in which the parts are *allured* to each other), but *complicated* systems which are fragile, and easily break down. (Nassim Taleb has written extensively on **our fragile systems, which emerge from this win/lose metrics rivalrous conflicts success story.**)

That's all a disaster!

So what do we need to do?

- We can't fix it based on changing governance structures by themselves. That's *social structure.*
- We can't fix it based on building more roads or creating more

jobs, although that's important. That's *infrastructure.*

Both social structure and infrastructure are trickle downs from what right Marvin Harris, the cultural theorist, called *superstructure.* **Superstructure is a fancy word for "story"** (although he wouldn't say it this way): **what is the story we are living in?**

In other words: **We need a new way of being human.** We need a new story of what the human being is. That is what we call the move from *Homo sapiens* to *Homo amor.*

WE HAVE TO WAKE UP FROM THE PSEUDO-ECSTASIES OF THE DIGITAL WORLD

Now, how do we *get* to this new story? **We have to *seduce* ourselves to the new story.** We do deep work here every week, and I just want to thank everyone for being willing to do the deep work. This is not light; we're doing deep work.

We are at the center of Reality.

We are taking our full responsibility.

We are refusing to turn away.

We are articulating these new source code structures.

Our job is to articulate them, to write them, to film them, and to download them into culture. We are adding something new every week, and right now we are talking about the need to seduce ourselves to a higher level.

We need to have a fluctuation point that jumps the system to a higher order, but we can only do that by *seducing* ourselves. Seducing ourselves means we've got to actually *arouse ourselves.* We have to take responsibility for our own arousal—that's the way the Zohar frames it in the 13th century.

Of course there's sensual arousal, which is very important, but our topic now is actually **the sensual arousal of sensemaking**—a kind of intellectual, spiritual, existential arousal. I need to be able to arouse myself to *see clearly*, and to *see through* the pseudo-eros and pseudo-ecstasies.

In the old world, the pseudo-ecstasies were about a dictator who whipped the mob into a pseudo-ecstasy. Then we went to democracy, and we were supposed to get over those pseudo-ecstasies, and be able to actually go deep into real Eros:

- The Eros of justice.
- The Eros of appropriate dignity of every human being.
- The Eros of fair courts and fair systems.

But we got lost, and we are actually back to pseudo-ecstasies. **Our pseudo-ecstasies now exist on Twitter threads**, in *madness of crowds*, in the web world determined by rules of pseudo-ecstasy, or pseudo-eros:

It's all about "likes" and "views": who got how many likes. You get "likes" based on attracting a certain kind of attention, and there's a negativity bias. **We've actually gone back to the madness of crowds**.

We have moved out of the normal democratic structures that were supposed to weigh evidence, and carefully make decisions, and cultivate discernment, into **a digital world that is driven by the pseudo-ecstasies** which has become a kind of new Roman Colosseum, where we throw some meat to the crowds, sacrificing people's lives—like they sacrificed the lives of gladiators in Ancient Rome for the sake of entertainment. That's a very big deal.

In order to arouse ourselves, and to seduce ourselves to a new order of Value, to a new story, we have to step out of the pseudo-ecstasies of the digital world—and reclaim the public square, and claim a new cultural enlightenment.

We have to reclaim a new vision of what it means to be human beings: to see each other face to face, to hug each other, to know each other, to feel each other, to learn how to do sensemaking, to learn how to cultivate discernment.

And to do that, **we have to arouse ourselves out of the torporific stupor of the pseudo-ecstasies of the digital.** We need to arouse ourselves from this torporific slumber, from the *comfortably numb* doldrums, from the automatic doomscrolling we do all the time.

A SENSUAL AROUSAL TO SENSEMAKING

We have to seduce ourselves out of that sleep, and awaken—or *arouse*—ourselves.

In the *Zohar* of the thirteenth century—the great doctrine of interior sciences—the word *arouse* and the word *awaken* are the same. They are deeply related. *To arouse* and *to awaken* is actually the same Hebrew root *er*: to rouse, or to awaken. To wake up.

To wake up means I've got to wake up out of the torporific slumber of the deadening internet, which destroys our ability to make individual discernments, to see people face-to-face, to feel each other, to cultivate judgment, to gather information properly. And we've got to be willing to actually wake up to a new Reality.

Today, we want to talk about the need for the individual and for the collective to seduce ourselves out of the sleepwalk, out of the trance-like, zombie internet state, into functioning, awake, alive, vibrant citizens in a democracy, who gather information, and cultivate discernment, and know how to engage in the art of evaluation. All of voting is based on that, and all the processes of democracy are based on that. That's what we are going to look at today.

We are going to try and talk in a surprising new way about what it would mean to actually seduce ourselves—to arouse ourselves—into a new public culture. That's our topic for today.

In the next couple of weeks, we are going to talk about more personal modes of seducing ourselves, what does it mean *to seduce thyself*. But this week, we're going to start in a surprising way—because seduction always requires surprise.

There's a distinction between **sacred seduction and unholy seduction. We are going to talk about the intellectual seduction, the collective intellectual arousal, the arousal to our own capacity to discern.**

The sensual arousal to sensemaking requires us to step out of the monological internet, and into a deep dialogical conversation with ourselves and with Reality to be able to cultivate our new public culture, our new commons.

The only way we get over the tragedy of the commons is to actually create a new possibility of *dialogue*, a new possibility of discernment, and a new possibility of sensemaking.

TO SEDUCE YOURSELF YOU HAVE TO HAVE THE CAPACITY FOR SENSEMAKING

Welcome to this place. This time between worlds. This time between stories.

In which we are here to articulate the new Story of Value based in First Principles and First Values. And to seduce ourselves and to arouse ourselves to this new story. This means we've got to step out of the torporific slumber of the pseudo-ecstasies of the digital. **Can we arouse ourselves out of the torporific slumber of the pseudo-ecstasies of the digital?**

We are going to do something unusual. We are going to look today at public culture and ask,

"How do we need to arouse ourselves in public culture to seduce ourselves to sensemaking?"

I want to start with the note that we sent out a couple of days ago. That's going to set our tone.

Seduce Thyself: **Taking responsibility for your own arousal.**

The old Delphic Oracle, in ancient Greece said: *Know thyself.*

27

In the sacred texts, *know* always means carnal knowledge: *and Adam knew his wife Eve.*

To know is to know the depths of Eros. **To know thyself means to know how to make love with yourself. To make love with yourself means to birth into Reality the most stunning, gorgeous, wildly unique and beautiful version of you.**

It is that version of you that Reality desperately yearns for, and that's what we call your Unique Self. Now, to be that—to seduce yourself into your Unique Self—you require this ability to seduce yourself. **To seduce yourself means you have to have the capacity for sensemaking.**

Because the society we are creating today is:

- A society of upgraded algorithms and downgraded human beings
- A society of human beings who are not aroused
- A society of human beings who have lost their access to authentic freewill
- A society of human beings who are manipulated by carefully programmed web algorithms, by personalized, micro-targeted campaigns—to hijack your attention and to form your opinion
- A society of internet silos and echo chambers

Unless you seduce yourself, unless you arouse yourself, unless you step in and cultivate your Unique Self discernment—you lose access to your own Eros.

IT NEVER OCCURS TO US THAT WE NEED TO DIE TO BIRTH OURSELVES

In our email, we asked, **what are you willing to die for?**

That's the piece I was most interested in. That's the instruction for who you want to be.

So, *what are you willing to die for?*

Say it softer, whisper it with quivering tenderness: *what are you willing to die for?*

- Because if there's nothing you are willing to die for, you're already dead.
- But once I am aroused to the realization of what I'm willing to die for, then I begin to live for it.

Now, what does that mean, *what am I willing to die for?*

Sometimes we're willing to die for a mother, a father, a partner, a son, a daughter, or even a friend—and that's beautiful. **But it never occurs to us that we need to die for ourselves; we need to die to birth ourselves. It also never occurs to us that we are willing to die for a value**—that if we are not willing to die for a set of values, then we are already dead.

We think that the people who are willing to die for values are Kamikaze Japanese pilots or Islamic fundamentalists who are suicide bombers or Christian Crusaders who attack a Muslim fortress—*dying for the glory of God.* **We identify the willingness to die for something as the mark of regressive fundamentalism, insanity, psychosis.**

When we hear, *What are you willing to die for?* it frightens us.

Of course, there *are* obviously regressive, fundamentalist, even psychotic versions of being willing to die for something. That's self-evidently true.

But there is also—not *pre-personal* but *transpersonal*—noble, wondrous willingness to die for something. In the Avengers movie (Marvel 2019–2020), Tony Stark finally gets to a place where he is willing to die for something—and he saves the galaxy. That's what it means to become a hero.

If I have a broader vision of death, if I understand that life is not over when it's over, if I have an understanding that I am part of a larger field of consciousness, if I understand that there's a continuity of consciousness—

which is the implicit knowing of the hero at the moment in which they sacrifice themselves—then **I wake up to myself, and I realize that there is something I'm willing to die for, that there are values I'm willing to die for.**

If there are no values I'm willing to die for, then I am basically in a race for immortality in this body and in this lifetime— which I will inevitably lose— and my life is pathetic. My life is a crumbling, pathetic failure, because I'm in a race for egoic immortality in this body—and it's a race that I will be defeated in, in a horrific way. That's a given. So, if that's my goal, then I have already failed. Instead. my goal is to live the fullest, most gorgeous, most stunning life, and to live for those values that I am willing to die for.

THE HERO IS WILLING TO DIE FOR A HIGHER VALUE

I know there are a bunch of strands on the table by now—and now we are going to start to really put this together in a deep way.

There is a very intense scene in Tom Hanks' "Saving Private Ryan." **It is about men being willing to die for something.** Watching this scene is part of our study, it is part of our meditation.

Can we *see* this, *feel into* it, and then talk about it? All of this is going to be a part of our own-self seduction, our own arousal to our fullest humanity, to the possibility of being new humans, to the sensuality of sensemaking. That's what we're looking for here.

In this scene, you see men being mowed down on the beaches of Normandy. Pretty much all of those men were killed. They knew going in that they were going to be mowed down, and they knew that at least half of them wouldn't walk out of that beach alive.

So why were they there, what were they willing to die for?

It wasn't win/lose metrics—**it was freedom**. It wasn't just that they were drafted. **No, actually, they were standing for something** (the same way as Ukraine does now, even with all the complexities of this war—*Glory to Ukraine and glory to the heroes*).

They were standing for the American way. They were innocent, and tragic beyond imagination. **And their willingness to die on the beaches of Normandy turned the tide of World War II, and defeated Nazism, and created, in many ways, the world we live in.**

So, what were they willing to die for?

They weren't willing to die for McDonald's.

They weren't willing to die for apple pie.

They weren't willing to die for baseball.

They were willing to die for the person next to them in the trench—but there was also an overarching cause.

My dear friend, Lori Galperin, her dad was on those beaches, and she has described her dad to me in very great depth and detail. Her dad was one of those 18-year-olds on those beaches. He couldn't have articulated exactly the Jeffersonian principles, and he didn't know the Federalist Papers. But **he got it, in his body, that freedom *matters* and that democracy *matters*.**

This is so insanely important. This is not about, *did they have a full cogent sense of this?* That's not the issue. The issue is, what this was really about. My sons were both soldiers at 18, and they have a deep sense of what being soldiers meant at 18.

There was a deep sense in American culture that we needed to oppose Nazism.

It meant opposing the gas chambers.

It meant opposing the Holocaust.

31

It meant opposing the worst tyrannies in the world.

Today, Ukraine is fighting for freedom. Beyond all complexities of Ukraine (we talked about them for four weeks), there is a second simplicity:

They are dying *for* something.

They are dying for the values of democracy.

They are dying for the values of freedom.

We've got to be really careful of this postmodern cynicism, where we are actually afraid to stand for value. Putin assumed that it had so infested the West that no one would stand with Ukraine, but Ukraine has reminded the West that there's something about standing for freedom, and that's a very big deal.

If there's nothing I'm willing to die for, I'm already dead.

I have shared this with you a couple of times.... I was with the Dalai Lama in his room in Dharamsala, we talked about the need for an army—**the need for an army of people that are willing to die for higher value**.

Now, I fully know in my body that when we die, we die into a higher order of consciousness, and we move from this dimension to another dimension. Nonetheless, the experience of dying is real, and whatever the next dimension is, there's an experience of death which requires great heroism.

The hero is willing to die for a higher value. And we're able to discern between a false cause and a true cause.

In CosmoErotic Humanism, we talk about six levels of pleasure, and the third level of pleasure is **the pleasure of standing for a cause.** But every pleasure has a counterfeit version, so the counterfeit version of this level of pleasure is a pseudo-cause, or a pseudo-value.

There's no question that there is a great danger in hijacking the human nobility to be willing to stand up for a cause, we can hijack that for a pseudo-cause, absolutely—but having said that, the willingness of these kids to storm the beaches of Normandy is huge!

WE NEED TO STAND IN THE INTEGRITY OF INFORMATION-GATHERING AND SENSEMAKING

Now, let's get to our core point.

Freedom and democracy are not apple pie.

It's not baseball.

It's not McDonald's.

Freedom and democracy are based on two principles:

- ◆ How do we gather information?
- ◆ What is the structure of Justice that operates in society?

So, what I'm going to focus on is:

- ◆ How do we gather information?
- ◆ What is the structure of justice that operates in society, and moves society? How do we evaluate a person? How do we form judgments in public culture? How do we form judgments in courts?

The process of information-gathering, the process of making evaluation—that process is the single most important process in democracy.

But more specifically, I am going to talk about public culture, because **public culture is where most judgments happen today—not in courts.** And that's where we are able to honor and uphold the integrity of information gathering:

We are able to cultivate discernment.

We are able to evaluate.

We are able to place value.

We are able to weigh competing narratives, not to get lost in the culture of "a balanced story", but actually **just stand for truth.**

And not to always be giving up our values, and distorting the truth, for some intended gain we have for whatever our own contribution is, **but actually stand for truth.**

We need to stand in the integrity of sensemaking, of information-gathering, of evaluating information.

When we don't do that, we get lost in the pseudo-ecstasies of the crowd. Charles Mackay, a Scottish journalist, called it **the madness of crowds** (I think it was in the 1840s).

Sometimes you'll go into a particular internet site, and it might even be an internet site that claims to have a high level of consciousness, but there's a madness of crowds there:

There's no actual sense of evidence, and conversation, and discernment.

There's a kind of politically correct *woke echo chamber*, where people reflect each other, and **the voices that are least enlightened, and least clear, and least loving, and least compassionate rise to the top.**

That's actually how the entire internet works today. The entire internet is actually geared towards the lowest common denominator—and information-gathering is taking place primarily on the internet today.

That's a shocking piece of information!

The internet is driven, as Douglas Murray correctly pointed out, by the madness of crowds. On the internet, we are often willing to engage in some version of sacrifice: **we sacrifice people.**

FROM SALEM WITCH TRIALS TO THE MADNESS OF CROWDS ON TWITTER THREADS

I want to just give you an example: the Salem Witch Trials—what were they about?

The Salem Witch Trials were about accusing a woman of being a witch, and hundreds of thousands of women were killed, many of them burned at the stake. **Because we were living in an era in Europe**—and then in Salem in America, but primarily in Europe—in which **the madness of crowds reigned**.

If there was a woman whose femininity threatened society—if she was a healer, or her sexuality may have been different from the classical structures of sexuality, or she didn't fit into church doctrine—**the easiest thing to do was to accuse her of being a witch—and that's what we did.**

Here is how it worked:

Within a period of a couple of weeks, you would have a *dozen* first-person testimonies as to her witchcraft. **There's never one complaint, there's always a dozen**, because there's a kind of infection, and a kind of contagion, in the madness of crowds.

So now we've got a dozen or a two dozen first-person testimonies, attesting to her witchcraft. Of course, as scholarship has pointed out, **there were often an entire set of hidden ulterior motives behind the accusations of witchcraft**—all sorts of political machinations, all sorts of rivalrous conflict and win/lose metrics—**tragic games of the worst kind of games that people play.**

Hundreds of thousands or millions of women paid the price—**because there was no ability to actually *gather information.***

Now, today, we don't live in a religious *Zeitgeist* on the internet, we live in a psychological *Zeitgeist*.

35

We don't call a person a witch, we call them a narcissist, or we call them a sociopath. But that's the same thing as calling the person a witch. We don't use the formal Salem Witch Trials, but we create Twitter threads in which people are very afraid of being called out. Because if you are called out in the wrong way in a Twitter thread—and then it comes up on the Google search about you that someone has accused you of something, that remains on the internet forever.

We live in the pseudo-Eros of Twitter threads, which are not about discernment, not about weighing information, not about face-to-face feeling each other, not about actually even reading or checking information in a serious way—*because who is reading nowadays?*

It is all based on an evocative, emotive madness of crowds with an automatic click-baiting, low level, tragic, lowest common denominator, human play. **That is actually how judgments are formed today.**

It's an unbelievable structure.

We haven't created litmus tests to actually *discern*, to tell the difference:

Is it internet abuse, the madness of crowds or an abandonment of principle? Is it a modern version of Salem Witch Trials or important issues that need to be looked at, and need to be weighed?

This is not a minor thing.

This is what those boys were dying for in Normandy. Yes, they couldn't quite articulate it—they were eighteen-years-olds from Kansas, and New York, and Montana, and San Francisco. But they *knew* it, and **culture knew it.**

- Today, culture knows that the way Putin is doing sensemaking is to remove all possibilities of people doing independent and serious sensemaking.
- But at the same time, in the United States, our own American group of oligarchs are controlling the internet,

and controlling the information flow, and creating micro-targeted, personalized advertising, forming opinions.

They are undermining our core essential ability to do sensemaking, and to arouse ourselves into our unique capacity to discern. That's a big deal. This is not nothing.

THE DREAM OF AMERICA IS THAT YOU CAN FEEL SAFE AND HELD IN THE ARMS OF LADY JUSTICE

What those boys were dying for on the beaches of Normandy was—and I am going to use an unpopular word here—*the American way*.

Now, **America is filled with flaws** (I read the book when I was a kid, *The Ugly American*, which critiques America's world policy—and there's a lot to critique in America). ***And* America is a great country.**

- It's actually the single most successful multi-racial country in the history of planet Earth.
- It's a dream in the making, as Barack Obama correctly says.
- **It's a dream that's unfulfilled. But we can't forget the dream.**

Because *what happens to a dream deferred?*—wrote Langston Hughes—*Does it dry up like a raisin in the Sun?*

> *The dream of America is that you can feel safe and held in the arms of Lady Justice.*

Lady Justice is the Divine Feminine.

I don't know if anyone has ever been on a vacation in the wrong part of Mexico, where when your goods are stolen, and you go to the local police, you realize they are probably involved with the people who stole them. That happens in Mexico tragically, all over the place. There is no sense of being held in the arms of justice, which is one of the tragedies of corruption in many parts of the Third World. It's obviously not true all over Mexico, but it's a demarcating characteristic of many, many, many towns.

We take it as an assumption that we are actually held, in the United States and other Western democracies, in the arms of justice—even if justice is imperfect, and it is often available only to people with disposable income, and not to lower socioeconomic classes (in which I include myself).

Justice is a dream in the making, but at least the aspiration is clear. *The aspiration is that we do justice.*

We look at every individual case.

We are not involved in a kind of identity politics in which we dismiss men, or Jews, or blacks.

We evaluate information in each individual case.

People are innocent until proven guilty.

And that's a big deal. This is what those boys were dying for on the beaches of Normandy.

THE DESTRUCTION OF THE AMERICAN DREAM

There is a new word in the press, and the word is **'credibly accused.'** It has found its way into culture, as one of *woke downloads*.

- We used to say a person is *innocent until proven guilty*.
- Now, we say a person is *credibly accused*.

Credibly accused is a very, very subjective term, invented by journalists, and it is deployed unevenly. Often, *credibly accused* also adds an enormous amount to how the public responds to the accusation. A whole set of assumptions that need to be challenged exist in this word, *credibly accused*.

Because the second a person is termed *credibly accused*, that's it. They're credibly accused!

- There has been no process.
- There has been no evaluation of information.
- There has been no fact-checking.

But the person is credibly accused, so that's it, end of conversation.

That's the destruction of the American dream.

The second that we are lost in the pseudo-ecstasies of internet hysteria—

I'll say this again, *the Roman Colosseum is re-enacted on the internet*. That's exactly what we stood against, in Lady Justice: **the pseudo-ecstasies of sacrificing innocent victims**.

Because when we sacrifice innocent victims, we literally rip their hearts out, and we throw them into the flames, and all the while, we pray that it's not us.

Imagine it happened to your daughter. Imagine it happened to your mother. Imagine it happened to your beloved.

This is the culture we are living in.

There is a scene in "Indiana Jones and the Temple of Doom" that shows **the pseudo-ecstasies of the premodern**, where there is no justice, and the crowds go wild when a heart is ripped out, and the human being is sacrificed.

I want you to catch that: *that is a Twitter thread*. You just watched a Twitter thread. Ripping someone's heart out.

That person is demonized.

That person is dehumanized.

Their heart is ripped out.

Do you see the crowd going wild, the kind of ecstasy of the crowd?

The ecstasy of the crowd is being manipulated by the high priest, but the high priest in this case is not one high priest, it's an algorithm. It is an algorithm that's geared to generate profit and power for about five or six companies run by about 15 people.

People and lives are regularly ruined, and families are destroyed, in Twitter threads and in Facebook threads, in ostensibly sacred places and lots of not sacred places. Because people are caught up in the pseudo-ecstasy of the crowd. The madness of crowds is subtle, and people are caught in the excitement of the crowd. **This is exactly what democracy stands against.**

Democracy stands against the notion that we do judgments based on processes that are about arousing feeling, where we arouse the feeling by hijacking a legitimate issue, and then whipping up the crowd in fear of that issue.

So, the question is: **am I willing to die for justice?**

If you are willing to die for justice, don't die for it, but live for it!

MCCARTHYISM IS A VIOLATION OF THE GODDESS

I'm going to give you another example: McCarthyism.

McCarthyism was against communism—and communism was a hugely important issue to be against. Communism had killed tens of millions of people in the world. Communism, in various forms, had been the single most brutal, repressive force in human history.

- ◆ **Communism was built on noble goals.** Most of the Jewish intellectuals in New York were communists in the 1930s, and they were affiliated with the Communist Party, because **the**

rhetoric of communism was beautiful, and seemed at least similar in part to the rhetoric of the prophets).

+ But **the actions of communism were pure brutal Stalinesque horror,** repeated again and again (in Ukraine, for example, killing 5 million people in forced starvation, in the process of *collectivization* of their land and farms).

McCarthy, who was a United States senator, takes this legitimate issue, and uses it to whip up the madness of crowds (using the newspapers—this is before the internet). **But what's actually driving him is all sorts of personal pathology, all sorts of personal agendas, all sorts of power issues.**

The entire McCarthyite attack on many, many, many people takes place in a democratic society—because everyone steps back, and no one's willing to stand up to it.

Why is no one willing to stand up? **Everyone steps back to protect themselves, and no one actually takes a stand.**

Now, there's a new term, *sexual McCarthyism,* when we use, for example, our correct fury at sexual harassment, and our correct fury at patterns of sexual abuse—and we create **Sexual McCarthyism.** In other words, **just like we used the fear and anger and outrage against communism, we use the legitimate outrage against, let's say, sexual harassment, to whip up the madness of crowds, and to actually become McCarthyite.** Meaning, we hide all sorts of hidden agendas, and all sorts of hidden motivations, under the veneer of protecting victims, or whatever the veneer is. That's called Sexual McCarthyism.

McCarthyism means you take a legitimate issue, you hijack that issue and you use it for the most abrasive human motives, to suspend the process of evaluating information, to suspend the process of evidence, and to suspend the process of justice.

All of this is a violation of Lady Justice. This is a great violation of the Goddess.

41

CULTIVATING DISCERNMENT: WE NEED TO AROUSE OURSELVES TO CREATE A NEW PUBLIC COMMONS

How do we now seduce ourselves, and arouse ourselves, to be able to do **discernment**? We have to arouse ourselves to sensemaking.

First, I've got to know: *What am I willing to die for?*

That was our first step. We saw on the beaches of Normandy, these boys—Lori's dad being one of them—being willing to die for justice. It wasn't quite coherent in their mind, it was more of a visceral knowing, and it was a cultural knowing.

I'm not talking about each individual boy from Montana, but **these boys were willing to die for justice.** That's unbelievable, and we are in their debt. Their willingness to die for justice defeated Nazism, and created this world that each one of us live in.

So that's step one: I've got to now identify what am I willing to die for? *I'm willing to die for justice.*

Two, **then I don't *die* for it, I live for it.** So I've got to *live* for justice.

But justice—that's the core of the American way—means:

- How I gather information
- How I do evaluation
- How we actually create fairness and integrity in our public spaces

That's number two.

Number three, **we don't get lost in the pseudo-ecstasies of the Salem Witch Trials, but do careful, case by case, information-gathering.**

We are careful not to get caught in these contagious memes, in which we accuse a woman—who is sexually or intellectually or spiritually postconventional in some way, or who's threatening to the community—and then burn her at the stake.

We prevent people with hidden ulterior motives from arousing witch hunts.

Because we begin to cultivate discernment.

Cultivating discernment is such a big deal. It is a move from the premodern pseudo-ecstasies of the pre-rational, into this evolutionary leap into the rational.

Here's the thing: around the world, both the far right and the far left:

- They are abandoning civil discourse
- They are abandoning a baseline of facts
- They are abandoning how we actually *talk* to each other, and do point-counterpoint, and actually evaluate information

Of course, we don't call people witches now, we call them sociopaths, because we are in a psychological world and not a religious world. **But we're actually destroying our public culture,**

- We are destroying the conversation of public culture
- We are destroying the public commons

That's the true tragedy of the commons today. And we need to arouse ourselves to create a new public commons.

A new public ethos.

A new public culture.

We need to evolve public culture in a real and substantive way.

THE MURDER OF EROS

Now, I'm just going to do one last step, just to complete this for you, so we can actually *see* this, and *feel* this, and *know* this.

I want to give you an example of discernment.

We have talked a lot about it, I want to do just this last second of it. Just going to give you one example. I actually took some notes this morning, I wrote like 10 pages, I'm just going to do one.

How do we discern? How do you know the difference between:

- something that seems to be a legitimate issue, and
- something that is *disguised* as a legitimate issue, but actually, there's a whole set of ulterior agendas that are behind it; a whole set of motivators, a whole set of players, which stay invisible?

It's very hard to know. How do you know that?

We live in a world which is filled with attack and scandal, so how do you know when these things happen?

I am going to give you an example which some of you are not going to like, and I apologize for it, but it's a very good example.

Andrew Cuomo, who was the governor of New York—he's a complex politician. He was a kind of hard ass, tough, disliked by an enormous amount of people. Other people thought it was enormously effective. A complicated politician with a long record of service, and a long record of controversy.

Andrew Cuomo, during COVID, became really a symbol, and an American hero. He did these incredible press conferences, he was unbelievable. They were famous in Holland as well, they were just wild.

He was unbelievable, in an unbelievable moment. Lots of people wanted him to run for President. He was talking to his brother Chris Cuomo, who was an anchor on CNN, and there was an enormous sense of warmth, and love, and all of that. About a year later, Andrew Cuomo was no longer governor of New York—**and there had been a spate of accusations of sexual harassment, from 9–10 people.**

If you look at those accusations clearly, they were not substantive—most of them have been thrown out already. He had very clear and cogent responses to them.

But where did they come from? Did they just appear?

He had been a politician for several decades, he was known to hug people, and to kiss people at weddings, etc. Everyone knew who Cuomo was, everyone knew his classical old school style. Most people thought he had great integrity. He clearly wasn't known as a womanizer, but he was known to have a certain kind of interaction which was not politically correct in the modern world, but which should in no way be termed "sexual harassment".

All of a sudden, he becomes this major hero in the United States, madly loved. **He incarnates Eros.** Then a process kicks in, which is called **the murder of Eros.** He has to be taken down! Those 10–12 complaints did not appear out of nowhere; they were organized. There was a campaign; people were in tandem with each other, people checked with each other, people talked to each other.

It was a carefully organized spontaneity that went to take Andrew Cuomo down.

Now, I am not Andrew Cuomo's press spokesperson. I have not investigated each of these cases, although I read as much information as I could on every one of them. But we in the United States, lost one of the best Democratic politicians, who could have effectively articulated democratic politics, and who could have challenged the Trump MAGA move that's happened in the United States.

But he got destroyed. He got destroyed on what most commentators at this point feel were either trumped up or close to absurd claims.

Now, was there one person, or were there a dozen?

There's always a dozen—because people are in touch with each other.

Because you find the disgruntled people, because you find the angry people, because you find the disaffected people. **The person who wrote the report about Cuomo, the Attorney General of the State of New York, announced her intention to run for governor against him—and yet she's writing a report about him!**

It's kind of a strange situation… The assumption was that once Cuomo resigned the governorship, he cannot come back. *There is no redemption, we can never allow Cuomo to come back again.* It's like, wow!

You have to cultivate discernment to see what's actually happening here.

There was no trial, there was no genuine point-counterpoint that was allowed.

There was a process, and the process was evaluated based on public opinion, based on Twitter threads and Facebook threads.

It was based on trying to create a certain kind of pseudo-eros explosion of anger in the public sphere. And we lost a very, very important public servant! Now, I am just giving you one example. **But no one points out that this was not spontaneous, that this was organized and careful.**

HOW DO WE DISCERN?

To cultivate discernment, we need to ask:

- How is this happening?
- Where is this coming from?
- Is this a false flag?

Not to be conspiratorial—but not to let your opinion be determined by Twitter threads either. **I want to offer you four litmus tests that are tried and true, so that you know how to discern whether what's going on in the public culture is real, or whether it's a madness of crowds.**

46

Here are the four litmus tests. When people are attacked in the public sphere, you have to ask:

1—Before action was taken, was there a fair process of fact-checking, investigation, talking to both sides, before the person was fired?

Johnny Depp was fired *immediately*, as socn as Amber Heard wrote a column about him a few years ago. No one checked, there was no interest in checking. Once she wrote the column, the assumption was *Johnny's an abuser.*

Obviously, Johnny Depp is a complex person, so it played into his complexity, and Johnny Depp lost an enormous amount.

Now, I don't think we need to cry for Johnny Depp. But the point was, **it all happened before there was any fair checking of information.** That's one.

If something happens before there is fair checking of information, and before evidence is considered on both sides—that's the first thing you have to look for.

2—What if new evidence comes to the fore?

If new evidence comes to the fore, are people willing to consider it, or are people uninterested?

For example, with Andrew Cuomo: an enormous amount of new information gradually started to emerge, and his stance became much more deeply supported. But once he's gone, **no one's willing to look at it again, there's no willingness to consider new information.**

3—Is the person who's being attacked being demonized?

Is there a **demonization** happening?

Is there a **dehumanization** happening?

Do we begin to talk about the person as if they're not a human being, so that we actually cannot feel them?

4—Is there the assumption in the public space that there is no room for resolution, it can never be resolved?

Is there an assumption that whatever "judgment" occurred in the "court" of the pseudo-ecstasies of the digital, or what we now call "public opinion", there's no ability to return?

It can never be resolved?

There's no redemption?

There's no liberation?

It is never over.

So, these are four litmus tests:

1. Judgment and action taken before there is a fair process of fact-checking.
2. If new evidence emerges, no one's willing to consider it.
3. Demonization or dehumanization.
4. No possibility for it to be ever healed or solved.

Those are four discernments we can use to understand what's going on—a legitimate public outrage, which sometimes has enormous importance in a democracy, or is something else happening under the veneer of public outrage. That distinction is enormously important.

A PRAYER FOR JUSTICE

I just want to ask a question here.

How many people have a sense of why this matters, what it means to arouse ourselves to discernment and creating a new public culture? **And why this matters so much?**

The boys on that beach in Normandy, they died for this.

It's very easy to lose track of what they died for.

They died for this! They died so that we could actually do discernments in a democracy, that we could stand for Lady Justice, that we could be in service of the Divine Feminine, who is Lady Justice.

If we get lost in human potential platitudes, or woke platitudes, or far right platitudes, if we lose track of just our core ability to arouse ourselves to justice—to do careful judgment, and to do careful information-gathering— **then we have defaced the Goddess.**

That's where I wanted to get today, and—paradoxically—**that's the beginning of self-seduction.**

I've got to seduce myself out of my torporific slumber, out of my sleep, and arouse myself to discernment.

I just want to thank everyone for staying with it, and for being inside, and for just showing up in the beautiful way that we do.

Let's just have, for a second, a prayer for justice.

Let's just pray for justice for all the people who don't have justice.

There's a project called the Innocence Project.

There're so many people who can't afford lawyers, so many people who have been murdered in the court system, and murdered in the public culture system.

All of them, their hearts have been ripped out.

This is a moment I feel we need to stand for justice:

- We need to stand for fact-checking,
- We need to stand for Lady Justice,
- We need to stand for the Divine Feminine.

So I'm just offering a prayer:

> To give power and hope to all the people who've been mis-judged,
>
> To give power and hope to all the people who've been demonized,
>
> To give power and hope to all the people whose hearts have been ripped out,
>
> To give power and hope to all the people who've been dehumanized.
>
> To commit to those boys who died on the beaches of Normandy, and who died in in Europe, to stand against Nazism.

For the boys in Ukraine, the men and women in the Ukraine, who are fighting for freedom, and fighting for the fair processes of information-gathering, who are standing for us.

Glory to our heroes—we're in your debt!

This episode of *One Mountain, Many Paths* was for you.

We pray for you, and we stand for you, and we're holding hands with you all the way.

CHAPTER THREE

EROS AND EXISTENTIAL RISK: 21 STEPS TO HOMO AMOR— MY TRANSFORMATION IS THE TRANSFORMATION OF THE WHOLE

Episode 296 — June 12, 2022

THE HOLY BAND: A VISION OF A PLANETARY AWAKENING IN UNIQUE SELF SYMPHONY

I am so madly delighted to be here. I have tears in my eyes. We got together right before the broadcast with the inner team that does so much fantastic creative joy-work-vision in creating *One Mountain* and I was just so happy to see everyone and in the choice that we make to be here together.

To know each other, to love each other, to be together, and to be the revolution.

And to stand at the very core of the revolution as a band of Outrageous Lovers, and to envision what's possible in the world.

In every generation, there has been what the interior sciences call the *chevraya*. **The *chevraya* means the holy band; the band of Outrageous Lovers.**

53

Sometimes it is translated from the Aramaic as *the companions*. The companions are usually a group—sometimes it's three people, sometimes it's eight, sometimes it's a few dozen—**who are at the core of a transformation of consciousness that is living at the periphery of society.** It is not in the center of the mainstream, it's at the periphery.

Imagine: at the time of Jesus, in Jerusalem, the center of society was the Roman procurator Pontius Pilate. The wealthy and the powerful, even in the Jewish community, were very much Hellenistic—meaning, they had, in some sense, assimilated and abandoned the vision of the revolution for the sake of power. For the sake of ephemeral, but seductive—in the sense of *unholy seduction*.

The seductive call of the siren—of superficial status, and superficial success, of instrumental climbing—which actually can never bring us joy.

It leaves us empty. It leaves us hollow—a form of pseudo-Eros which leaves us with incessant cravings that cannot be filled by the pallid fare— un-nourishing, almost repulsive in its aftertaste... The utter, bloated consumption of pseudo-Eros.

And then there was this band in Jerusalem—it happened to be a bunch of Jews—gathered around a teacher. They were all teachers, actually. In the new vision, they were all teachers, and they gathered, and there was a crucifixion.

At the crucifixion, how many people were there?

So few, right? The parties were going on, and the revelry went on, and the powers of Rome went on, and that band held strong—they had a vision. **They had a vision of a planetary Pentecost, to use the Christian word.**

We call it today a planetary awakening in love through Unique Self Symphonies. Barbara Marx Hubbard, my dear evolutionary whole-mate— and I know you're listening right now, Barbara—together, we called that planetary Pentecost **a vision of a planetary awakening in Unique Self**

Symphonies. That group of people, those few dozen people, they come together—and they hold a vision.

They hold a vision of something that's possible.

They hold the vision of the possibility of possibility, of a world that can't quite yet be seen, of a fragrance of a new human and a new humanity, of the possibility of *Homo sapiens* becoming *Homo amor*.

It's a vision of Eros, because **pseudo-Eros itself is the very source of existential risk**.

I want to share with you in, a couple of minutes, a vision of this Eros. But before that, I just want to feel if I can, with permission, everyone, *what it means to come together.* **What does it mean, to come together, and why are we coming together?**

We are coming together because we are poised in this moment between utopia and dystopia, between a world more beautiful than we could possibly imagine—and a world that's crushed, in which upgraded algorithms control everything in dystopian metaverses, as Facebook becomes Meta.

The world decided Facebook is not a good thing, and Facebook decided the world is not a good thing. Facebook's response was: *"Well, actually, the world is not a good thing. Let's actually get rid of the world and go virtual."*

Think about that, what does it mean to enter a metaverse, which is disembodied *at its core*, in which every single movement is measured computationally, so **you have literally commodified all of Reality?** *Every move you make, and every breath you take, we'll be watching you, we'll be tracking you; we'll be computing, and measuring, and quantifying.*

Every single move you make becomes transactional in the service—not of a greater good, but in the service of direct or indirect profit for the people who are actually controlling the metaverse. **Pseudo-Eros in the extreme!**

That's one dystopian vision of the future.

But there are other dystopian visions which involve actual **existential risk, which means there is actually no future at all,** and we are at the last generation of humanity. Those dystopian visions are real.

Then there are other visions that involve catastrophic risk, and **catastrophic risk means massive suffering or death to billions.**

At the core of these risks is a set of structural factors that are happening right now:

- Extraction models—extracting resources from the earth that it took billions of years to create.
- Exponential growth curves, which are in place in order to meet rivalrous conflicts governed by win/lose metrics.
- Developing certain forms of AI (Artificial Intelligence) technology that should not be developed, which are being developed anyways because there's a race to the bottom. Multipolar traps: "I know you're going to develop it, so I better do it so that you don't." Win/lose metrics.

All of it is happening as everyone is focused on the short-term. **All the long-term structural things are at play in creating the seeds of potential destruction, and everyone looks away.** Everyone looks away—not because they are bad, but because no one quite knows what to do about it.

No one quite knows what to address, because there is no shared grammar of value.

Because we are not living in a shared Story of Value that would allow us to overcome the global intimacy disorder, which undermines our ability for global resonance, which then undermines our ability for global coordination—which is what we need in order to enact global solutions to every one of these global existential risks.

But at the core, what is driving it? Underneath all of it, what is driving it?

What's driving it is a collapse of Eros.

56

EROS MEANS THE UNBEARABLE GOODNESS OF BEING AND THE UNBEARABLE NEED FOR ME, FOR MY LIFE, FOR WHO I AM

Eros means that I live in a shared Story of Value in which I *experience* that shared Story of Value:

- I have an immediate and direct experience of the **goodness** of Reality
- I have an immediate and direct experience of the **beauty** of Reality
- I have an immediate and direct experience of the **truth** of Reality

I understand that everything is connected to everything, and that those everything-s that are connected are not interconnected *its*, but it is **an interconnected, pulsing, throbbing, living organism.**

That every one of us is a cell in that organism, even as **we are irreducibly unique and individuated.**

That each of us are individuated expressions of that organism with irreducible dignity, and **each of us have a gift to give** that addresses a unique need in that larger organism. That unique need lives in **our unique circle of intimacy and influence**, a need that could be addressed directly by us. And that addressing—that gift that's ours to give—is **the great joy of our lives.** That's what Eros means. Eros means the experience, number one, that is good right now; and number two, that I have purpose, that I have need, that I have meaning, that I have a gift to give that's desperately needed by the whole. These are the two dimensions of Eros:

- Number one: the irreducible goodness of being, the unbearable goodness of being
- Number two: the unbearable necessity, the need, for me, for my life, for who I am. I'm desperately needed!

That's what Eros means.

When Eros isn't there, you have pseudo-Eros. When you can't live in that Story of Value, you have pseudo-Eros.

Are you willing to step into the mystical interior scientific significance of your life, in which you say:

I'm joining the band of Outrageous Lovers. I'm going to make my life matter so much, because I understand that I live in the field of the whole, and I actually have a glimpse of fragrance of enlightened consciousness, which every great system of interior science realized, which means I actually experience that the whole lives in me. I live in the Intimate Universe, I live in the whole; it's all interconnected. But I have this realization, the sense that the whole actually also lives in me. **It's all in me, so I can feel the whole.**

That's why you can do mathematics. The unreasonable effectiveness of mathematics—how a mathematician can stretch and feel the whole Cosmos backwards and forwards, and express it in a mathematical formula—is because **the whole lives in me.**

I live in the Intimate Universe, and the Intimate Universe lives in me.

That's what *Homo amor* knows. That's what the Outrageous Lover knows.

So, I just wanted to gently ask you: *Are you willing to play a larger game, but for real?*

To actually step in and say:

I am in this band of Outrageous Lovers, and I am going to go out of my way.

I am going to inconvenience my small self, I am going to inconvenience my contracted self, I am going to inconvenience my ego self.

I am going to get underneath the public game that I am playing.

I am going to get underneath my attacking.

I just saw a blog of somebody, who basically spends his time attacking influencers in order to become one. But he doesn't tell that he's trying to become an influencer. In other words, the pseudo-Erotic craving for attention, as the person self-righteously (Joseph McCarthy style) attacks influencers; dog-piles information, distorts, lies. But really what they are doing is—it is actually a desperate move of pseudo-Eros: *I'm going to attack, and I'm going to attack influencers because I desperately crave to be like them.*

Everyone's got their hidden little strategy.

Can I give that up?

Can I give up that small, contracted, coiled, desperate craving—and actually step into the goodness of my life?

The goodness of my Unique Self, the unbearable joy of my existence, and the knowing that actually, I *do* have a gorgeous contribution to make.

I've got a song to sing, a poem to write.

I've got a way of laughing, living, loving, and being and becoming in the world, that never was, is, or will be, other than through me.

My instrument is desperately needed in the Unique Self Symphony, as I play and listen to all the other instruments, and feel the interconnectivity of all with the All.

That's Eros.

We get a fragrance of it in sexuality.

We get a fragrance of it in creativity.

We get a fragrance of it in transformation.

We get a fragrance of it in innovation.

We get a fragrance of it in service.

So, are we ready? I want to ask you, band of Outrageous Lovers—tears in my eyes: *Are we ready?*

Where are we in Jerusalem?

- **Are we with the Roman procurators in the games of politics and surface power?** Often, we're disguising ourselves as the righteous rescuers when actually, we are the predators. Are we speaking pretty words, and dressing ourselves up with the charades of pretty costumes of righteousness, but actually, we are driven by a kind of naked emptiness?
- **Or are we willing to step into our Eros, and feel the pulse of Reality quite literally moving through us?** To go on a psychedelic journey of unbearable joy, where we feel the joy pulse of Cosmos awake and alive in us?

When I'm no longer in pseudo-eros, I step into Eros. And when we democratize that experience, it's not just the experience of *a master here, or a master there*. All masters are, by the way, broken, and all masters are imperfect vessels for the light.

So, when I say "master", I don't mean the perfect one. I mean **those who are willing to lay their lives on the line to feel that pulse, and that's all of us.** It's not one master, it's not two. We've got to move beyond the old vision of the master, we've got to become masters together. We've got to create a Unique Self Symphony.

It's not about Jesus anymore. It's about the Unique Self Symphony.

But the Unique Self Symphony is often at the periphery of culture. Are we willing to move from the feasts in Jerusalem, 2,000 years ago?

The Jerusalem of today means you're *Shalem*: full consciousness.

Are we ready to stand by the cross, or the Magen David, or the Buddhist symbol, or the secular humanist symbol?

Are we ready to stand in value?

Are we ready to join the band of Outrageous Lovers, to know that *my transformation is the transformation of the whole?*

That's the experience, that's the knowing of *Homo amor.*

TWENTY-ONE STEPS TO HOMO AMOR

The *knowing* of *Homo amor*, here it is:

1. Reality is evolution.
2. Evolution is the process of becoming.
3. Underneath becoming is being, the utter goodness of Cosmos.
4. Becoming is the process of transformation.
5. Reality is a series of transformations.
6. We've come now to the human level of Reality, and the human level of Reality has gone through transformation after transformation, many of them have brought unbearable joy. **But our exponential technologies have also brought us to a place of unbearable risk to our very existence.**
7. This requires a new transformation. Like always, **a crisis is an evolutionary driver, and a crisis is always a crisis of intimacy.**
8. The crisis of intimacy today, **this global intimacy disorder, is that we are not living together—7.8 billion of us—in a shared Story of Value.**
9. We are clashing into each other in win/lose metrics, in desperate moves to be seen, desperate gambits for power and status— but we are doing it now with exponentialized and weaponized technologies.
10. Those technologies are available to rogue players, to non-state actors. **There's a race to the bottom, we are producing that which can destroy us.**
11. How do we shift that? **We shift that by articulating a new Story of Value**, and that new Story of Value is not held by an elite.

12. The new Story of Value lives in the new human and the new humanity. **We actually birth a new structure of consciousness in the world.** That's what we did with democracy. A thousand years ago, democracy didn't exist, it was a joke. There was no possibility that there would be governance through something called *democracy*. But today it exists. That's how the evolution of consciousness takes place.

13. This new Story of Value is the emergence of *Homo sapiens* as *Homo amor*, where we understand that **the whole lives in us even as we live in the whole**, and that, actually, my transformation is the leading-edge of evolution.

14. Because who am I? **I *am* evolution.** Evolution is not a fact out there. Evolution is a process that is the actual structure of Cosmos, which I am an expression of. **The evolutionary impulse doesn't live out there, the evolutionary impulse lives in me.**

15. I am a unique expression of the evolutionary impulse, and so the process of evolution which is a series of transformations is taking place in me.

16. **My transformation is the transformation of the whole.** My transformation transforms the whole. *Like, wow! Can we begin to feel it?* My transformation actually transforms the whole.

17. I am willing to be one of those who joins the band of Outrageous Lovers, and says, "I'm willing to lay my life down, not to give it up, but to live it in a way where I actually understand that I'm the superhero. I'm actually the superhero. It's not Superman, I'm the superhero." One of the things I love about superhero movies is that superheroes are becoming more human, more flawed, more complex. They are holding the holy and broken Hallelujah.

18. *I might have skipped 18, but let's make it 19.*

19. I am the superhero, I am in the band of Outrageous Lovers. **I'm stepping up and stepping in. I'm waking up, I'm growing up, I'm showing up.** And I understand that, as *Homo amor*, my transformation matters.

20. My transformation is the transformation of the whole. Now, when that realization moves from a very small band of the elite—the masters in every generation who understood that they were *axis mundi* (what the Sufis called "the pole that connected heaven and earth")—so when that realization moves beyond an elite group of masters, **we actually manifest together this new human and a new humanity, which expresses itself as a planetary awakening in love through Unique Self Symphonies.**

21. This means the democratization of enlightenment. **When we join the band of Outrageous Lovers together, existential risk disappears.**

Because the extraction model recedes.

Because the multipolar traps, all of a sudden, seem ridiculous.

Because we step into a shared Story of Value.

Because we can actually stand in value and challenge that which is against the greater good.

We can, for example, create a new Digital Communications Act, like we did a hundred years ago when radio began in the world, which would transform social media into what the old legal precedents demanded. Brandeis's decision and Frankfurter's decision in the courts in America— just like radio needed to be for the public good, **social media is not just a privatized, neutralized effort at technology, it is a public service that has to be for the public good.** We can actually create a Digital Communications Act, adopted universally around the world, which changes social media from the divisive polarizing force, into a force that's for the public good. It is complex maneuver, and utterly necessary, Digital Communications Act.

There's a thousand things we can do when we have a shared grammar of value. We can do this!

So, every week we come together here on One Mountain to speak this revolution.

63

Are we ready to play a larger game? Are we ready? Are we ready to actually be the band of Outrageous Lovers, and to participate together in the evolution of love?

That's what we are here for.

In this generation, this is ours to do. When I say "ours to do", I mean in concert with all the great people and forces around the world, the wonderful, gorgeous people. But there's not a lot of us. There are few people who can actually see around the corner. This is not a grandiose claiming. **This is a desperate, beautiful, radically joyous, awake realization, that we need to be like da Vinci in the Renaissance.** I have pointed out a thousand times what Paul Tillich, the cultural critic and thinker, points out—that there were about a thousand people at the core of the Renaissance.

This is the moment in which there's a crisis of intimacy, and that crisis needs to be met by a new evolution of intimacy. The crisis is an evolutionary driver, and the new emerging needs to be *Homo amor,* a new experience of what it means to be a human being. The move from pseudo-Eros to Eros, where we all gather in the public square, and we seduce ourselves to our own greatness.

We seduce ourselves to our own greatness! We confess our greatness

---

This is the core of One Mountain. It's the core of the band of Outrageous Lovers. It's the core of the *chevraya*: the companions, again, translating from the Aramaic. It's the core of what Philip Wexler, in a wonderful book, calls the mystical society.

ODE TO JOY: AN ACTIVE MEDITATION

I want to show you a vision of it, which we looked at about a year or a year and a half ago. I thought about it this morning when I was thinking about *One Mountain*, and it really captures everything.

We are going to go to a scene in Italy. I want to take a look at the relationship of Eros to pseudo-Eros, and how Eros responds directly to existential risk. How do you invoke Eros?

Remember, there are two parts to Eros. One part of Eros is the experience that it's already good right now; the intrinsic goodness of being, the unbearable goodness of being. That's one. It's the opposite of Milan Kundera's *Unbearable Lightness of Being*, it's the **unbearable goodness of being.** That's number one. Number two: **I've got a unique gift, and that unique gift makes music in the Unique Self Symphony.**

I want to ask everyone, if you can—we are going to do this as a practice—to watch every face carefully, and then we are going to have a discussion in the chat box about what happened. Then we are going to go into prayer, and Krista is going to take us into a particular song, a particular way of making this alive.

So who is ready to go to Italy?

Let's take a journey. Let's go to Italy.

I'm going to ask everyone, as we go to Italy: *Hold your attention.*

Hold your attention.

Place your attention in the center.

Don't get distracted.

Be the master of your attention.

Step inside.

We are doing a meditation here, it's what is called *an active meditation.*

It's not that we are going into silence, **we are going into actually *watching*, actually *seeing* what's happening in front of us.**

We are going to Italy.

We are going to meditate in Italy.

It's what Dalai Lama said to me, he said, *it's an act of meditation: watch every face, watch what happens.*

We are on the inside together, band of Outrageous Lovers. Here we go. Italy, coming at us.

[Clip: Flash mob—Ode to Joy]

WITNESSING THE EXTERIORS

Now what just happened?

But stay close, what was that?

They are sitting there in a square in Italy, maybe near Firenze. What happens?

I'm going to track the chat box. What was that?

Don writes: *music carries the words, hearts opened, joy, connection, allurement, symphonizing; Unique Self Symphony.*

Yes, totally. But we are going to practice now slowly.

Let's go one step at a time.

In order to know what happened, you have to start on the outside, and then go to the inside.

There are exteriors and interiors. First, just start in the beginning, **what were the exteriors?** How did it start?

A child puts a piece of money. Just the facts, what happened?

The child, who was the child, was it a boy or a girl? It was a girl.

About how old was she? *Let's collect the moment.* She was about five, six, seven, or eight.

She goes up to a man. *Go slow.*

She goes up to a man: he is bald, about middle age.

What was he wearing? A man 50–60, dressed kind of classically.

He was the one person in the whole place who wears a tuxedo, so you know that something is happening.

She puts a little money in his hat, and she looks: what's going to happen?

That little girl lives in us.

That little girl is us who puts a little piece of money in the hat and wants to see what's going to happen, what's going to come out of that hat?

Now, did you see?

She is curious, someone wrote, *and he was already playing his instrument.* Did you see the little twinkle in his eye? There was a little light. **There is a twinkle in his eye, and it begins.**

Then, who was the second person who joined, anyone saw the second person?

A lady. A woman with a cello.

She joins, and she does it very quietly. About how old is she? She's probably also about 50. She joins, and then she starts playing. She joins.

Now, is she wearing a tuxedo? No, no tuxedo there.

Is anyone else in the whole scene wearing evening clothes that you wear to Symphony? Nope, everyone's wearing these very ordinary clothes.

Then one person joins, and then another person, and then another person. Then you see people watching, somebody looks up.

A young child looks up.

An old woman looks up.

A group of boys: *wow, what's that?*

Slowly, another person, and another person joins, and another person and another person looks up and they see: *wow, what's this?*

Now, **lots of people didn't quite** know how to be there, so they did what people do today.

When you don't know how to be there, what do you do? You take a picture.

You hold up your phone to watch it—which is actually sweet and beautiful. Not bad people, beautiful. ***But it is a way of not being there.***

Does everyone get what I mean?

- ◆ We think that if we didn't record it, if it doesn't appear on social media, if we cannot forward it to somebody else, it didn't happen. That's the tragedy of the commodified society. We are never here in the fullness of the moment.
- ◆ We are actually asking ourselves a question: did we create a social media post, can we forward this?
- ◆ We are actually never *present*. And a life that's not public, and recorded, and doesn't get a certain number of likes, and a certain amount of attention, is considered to be not a life.

That's how you get to the *Metaverse*, in which you live in a truly commodified Reality. Does everyone get this? Like, wow!

That's why, **when you travel, leave your camera behind! Show up in the eternity of the moment.**

MUSIC IS A KEY TO EXPERIENCING THE INSIDE WHICH IS JOY

Let's go back to our square in Firenze. There we are, everyone is there.

Slowly, everybody comes together. And what do they experience?

... Schiller's words to Beethoven's Symphony, *Ode to Joy*.

An die Freude	Ode to Joy
Freude, schöner Götterfunken, Tochter aus Elysium, Wir betreten feuertrunken, Himmlische, dein Heiligtum! Deine Zauber binden wieder Was die Mode streng geteilt; Alle Menschen werden Brüder. Wo dein sanfter Flügel weilt.	Joy, beautiful spark of Divinity [or: of gods], Daughter of Elysium, We enter, drunk with fire, Heavenly one, thy sanctuary! Thy magic binds again What custom strictly divided; All people become brothers, Where thy gentle wing abides.
Wem der große Wurf gelungen Eines Freundes Freund zu sein; Wer ein holdes Weib errungen Mische seinen Jubel ein! Ja, wer auch nur eine Seele Sein nennt auf dem Erdenrund! Und wer's nie gekonnt, der stehle Weinend sich aus diesem Bund!	Whoever has succeeded in the great attempt, To be a friend's friend, Whoever has won a lovely woman, Add his to the jubilation! Yes, and also whoever has just one soul To call his own in this world! And he who never managed it should slink Weeping from this union!

Freude trinken alle Wesen An den Brüsten der Natur; Alle Guten, alle Bösen Folgen ihrer Rosenspur. Küsse gab sie uns und Reben, Einen Freund, geprüft im Tod; Wollust ward dem Wurm gege- ben und der Cherub steht vor Gott.	All creatures drink of joy At nature's breasts. All the Just, all the Evil Follow her trail of roses. Kisses she gave us and grapevines, A friend, proven in death. Ecstasy was given to the worm And the cherub stands before God.
Froh, wie seine Sonnen fliegen Durch des Himmels prächt'gen Plan Laufet, Brüder, eure Bahn, Freudig, wie ein Held zum Siegen.	Gladly, as His suns fly through the heavens' grand plan Go on, brothers, your way, Joyful, like a hero to victory.
Seid umschlungen, Millionen! Diesen Kuß der ganzen Welt! Brüder, über›m Sternenzelt Muß ein lieber Vater wohnen. Ihr stürzt nieder, Millionen? Ahnest du den Schöpfer, Welt? Such' ihn über›m Sternenzelt! Über Sternen muß er wohnen.	Be embraced, Millions! This kiss to all the world! Brothers, above the starry canopy There must dwell a loving Father. Are you collapsing, millions? Do you sense the creator, world? Seek him above the starry canopy! Above stars must He dwell

What happens?

All of a sudden, this square is transformed into shimmering joy.

- ◆ Now, did anyone in the square win the lottery?
- ◆ Did anyone solve a relationship issue happening at home?
- ◆ Did anyone have great sex?
- ◆ Did anyone get a promotion at work?
- ◆ Did anyone have some problem in their life solved?

None of that happened! Does everyone get that? None of that happened, and yet, everyone stepped into joy.

Let me ask you a question.

Was there only a particular group of people that stepped into joy?

No. Everyone, everyone, everyone stepped fully into joy.

It is so beautiful, *Ode to Joy.*

We enter, Daughters of Elysium, which is the great mystery in the Greek tradition. *We enter, drunk with fire. Heavenly one, thy sanctuary! Thy magic.* It's complete magic! *Thy magic binds again*—your magic binds means "brings us together"—*what custom strictly divided.*

Does everyone see what happens in that? *What custom divided*—meaning all of the win/lose metrics, all of the conventions that divided everyone in the square. Everyone was locked in their own rivalrous conflict win/lose metrics, contracted, Separate-Self life. Then,

... drunk with fire,

> *We enter again your sanctuary.*
>
> *The magic binds what custom divided,*
>
> *and all people become brothers and sisters*
>
> *where your gentle wing abides.*
>
> *Whoever has succeeded in this great attempt,*
>
> *to be a friend's friend.*

This is what it's about—it is about a jubilation. That's what we do every week at *One Mountain.* We are actually stepping into this union.

THE JOY WAS ALWAYS THERE

Now, what stepped them in? How did they get inside?

They were seduced.

It was a seduction. It was a holy seduction.

That's what we're talking about here: *it was a holy seduction.*

Imagine Reality. Reality has its exteriors. But in every second of Reality, in every moment, there's a door. It's an invisible door, but it's always there. **That door has a key, and you can open that door, and music is one of the ways to open that door.**

Music is a key, and Outrageous Love is a key. You place the key of Outrageous Love, or the key of music, or the key of practice through meditation, or the key of studying a sacred text, or the most powerful key—which is the key of coming together as a band of Outrageous Lovers, and loving each other outrageously for the sake of the evolution of love.

You place a key in that door, and you open the door, and you step inside, and **you realize that joy was always there.** You open the door, and you realize that you have always been inside!

- That it has always been an Ode to Joy.
- That every place you've been, you needed to be.
- That no one is an extra on the set, and no action was unnecessary.
- That all of eternity resides in every moment, and every human being participates in the continuity of consciousness and an immortality.
- That all of Reality reaches for its own wholeness in every second, and that is the true nature of what is.
- That we don't need to look for the meaning of life—because there's nothing to search for, it's right here, and available right now in its utter fullness for its own sake.
- That all men and women are brothers and sisters.

Was anyone excluded from that circle?

I ask you, my friends, *was anyone excluded from that circle?*

No one. Did anyone in that circle win anything in the win/lose metrics? Was there one thing in the rivalrous conflict governed by win/lose metrics, in that square in Firenze, or wherever it was? Nothing! Yet, **everyone opened the door and stepped into the Infinity of Intimacy, the field of joy.**

That is what we are here together to do. We are here together as a band of Outrageous Lovers. We are coming together this summer at the Festival, to enact a Story of Value, which democratizes enlightenment, which invites every person to take up their instrument in the Unique Self Symphony.

You might think that the only people playing their instrument in that square were the musicians. But **they were actually infused with love, blown open with love, by everybody around them.** Each person who opened their heart made the music more clean, and more pure, and more wonderful.

Can you imagine, could they have done that piece of music in a basement someplace by themselves? No, they couldn't have done it the same way. They could have played the music. **But this piece of music, this moment, this joy, needed every single person, every child.** Did you see that child who was on the pole? Did you see that guy, that older guy who was kind of unshaven, who said, *wow*?

Then *everyone was weeping from this union*; tears of joy, weeping from this union. We need to create that Symphony in every city, in every town, in every language. But we cannot just do it through Beethoven's *Ode to Joy*.

IT ALL DEPENDS ON ME, AND IT ALL DEPENDS ON YOU

We have to write the Story of Value that creates that joy, which is **the story of Unique Self, which is the story of realizing that I am a unique expression of the Eros, the evolutionary impulse, that lives in me, as me, and through me.**

73

That my instrument, playing with other instruments, in a planetary awakening in love in Unique Self Symphony. That my transformation transforms the whole thing.

There are no evening clothes, there are no ordinary people—each one a superhero, each one gorgeous beyond imagination. Wow!

Then at that moment, every single person in that audience could look at each other and say, and know the truth of the following.

How could anyone ever tell you that you are anything less than beautiful?

How could anyone ever tell you that you are less than whole?

How could anyone fail to notice, band of Outrageous Lovers, that our loving is a miracle, and how deeply we're connected to each other's souls?

That's prayer!

Sometimes prayer is when I ask for everything, and we need to do that. We need to turn to the Infinity of Intimacy, and ask for everything. But there's another kind of prayer, which is called in the interior sciences, *v'ani tefillah*: **I am prayer**.

> *I just become prayer myself.*
>
> *I become prayer myself when I'm playing my instrument in the Unique Self Symphony,*
>
> *I am giving my gift,*
>
> *and I am in the unbearable goodness of being in this very moment.*

I want to ask everyone—if you're up for it, if you can, if you're willing—to weep from this union, and say:

It all depends on me.

It's a big deal!

That's not narcissism. It is knowing that you have a unique instrument in the Unique Self Symphony, that you and I together are *Homo amor*. That there is no guru. There could be teachers (I need a job)—but **the ultimate teacher is the Unique Self Symphony, it's all of us together**.

Knowing that my transformation is the transformation of the whole. So our symbol for that today is: *it all depends on me.* Then, the next sentence: **It all depends on you.** That's what it means. *It all depends on me, and it all depends on you.*

CHAPTER FOUR

ROE VS WADE: EVOLUTIONARY SENSEMAKING FROM POLARIZATION TO PARADOX—RE-ENTERING THE FIELD OF VALUE

Episode 298 — June 26, 2022

It's such a good moment, my friends, to be together.

In this good moment, there is Outrageous Pain, and in this good moment, there's Outrageous Love, and in this good moment, there's Outrageous Beauty.

I want to just share for a moment what we mean when we say "Outrageous". Because the word *Outrageous* is part of the core structure of the new Story of Value rooted in First Principles and First Values that we are formulating, articulating, and sharing as the primary response to existential and catastrophic risk in this moment of time between utopia and dystopia, as existential risk hovers in multiple vectors and as we need to respond. But first, let's look at the root cause of existential risk.

THE BREAKDOWN OF STORY OF VALUE IS THE ROOT CAUSE OF EXISTENTIAL RISK

We understand that, although infrastructure responses are important and valid, and social structure changes of laws, etc. are important and valid, they depend on *superstructure*.

This is a distinction from Marvin Harris, a Marxist theorist (Marxism is complex. And this distinction is excellent). **Superstructure is the worldview that society is rooted in. Superstructure is what we're calling the Story of Value that a society is rooted in.**

So, what we've done in the Think Tank of the Center for Integral Wisdom, is trace every major vector of existential and catastrophic risk to a breakdown in superstructure, meaning to a breakdown in the core Story of Value that animates society.

- ◆ For example, we looked at *MeToo*, with all of its beauty and all of its excesses
- ◆ When we look at masculine sexuality, with it's wild beauty and its excesses, which have expressed themselves for some men in sexual harassment
- ◆ When we look at the acting out that takes place within the context of feminine shadow in sexuality

Whatever the sexuality story is, if you look at the larger issues in culture(for example on college campuses),both in actuality, and the way it has been misreported—all of those issues are rooted in a fundamental breakdown in a Story of Value, which is: **we don't have a sexual narrative that meets our experience.**

That's just one example.

Therefore, the sexual experience causes enormous shame, and only by retelling the sexual story can we address those issues.

For example, in the Think Tank, we have spent several years on a project (it is now in the final stages). We have written 16 volumes on the phenomenology of sexuality. We have written what we hope is the great work in this generation on Eros, and Eros' relationship to love and to sexuality. Why? Because we have to retell the story.

This need to retell the story is not just true about sexuality.

- It's true about economics.
- It's true about immigration policy.
- It's true about methods of governance.
- It's true about how technology is enacted (technology is not merely a tool, but an environment, and how those environments of technology are enacted).

All of these dimensions are dependent on a prior Story of Value, and how we live in that Story of Value is how we show up, how we make policy, how we engage. **You can't just change policy, it's not going to work.**

Policy, in general, is about social structure, and often infrastructure (infrastructure is the structure of how things work; roads, technology environments are infrastructure). For example, healthcare programs are a mixture of infrastructure and social structure (because they're governed by a set of laws).

- Social structure is laws and contracts in society.
- Infrastructure is the actual planetary stack of society, how it works, transportation and technology in all of its forms.

So what we are saying is you cannot change the world based on infrastructure and social structure, *you need superstructure.*

And we are saying this differently than Marvin Harris would have said it, because he didn't understand the intrinsic nature of value.

But we are emerging out of his notion of superstructure and saying:

There is a story we live in.

It is a Story of Value. It is rooted in First Principles and First Values.

And we have to retell that story, because the story is what has broken down:

- Premodernity had stories of value connected to each of the great religions, which each claimed that its value was exclusive.
- Then, premodernity breaks down. We realize all the **religions are claiming a mutual exclusivity, it doesn't make sense to us**. Each one is saying that they've got the only source of value. Then, we go to modernity, and **modernity rejects these claims of intrinsic** value and many of its major expressions, and begins the articulation of value being as merely a social construction (that was the major strain in modernity, although not the only one)
- Then, that explodes in postmodernity, in which postmodernity argues for a complete deconstruction of all value.

For example, one popular historian parroting (or echoing) postmodernity says: *all value is a figment of your imagination, a social construct, a fiction.*

That's where we are today. We are at a moment in which the very notion of intrinsic value has been fundamentally undermined and fundamentally questioned.

Our own experience of value has been challenged as being but our own, coincidental, random, and ultimately meaningless—in any ultimate sense, meaningless—human projection. In a world which, ultimately, is *a tale told by an idiot, full of sounds and fury, signifying nothing.*

This breakdown of a Story of Value is the root cause of existential risk.

If we don't go to the root cause…

If we don't go back to source and actually reclaim a Story of Value…

A post-postmodern, meta-modern, Integral, a kind of new Story of Value, which can actually:

◆ Be told

◆ Be articulated

◆ Be scaled

◆ Be shared

◆ Reshape education, commerce, economics, politics (once it is shared)

That's the way it has always happened.

When da Vinci and his cohorts were in Florence in the Renaissance, and the Black Death pandemic had swept Europe, they understood that the only response that would be effective was to tell a new Story of Value.

That's what the Renaissance did.

The Renaissance was like today; we are at a time between worlds, a time between stories.

And what did da Vinci and his cohorts do, about a thousand of them? (As I have mentioned probably a thousand times here, as Paul Tillich has pointed out, there weren't more than a thousand people involved at the inner core of the Renaissance.)

There was this band that got together, and what did they do?

They made attempts at infrastructure, and they made social structure attempts, but at the core, they told a new story.

They realized that the Story of Value that was pre-modernity, the traditional Story of Value, had broken down, and that we need to tell a new story.

They told the new Story of Value which was modernity.

Now, to the extent that modernity adopted genuine core values and articulated them, it articulated and evolved the great dignities of modernity: feminism, universal human rights, third-person gnosis which created science and possibilities for measurement; for moving from mere classification in the Middle Ages, to measurement.

All of these are the great dignities of modernity.

But to the extent that the deeper philosophical understanding of modernity claimed that value wasn't actually real—that even as modernity was articulating values, it was saying in the same breath: *we're making these up, these are not actually real*—**they couldn't find a way to root the values in Cosmos once they were no longer rooted in a revealed scripture.**

That was modernity's great collapse, and that exploded in postmodernity.

Postmodernity was really modernity on steroids. It formally deconstructed all value, and created a world in which the political leadership of the world, in their core—from Putin and Xi in China, to I'd say even most of American leadership and American political leadership, and European political leadership—actually do not believe in intrinsic value.

Either they don't believe in intrinsic values, or they make a premodern regressive traditional move, that the only value is our particular version of value in our particular religion—so that premodernity comes back online. For example, the Catholic view of abortion in America is coming back online.

You cannot understand Reality without understanding that the entire question is, *are we living in a shared Story of Value?*

WHAT IS OUTRAGEOUS BEAUTY?

Now, I began with the words: Outrageous Love, Outrageous Pain, and Outrageous Beauty.

We live in a world of Outrageous Pain. The only response is Outrageous Love.

We live in a world of Outrageous Beauty. The only response is Outrageous Love."
We live in a world of Outrageous Beauty.

But Beauty is a value.

Beauty is not nothing.

Beauty is not just a beautiful man, a beautiful woman, or a beautiful sunset. It's all of those.

Beauty comes in a beautiful old woman of 97, and a gorgeous, beautiful man's face who's 93, and you just see amazing Beauty on their faces.

Beauty comes in many shapes and forms.

But Beauty is something deeper, as Alfred North Whitehead talked about, and as the Zohar (a 13th century Hebrew interior science document) talked about.

Whitehead writes about this in *Adventures of Ideas* and in *Process and Reality* (and this is not a direct quote):

Beauty is the ability to contain oppositions.

Beauty is the symmetry that happens when diverse threads come together, and then something new is manifest.

That's how Whitehead talks about Beauty. **Beauty is that which, as Walt Whitman said, *contains multitudes*, and what synergizes from those multitudes is something new which is unimaginably beautiful.** For Whitehead, Beauty is the primary experience, and Goodness and Truth are both expressions of Beauty.

That is similar to the interior sciences of Hebrew wisdom:

Tiferet is the lumination of the Divine. And *tiferet* means Beauty. *Tiferet* is the lumination which is also called *shalom*, which we translate as *peace*, but it means *wholeness*.

Wholeness means that diverse values, which oppose each other, come together and live together, and they synergize and they create a larger whole of stunning symmetry, which generates a whole greater than the sum of any of the parts.

That's Beauty.

So, Whitehead and the Zohar actually experienced Beauty in the same way.

That's what Beauty is.

A *beautiful person* doesn't mean Beauty in some plastic, superficial sense.

It is this depth in which the entire person, interior and exterior, shines together, whether it's the Beauty of a person, or an idea, or a landscape, or a color that integrates different colors.

- We live in a world of Outrageous Beauty.
- We live in a world of Outrageous Pain, and Outrageous Pain is the *opposite* of Outrageous Beauty.

Outrageous Pain comes from this experience where I take one value, and I reject other values. I take one experience, and I reject other experiences. I take one insight, and I reject other insights and then I build my worldview based on that one value or that one insight.

I allow my value to stand by itself, I decontextualize it from the larger Field of Value—and no longer do you have outrageous Beauty; you always get Outrageous Pain. Whenever you decontextualize a value from the larger Field of Value, and it doesn't live in creative tension with the other values that creates a new whole, you create Outrageous Pain.

THE ONLY RESPONSE TO OUTRAGEOUS PAIN IS OUTRAGEOUS LOVE

In America this week, we have seen Outrageous Pain, as Roe vs. Wade (which I'll talk about in a second) was overturned.

Our response to Outrageous Pain is:

We live in a world of Outrageous Pain, the only response to Outrageous Pain is Outrageous Love.

What is Outrageous Love?

In this new Story of Value we are telling, one of the qualities is **Eros or love as perception**, which is the ability to see the whole (you can take a look at in a book called Mystery of Love, there is a chapter on perception.

Then in our book called A Return to Eros: The Radical Experience of Being Fully Alive, where there's also a chapter on perception, where we unpack the qualities of Eros).

Outrageous Love means *I love you* means *I see you.*

I don't identify you with *one* part of you, and then identify *that* as *all* of you—and therefore dismiss you—that's what hate means.

Hate means: I see one narrow part of you, it might be a shadow part of you.

I identify you with that shadow.

I identify you with that scandal.

I identify you with that place that you fell, that place that you yelled, that place that you were enraged, that place where you made a mistake and I say *that's who you are.* No!

I can see all of you.

To be a lover is to see with God's eyes.

It's to see the landscape. It's to see the thought-scape. It's to see the mindscape. It's to see the heart-scape with God's eyes, **and to know that it contains multitudes.**

Love is perception.

Outrageous Love is Outrageous perception. It is to see. And when you see, you see Beauty.

ROE VS WADE: THE SECOND YOU DEMONIZE THE OTHER SIDE; WE ARE OUT OF BEAUTY AND WE ARE IN OUTRAGEOUS PAIN

Now I want to apply this. And we are just setting the intention, but the intention is important to set today.

Because with this setting of intention, I just want to look at what happened in America last Friday, June 23rd, 2022.

- There was a constitutional right to abortion that was enacted in the United States some 50 years ago, by the Supreme Court.
- The Supreme Court just overturned that constitutional right, and there is a huge divide in America.
- There is an enormous celebration by pro-life activists, and there's enormous mourning by pro-choice activists.

Both sides are filled with intelligent people, not evil people.

I want you to get this. The second you demonize the other side, we are out of Beauty and we are in Outrageous Pain.

Fabulous, beautiful people, filled with a sense of value, are on one side.

Fabulous, beautiful people, filled with intelligence and a sense of value and goodness, are on the other side.

So what happened?

I want to really get this, this is so deep.

I know this is really subtle, what we're about to do.

This is super-subtle.

We are here to actually say the things you cannot read in the news. We are here to go deeper, we are here to get underneath.

I want to see if we can capture this, what is actually happening here. I want to see if we can find it deeper than deep and actually do *evolutionary sensemaking*.

WHAT IS HAPPENING IN THE PRO-LIFE VERSUS PRO-CHOICE CLASH?

So in the clash between the pro-life position and the pro-choice position, several things are happening that need to be pointed out, that are beyond important.

In the pro-life vs pro-choice clash each side is claiming a value as the ultimate value—dismissing the value of the other side.

The pro-life people are saying the value is life, but particularly they mean the life of the unborn baby—that's the primary value, protecting the value of the life of the unborn baby is the primary value. Therefore, they call themselves pro-life.

But actually what they're doing is, they are hijacking the value of life, turning that into an absolute value and ignoring a second value, which is the value of choice.

87

Now, the pro-choice people are doing the same thing. They are picking a value, choice. It's the woman's right to choose, that's what they're talking about; choice. They are calling themselves pro-choice.

But actually, in doing so, they are decontextualizing *choice* from the larger Field of Value which includes life, and making choice the primary value, and in some sense, the only value before which all other values must bow.

Now, again, the pro-life people are doing the same thing. They are decontextualizing life, in this case, the life of the baby, from the larger Field of Value, which includes life of the mother and includes choice (and those are related) and saying their value reigns supreme.

But here's the thing, it's very beautiful.

The word value in Hebrew is *erech*. Now, *erech* means value, and *erech* also means context. *Erech* means *constellation*, or *field*—meaning **the value in a larger context of values, or the constellation of values, or the Field of Value.**

The word *value* in Hebrew means context or constellation, or the larger field, because **no value exists independently of the larger field.**

Whenever you **isolate a value from the larger Field of Value** and you transpose it into an **absolute** value, before which all values must bow, at whose altar you worship and bend your knee slavishly, then you create **idolatry**, then you create **Outrageous Pain**.

EACH SIDE CARICATURES THE OTHER'S POSITION IN ORDER TO HIGHLIGHT THE ABSURDITY OF THE OTHER'S VALUE

In the pro-life vs pro-choice clash each side caricatures the other side to highlight the absurdity of the other's value.

In this great argument between pro-life and pro-choice, the way they've framed the arguments is absurd.

They've each claimed a value, they have then rejected the other value. They have caricatured the other's position in order to highlight the absurdity of the other's value.

I want to go slow here for a second, and go deeper.

I want to get both sides of it, so I'm going to actually cite two texts here:

- One is a *Washington Post* article that I read yesterday [June 25, 2022], which is one of the two key liberal papers in the United States.
- The second is a post (number 68 posted on February 6, 2019) by a colleague of mine. We've actually chatted a whole bunch of times. We did a big public debate back in 2005 and we got about a thousand people there. We are about to have a second one in Los Angeles. His name is Dennis Prager, and we've had dinner a couple of times. Dennis Prager, in what he calls his *Fireside chats*, in number 68, does a chat on abortion, which is highly relevant.

Dennis is clearly articulating some version of a pro-life position, and the *Washington Post* was articulating some version of a pro-choice position.

Now, I want to watch this carefully.

So Prager, correctly and wisely, at least in part (when I say correctly and wisely, I mean not in an *ultimate* correct and wise sense, but I mean from a polemical perspective, for the sake of argument) he opens (Editors note: Prager posted this on February 7, 2019). He speaks about a number of bills being presented to legislators. He presents them to actually argue that abortion should be a woman's choice, because after all, we need to have control over our own bodies. **Particularly abortion should be a woman's choice in the third trimester (between six and nine months), when clearly there's fetal viability.** That's what he makes the subject of his piece.

- Then, with that context—so he's now evoked the context and the vision of a baby that's clearly alive in the mother—he then makes the second point, and **from that perspective of the last trimester, he essentially mocks the notion that women should be responsible for their bodies.**

♦ Because, he says, the notion that women are responsible for their bodies is not the issue. The issue is not the body of the woman, the issue is the body of the baby. Now, in the third trimester, that's fully true.

♦ Then he goes on to say, if in fact that baby in the third trimester was born prematurely and the mother killed the baby, would that be okay? Well, obviously, that wouldn't be okay. So then one becomes emotionally invested in the pro-life position, and it seems to be patently obvious.

He makes the point that actually, it's not just about the woman's body, it's about a baby inside the woman's body (that's why we don't ask the woman *how's your body,* we say, *how's the baby doing?* during pregnancy). Clearly, there's a sense of the baby, and that we're talking about protecting the life of the baby in the third trimester.

Now, when we're looking at an extreme bill, which Prager mentions. I haven't researched all of these bills, I'm actually citing Prager about these bills. But I'm going to actually ask one of the researchers to actually find those bills. [Editor's note: Prager gives no specifics about which bills he has in mind, but, at the time, the governor of Vermont signed a law which puts no thresholds on abortion. There are other states that put no legal threshold on abortions, effectively allowing abortion in the third trimester, leaving the decision to the woman and her doctor: Alaska, Colorado, District of Columbia, New Hampshire, New Jersey, New Mexico, Oregon, and Vermont. In many other states, late-term abortions are allowed when the mother's life is threatened, or there is a danger of significant health issues].

90

But Prager, he is referring to these bills, and Prager is trustworthy in that sense; he's a trustworthy source. So I trust him in that sense, I don't think he'd talk about bills that didn't exist.

Now, what he's doing is he is taking the position of choice, the pro-choice position, and he's showing its expression in its most extreme form, almost a caricatured form, which is absurd.

That bills like that were put forth, I have no doubt, and I believe that those bills are on the face of it, other than in extreme circumstances, absurd.

As does virtually everyone, because everyone agrees that if there's full fetal viability, and we're in six or seven months, the notion of an abortion takes on an entirely different meaning. It's not just about the woman's body, but it's about the baby.

Okay, that's clear. But what has Prager done?

He has caricatured the choice position and made choice into an independent value that stands by itself, and then showed it to lead to Outrageous Pain.

Now, again, when I say Prager has done it, it's not actually Prager who did it. It's actually the bills that were introduced on the pro-choice side that argued for this radical notion of choice being the exclusive value.

But Prager intentionally picks up on that in order to characterize the pro-choice position, and that is a distortion of an extreme kind on Prager's side.

Here's the other side, *Washington Post*.

Washington Post is reporting on the overturning of Roe vs. Wade, and a number of other major outlets did the same thing that the *Post* did.

They interview any number of people and any number of abortion clinics that are immediately shutting their door and refusing abortions based on how they understand the law.

Indeed there are "trigger laws" in certain states that are in place that say that right after Roe vs. Wade is overturned, then state laws are passed on

91

abortion, and some of those state laws—Oklahoma, for example—will prohibit abortion immediately [Editor's note: Indeed, there are many states in which abortions are now banned absolutely, the ban is expected to come in effect soon. This can be tracked here]. Meaning, as soon as there's fertilization, abortion should be immediately prohibited.

Now, let's go slow.

The position that abortion should be immediately prohibited as soon as there's fertilization is an extremist pro-life position, just like the position that would allow choice in the third trimester is an extremist pro-choice position.

In other words, a position that would say that we ignore the body of the woman, we ignore woman's choice, let's say in some time in the first trimester, let's not talk about what that dimension should be, is actually a fundamentalist position of the worst kind that actually denies the depth and the wisdom of most of the great traditions.

For example, there are important Upanishads in the great Hindu tradition that talk about the soul entering the baby much, much later.

There are actually even Upanishads that talk about the soul entering the baby at the end of the second trimester. That's dramatic, but let's not get that dramatic.

There are major sources in the Judeo-Christian tradition, and particularly in the Talmud, that argue for the possibility of abortion in any number of quite a wide range of possibilities, within at least a certain dimension of the first trimester.

Now, in the period of time in life in which I functioned formally as an orthodox rabbi, within the Orthodox Hebrew wisdom tradition, in accordance with the laws of the Talmud, I was in touch with the leading decisis of the day; the great saints and sages with long white beards, who were experts in decision-making of the day, including Moshe Feinstein, one of the greatest sainted decisis of the day.

And we allowed abortions, meaning we decided the law, we adjudicated the law, and many women are involved in adjudicating this law. It's about the law, it's not about the people.

The law was adjudicated in favor of abortion within a certain dimension of the first trimester within orthodoxy, meaning within the most stringent form of the interpretation of Hebrew law.

The question is: *When does the fetus step into being a person who is, in some sense, independent, and needs to be considered as a person*, and that's a very real question.

Actually, there's no monopoly on that.

The great traditions of spirit had an enormous range of conversations about that.

When we integrate the best of premodern, modern, and postmodern, in order to create a new Story of Value, we have to integrate the best wisdom of the great traditions that actually had a very sophisticated position on abortion, that actually allowed and integrated two values.

- One value is choice, and the woman's health, and the woman's wholeness, and the woman's wellbeing, and the woman's possibility for expression in the world.
- Another value articulated protection of the baby and the life of the baby.

Clearly, those are both values, and those are both critical values.

The second we step out of the Field of Value, and this is critical, there is no possibility of coming to a higher synergy and higher Beauty.

To be clear, these decisions need to be made from the depth of understanding, not by men or women, not by patriarchies or matriarchies, but by men and women working together, particularly within Hebrew wisdom.

I'm now functioning in a more universal world, but when I was in within the Orthodox Hebrew wisdom tradition, I long argued that women who are expert in law and tradition, and in compassion and love in this particular field, should be the ones who are adjudicating the decisions on abortion.

There are many, many women who are brilliant experts at the text and at the medical issues, and at the embodied experience level.

And clearly, **we are in a generation where we shouldn't have men deciding these issues for women.** We should have, within each tradition, great women who are involved in adjudicating these decisions, who experience these realities in their body.

We're at a new moment in time.

So although patriarchy is a complex word and it's overused and misused, it also has some legitimacy and some importance. But let's take patriarchy out of this conversation.

So let's find this, friends.

This is a big deal.

In order to actually engage in this conversation, we can't caricature the other side.

We cannot do the *Washington Post* caricature, which says that actually the intention of all pro-life legislation on abortion is to disallow abortion at the moment of fertilization. That's actually not the case, nor should it be the case.

Although, the *Washington Post* is absolutely right that there are states that have articulated trigger state laws, in which a law is going to be triggered 30 days after Roe v. Wade is overturned; they've been on the books for many years.

In some of them—I've got to check each one of them, at least one of them I know right now—it actually triggers a law which makes abortion immediately illegal.

So we will have to look, I haven't had time to research all of the detailed legal issues.

THE DECONTEXTUALIZATION OF VALUE IS IDOLATRY

But clearly, there *are* serious voices in the pro-life camp that are doing what the *Washington Post* is claiming.

That is a complete fundamentalist move which idolizes; it's the idolatry of one value, which is the idolatry of the pro-life vision.

It says we have to protect the life of the baby, which they argue, gratuitously against the great traditions of most of the religions, begins at fertilization.

That's extremism!

Extremism means you pick one value, you decontextualize your value from the larger Field of Value, and then you say you can never have enough of your value.

Does everyone get that?

That's not Outrageous Beauty.

Outrageous Beauty incorporates and integrates contradicting values.

And there are real laws in real states right now that are claiming that position, which is a complete violation of Spirit. I want to say that really clearly.

There are real states and real laws that are making that claim right now, not the entire pro-life movement, but there are clear powerful expressions of it happening right now, and that is idolatry.

I just want to say it clearly: **that's idolatry**.

It is an extremist fundamentalist position: the taking of one value, and decontextualization of that value from the Field of Value, and then propping it up as an absolute for which we must all bow.

So that's one extremist position on the pro-life side.

But then, on the pro-choice side, and it's part of what has fostered this—not all of what has fostered this, it's been fostered by both sides, but part of what has fostered it—is the kind of bills that Prager described, which argued for a choice possibility even at the third trimester, which shocked, which sent ripple waves of shock through the pro-life community and created a counter-reaction.

So here's the thing.

The demonization of either side, which is the demonization of the other's value, or more specifically, the transformation of my value into an absolute before which all other values must bow—that is Outrageous Pain.

THE ONLY RESPONSE TO OUTRAGEOUS PAIN IS OUTRAGEOUS LOVE

Outrageous Love: love is a perception, love is knowledge, love is gnosis.

Martha Nussbaum correctly titled one of her books, *Love's Knowledge*.

Love allows me to see.

Love allows me to know.

And love allows me to perceive Beauty.

Beauty,

both as the Hebrew wisdom material sciences articulated it

and as Whitehead correctly articulated it:

Beauty contains multitudes.

Beauty contains contradictory values.

And from that contradiction,

paradox emerges and new synergy and new Beauty arises.

Now I want to go deeper. Let's see if we can go deeper one step. It's wild, and it's important and, it's critical. Can we go one step deeper, who's up for one step deeper?

This is so subtle, and it's beautiful, and it's important.

But it's not easy to get.

So let's go step at a time.

I'll be happy to take a couple of questions, but let's go deeper for a second.

BOTH PRO-LIFE AND PRO-CHOICE STEPPED OUT OF THE FIELD OF VALUE

Paradoxically, both the pro-life and the pro-choice position, I believe, in their own interior, have stepped out of what I would call the Field of Value.

I want to explain what that means, we're going deep now.

It's going to be paradoxical and surprising on both sides.

One, the position of much of the left, which is expressing the pro-choice position, is deeply entrenched in the postmodern matrix—and the postmodern matrix deconstructs value. Value doesn't actually exist, you're not in a Field of Value.

But no one can live without value.

So once you step out of the Field of Value, you choose one value, and you make that value not a value in the field, but your identity.

That value actually becomes your identity.

That value becomes your absolute.

That value becomes a kind of Puritanism.

That value becomes your crusade.

Because that value is no longer a value in the Field of Value, **that value becomes you**, entirely your identity, and **any compromise on that value is a compromise on your very existence.** Therefore, you become a rabid extremist; you become angry, **you can't have a real conversation, you can't engage in facts** because **your identity is that value**, and **that value is decontextualized from the Field of Value**, and therefore **that value brings Outrageous Pain**—and **there's no Outrageous Love to respond to it that will bring us to Outrageous Beauty.**

Now let's get to the other side, the other side is deep.

The other side, you would think *well, but the pro-life people, they are in the Field of Value.*

No, they're not.

The pro-life people have actually regressed. Most of the pro-life position is animated and funded by either fundamentalist versions of Christianity or particular Catholic versions of Christianity—let's catch this—which are **actually, in their core belief systems, *premodern.***

In premodernity, it wasn't a field of universal value with multiple values in the field. It was a Field of Value that was hijacked and colonized by one set of, in this case, often patriarchal interpreters. Here I will use the word *patriarchy*, although I often don't use it because it's overused and misused, as my friend Warren Farrell has pointed out. But here I will use it. In other words, men, who were not living in women's bodies (some of them were deeply sensitive to women in many ways, and some of them were definitely not).

There was a particular position on the role of women in society, and in most of Christendom, and that came together with legitimate life considerations of the baby, and formulated a set of laws of a particular extreme fundamentalist nature, both in Catholicism and in the sources of many of the fundamentalist Christ traditions that are happening in America, in their more kind of Baptist or fundamentalist forms.

What's happening now is, much of the pro-life movement is animated not by the Field of Value, but actually by a premodern position that's paradoxically not in the Field of Value.

How do you know the premodern positions were not in the Field of Value?

Because they actually claimed that only their position was value, and that all the other competing religious positions were not only wrong, but the competing religions deserved to be killed, as either infidels or heretics, burned at the stake, tortured by the Inquisition.

Let's get this really clear, that's not a position in the Field of Value.

So the pro-life movement is informed not by the Field of Value, the pro-life movement is informed actually by being out of the Field of Value; they've stepped out of the Field of Value, they've caricatured the Field of Value, and hijacked it. So therefore, now their identity is bound up with their parochial, self-aggrandizing, essentially narcissistic position: *it's us, and it's no one else.*

Therefore, it can't consider other very substantive saintly religious positions on this issue of abortion, that take fundamental issue with any of the extreme expressions of it. For example, no allowing of abortion to at least some segment of first trimester, which is utterly absurd.

To be clear, I myself have adjudicated abortion cases with women who are experts in the law, together in which I encouraged the women in those conditions together with her husband to get an abortion, because having the baby—it would have actually destroyed her life.

Did I think I was destroying a baby's life? Absolutely not.

There's very, very saintly reasoned, stunning positions of some of the deepest hearts and minds, looking at the law in the Talmud, that supported that ruling.

All of that has been thrown out by the pro-life expressions in their extreme forms, which are decontextualizing one value from the Field of Value in a premodern way, in which only their interpretation of that value is considered in any way legitimate.

Wow! Does everyone begin to see it? In other words, you begin to see what we mean when we say that…

In order to evolve the source code of consciousness and culture, in order to move beyond polarization, we have to tell a new Story of Value, which is a story of Outrageous Beauty.

Outrageous Beauty means that we have articulated a Story of Value rooted in First Principles and First Values, in which choice and life are obviously both First Principles and First Values, out of which synergy emerges, which generates, in response to Outrageous Pain— through Outrageous Love— Outrageous Beauty.

Now remember, and this is really important… When you step out of the Field of Value, and you choose one value, an idolatry before which you kneel, your identity which you can't compromise on, you create Outrageous Pain and you create polarization.

You create polarization because you've stepped out of the Field of Value so the two values clash with each other, and each side thinks they're representing value. They're not, they're representing narcissistic identity or idolatry. Now let's go one last step, and it's really beautiful.

IF BOTH SIDES STEP INTO THE FIELD OF VALUE, THEN THEY SHARE THE FIELD OF VALUE TOGETHER

I want to get this really clearly, and this is a big deal. This is a whole new notion. So imagine you step into your true identity. What's our true identity?

So we know, as Albert Einstein correctly pointed out, that separation is an optical delusion of consciousness. The notion that *I'm a separate self* is an optical delusion of consciousness, it's not true. There is no ultimate separate self. Separate self is real, of course. I should experience myself as an individuated, separate self with appropriate boundaries, that is of course real.

But that's not my deeper identity. **My deeper identity is that my separate self is located in a larger field.**

  ◆   I don't exist, for example, without certain microbes at the bottom of the sea; I actually have no life without them.
  ◆   I have no life without the coral reefs.
  ◆   I have no life without the larger field of the biosphere.
  ◆   I have no life without the larger field of consciousness.

My consciousness is not a separate consciousness; I'm living in the Field of *LoveIntelligence* and *LoveBeauty* and *LoveDesire* and *LoveConsciousness*.

We call that True Self. Now, **True Self is in that Field.**

So in that field of True Self, is there any difference between Marc and Elena, or Chahat, or Marc and Larry? None, we're all the same in True Self! In the field of True Self, there's one True Self; the total number of True Selves in the world is one.

- True Self is the singular that has no plural.
- It's the *seamless coat* of the universe.
- It is the one heart.
- It is the one Eros,
- It's the one consciousness that animates the four forces of physics, that is, as systems theory points towards (in its deeper expressions, not in its surface expressions) the one Cosmos, if you will.

That's why it's a uni-verse. It is one text. That's True Self.

Now, this is subtle, and it's beautiful. True Self is the same as the Field of Value. Value is True Self. Value is consciousness. Consciousness is value. In other words, **value is everywhere.**

A lot of times today, post Claude Shannon, we talk about information. Claude Shannon is one of the fathers of information theory, but Claude Shannon actually wrote a paper with Warren Weaver, where he pointed out that what information is at its core is not bits and bytes, which is how it was used in information theory.

But actually, as Warren Weaver writes with Shannon, in about 1948, **information, at its core, is meaning or *value*.**

In other words, when three quarks associate with each other—two down quarks and one up quark, two up quarks and one down quark, one's a proton and the other's a neutron—that which brings them together to create a proton and a neutron, that's value.

There are values that exist from the first nanoseconds of the Big Bang, when gazillions of quarks reign, and there are only 16 kinds of particular configurations of value which create 16 forms of quarks.

I mean, it's wild!

The universe is not random in any sense, shape, or form.

The universe has a dimension of spontaneity and contingency and freedom in its core, that's in the context of enormous beauty, in which opposites synergize in fields of value in configurations of intimate coherence.

So the Field of Value is like the field of True Self.

I may have lost a couple of people here because I know it's a deep dive, let's see if we can get it.

True Self is the singular that has no plural, it's the field of one consciousness.

Consciousness is the same as value; consciousness and value are inextricably entwined with each other.

Just like there's a field of consciousness, which we are all part of the same True Self, there is no distinction between Marc and Chahat or Marc and Elena in that field of one consciousness, that field of one value. **The second we all step into the Field of Value, we recognize each other in the Field of Value; we are part of the same true value. We are part of the same True Self.**

Then Elena individuates, then Ben individuates, then James individuates; I individuate as Unique Self. Kohlene individuates as Unique Self. Does everyone get that?

Now there's Kohlene, Kohlene who is a beautiful artist in Europe doing gorgeous work, and has done 12 beautiful paintings on Eros. So True Self individuates as Kohlene, that's Unique Self.

The same way that True Self individuates as a Unique Self, the field of true value individuates as choice, or individuates as life.

It individuates as any one of the larger Field of Values.

103

In other words, a unique value is the same as Unique Self. That's beautiful.

Just like True Self individuates as Jacqueline, or as Kohlene, or as Elena, or as Marc, or as Sally, so **true value individuates as unique value.**

Now, True Self is not the same as Unique Self.

Unique Self is the individuation of True Self.

But stay really close now, stay really, really close.

But Unique Self is not the same as Separate Self.

Separate Selves are in what Hobbes called a state of war; there is a natural state of war between the Separate Selves. This is one of the things that Russian literature, when it's truly trying to stand for moral clarity, is grappling with: how do we actually create peace between separate selves, each one with their own rich inner texture, and how do you create a larger Field of Value?

It's very hard to do. Bracket those two sentences if you missed them, but here's the important point, stay close. Unique Self is not the same as separate.

I can only create harmony between Unique Self if Unique Self understands that I'm an expression of True Self.

If I'm an expression of True Self, then we're all True Selves.

We're all together in the Field of Consciousness.

We're all brothers and sisters in the one love and the one heart of Cosmos, and then we're uniquely individuated. Then we can create synergy, then we can create beauty, and then we can create outrageous beauty.

But if we're separate selves—what Hobbes calls in *Leviathan*, or in his earlier book, *Man and Citizen*—the natural state of war—which is nasty, brutish, and short, as our lives so often are—actually reigns. Wow!

Actually, as Leo Strauss pointed out, even John Locke was really Hobbes with a velvet glove, and the separate self is the core of Western society.

Now stay with me, the same thing is true about value. In other words: **If I never enter the field of true value—the field of True Self as it were, if I'm not in the Field of Value—then the value that I choose will be not my Unique Self value.**

It won't be a unique value, which is the same as Unique Self, in which those unique values that emerge from the Field of Value can synergize. It will rather be a separate value, just like separate self. Then we have separate value. And because it's a separate value, those two values will clash; they have to clash, because it's a separate self value, it's a separate value in the same sense of separate self, so now they've got to clash with each other, they can't actually find each other—because it becomes identity, just like in the realm of self, separate self becomes identity; it becomes an ego identity, which I have to defend at any cost. So too, **the separate value becomes my identity, which I have to defend at any cost.**

Paradoxically, both the pro-life and the pro-choice movement, in the ways we've outlined today, have stepped out of that Field of Value, so they don't recognize each other, they don't find each other in the field of one value.

If we found each other and experienced each other in the field of one value, then we'd be able to synergize, and we wouldn't come to this day of Outrageous Pain in America. This is deep, friends! This is what we mean by a source code evolution.

WHEN WE'VE STEPPED OUT OF THE FIELD OF VALUE, THERE'S NO INTIMACY BETWEEN VALUES

And what is intimacy? Intimacy is shared identity in the context of otherness; that's the intimacy formula.

So when you have intimacy between values, you can create a shared identity between two opposing values in the context of otherness, where the integrity of each value is honored.

That's huge! So actually, this entire conversation could be understood in terms of the Tenets of Intimacy.

Intimacy equals shared identity in the context of otherness.

Here's the full Intimacy Formula: *Intimacy= shared identity, in the context of relative otherness x mutuality of recognition x mutuality of pathos x mutuality of value x mutuality of purpose.*

You apply that intimacy formula to values, and you have our whole conversation today. It's wild!

Now you begin to see what the Center for Integral Wisdom is doing. This is what we're doing together. This is what we're doing as Unique Self Symphony, we're actually **articulating a new Story of Value.** Because right now, there isn't a Story of Value.

The superstructure has broken down.

We need what my friend Daniel, calls *the third attractor,* I call it the *new strange attractor.* I call it, in other writings, *a new allurement.* We say that a complex system is based on allurement. In a complex system the whole is greater than the sum of the parts.

And a complicated system which is fragile has no allurement. I shared that distinction with my brother, Daniel, about five or six years ago.

The core to generating a new Story of Value is to recognize and articulate a vision of value which is intrinsic to Cosmos and evolves. It's an evolving value, but there are intrinsic values. **Once we have evolving values that are intrinsic, then we're in a field of allurement**—because value allures; the nature of values is that value allures.

This is really important, and we'll finish with this.

Eros is value, and value is Eros. Eros generates allurement.

When you're not in the Field of Value, there's no allurement. So what happens is, you manage to find the position of your adversary not alluring, even ugly, and you caricature it as being ugly. You caricature the pro-choice position in an ugly way, and you caricature the pro-life position in an ugly way.

But when you step into the Field of Value, you're in the field of Eros, you're in the Tao. When you're in the Tao, then all values have a place in the Tao, and they're beautiful.

Now you're moving towards Outrageous Beauty; Whitman's I contains multitudes, or Whitehead's notion of beauty that contains more and more and more contradictions, in which **the contradiction** *becomes not only* **absolutely critical** *to our Eros theory, but to our CosmoErotic Humanism.*

CosmoErotic Humanism, for those of you who are new, is the overarching Story of Value that we're working on at the Center for Integral Wisdom, that everything's a part of. Unique Self theory, they're all part of CosmoErotic Humanism.

In the basic notion of CosmoErotic Humanism, we articulate a *vision of Beauty which allows contradiction*, not to turn into polarization, but to turn into *paradox*.

When you're in the Field of Value, which is the Field of Eros, which is the Field of Beauty, then contradiction becomes not polarization but paradox.

The Garden of Eden is not paradise, the Garden of Eden is **paradox.** From that paradox, we can love each other.

Because love always holds paradox. Paradox is uncertainty. From that place of epistemic humility and uncertainty, we can create new synergies and new beauties that are unimaginable.

Thank you, everyone.

CHAPTER FIVE

TWO EVOLUTIONARY PRACTICES OF HOMO AMOR: LIVE YOUR DREAM AND CONFESS YOUR GREATNESS

Episode 299 — July 3, 2022

CELEBRATION IN THE MIDDLE OF EXISTENTIAL RISK

It's great to be with everyone! Totally, absolutely, wonderfully, wildly great.

I'm on a movie set in New York, where we are doing some filming. So the lighting is not exactly right, and this is the only place I could find to do *One Mountain*. They told me, you can't do *One Mountain* this week, we are in the middle of filming. **But we can't miss *One Mountain*.** We're wildly excited to be here. But my light's not ideal, there might be a little background noise… I apologize for the not perfect circumstance, and madly excited and delighted to be with you! Oh, my God.

We are in Week 299. Can you believe that? Oh my God, we're in Week 299, which is shocking, and beautiful, and wondrous, and we are beginning to find our way in. **Next week is Week 300**. And so, I really want to invite everyone

109

to come, bring friends, and we are going to have this fantastic Week 300, which is a huge celebration moment.

Celebration is always with a sense of urgency, a sense of ecstatic urgency, a sense of Outrageous Pain, a sense of Outrageous Beauty, a sense of Outrageous Love. We laugh out of one side of our mouths, and we create out of the next side, we cry out of the next side, we manifest the new world, and we do it all together.

We are in the fullness of the beauty, and we are in the fullness of the pain together.

The other celebration that's coming up, that I really, really want to invite you—for your own unimaginable joy—to participate in, is this summer, August 6th through 12th, we're doing **the 10th Annual Dharma-intensive Outrageous Love Festival**. It's going to be in Belgium and online. It's seven days.

Oh my God, we *need* you there, and **you need to be there if you at all can!** Turn the world upside down to get there, it's going to be so stunning. It's this massive celebration. **It's a celebration, even as we're deeply aware that existential risk—a threat to our very existence—looms.**

This is really critical to understand. Someone asked me a few weeks ago in *Holy of Holies*: *Like, existential risk—how can I even breathe or do anything else?* This person is a fantastic human being, who is a dear friend, and a student and colleague, and partner, and pillar. So I want to answer that question.

How can we have a celebration when we are in the middle of existential risk, when there is a looming dystopia, when we are poised in this time between worlds and this time between stories, when we're poised between utopia and dystopia?

Shouldn't we just be shouting from the rooftops? Even to mention the word celebration, shouldn't that be obscene?

YOU CAN'T CHANGE THE WORLD UNLESS YOU ARE WILLING TO ALREADY LIVE IN THE WORLD THAT'S ALREADY CHANGED

We are at this critical inflection point in history, which people are, for the most part, unaware of.

The pandemic made people a little more aware of it, of what we've been talking about here for a decade: that our systems are not too big to fail, that **there are systemic structural weaknesses in the very fabric of how our Reality is built today**, which will cause it to collapse into a dystopia—or worse, into an imploded existential risk.

If that's actually the case, how can I even talk about celebration? Isn't that obscene?

Does everyone get the question? It's a big question.

I want to talk about that more at length this summer at the Festival, and maybe in a couple of weeks in a couple of *One Mountains*. But here, I just want to say one sentence. It is a sentence that clarified for me this past week, I just want to give you this one sentence. Here's the sentence.

You can't change the world unless you are willing to already live in the world that's already changed.

That sentence just emerged this week. It's a fantastic sentence. When it emerged (I was in a deep three-day seminar), I was ecstatic.

It's a beautiful sentence. *You can't change the world unless you're willing to already live in the world that's already changed.*

Can you track what that means?

What that means is:

111

If you are going to change the world, and you realize the corruption and the suffering and the betrayal and then you realize—even more deeply—the imminent potential catastrophic or existential risk in either the next 100 years, or 50 years, or 400 years, it's unclear, and you are not sure how to change it… then what happens?

You become bitter. You become broken. You dry up. Your soul shrivels. *You dry up like a raisin in the sun.* There is no place for laughter anymore. There is a kind of deep—not sadness, but a kind of cynicism, bitter cynicism that sets in. No!

I have met my friends, many beautiful people I'm close to today, who began as great visionaries, and are now bitter and cynical. You become bitter and cynical when you are so involved in transforming Reality—which we should be: *I'm involved in it 24 hours a day, even when I'm sleeping*—but when you are so involved that you stop living in the world that's already changed……

Meaning: *you have to live the dream!*

Langston Hughes, the black poet, writes:

> *What happens to a dream deferred?*
>
> *Does it dry up like a raisin in the sun?*

In other words, you *delay* the dream: *'The world is going to be great in the next world, in heaven, in the next millennium—but right now, it's broken, so we all have to just do everything we can to create that new world, and until then, anyone who is laughing, and anyone who is making love, and anyone who is celebrating is obscene.'*

No, it's not that way. It's not that way at all.

You have to be able to laugh even in hell. You have to be able to celebrate even in the midst of chaos, and breakdown, and intense suffering.

Because our capacity to heal the suffering, our capacity to transform Reality, depends *directly* on our having direct access to the taste of the liberated world.

Once we can't *taste* the liberated world, once we can't taste what it feels like to be *Homo amor*, to be the new human and the new humanity, who is not only omni-considerate for the sake of the whole, but who is in mad celebration of Reality, who is experiencing joy pouring through them—we cannot change the world.

Not that the joy occludes the tears. But **the joy is fundamental and present.**

You have to eat well—and you have to savor the food, and let the food love you open.

You have to live in your body.

You have to let colors blow you away—and great literature, and friendship, and song, and lovemaking, and massage.

You have to live the dream!

You can't change the world unless you're willing to already live in the world that's already changed.

That's a new practice, I want to call that practice: *Dream Time*, and the "verb" version of that practice is: ***Live the Dream***. Because otherwise:

> *What happens to a dream deferred,*
>
> *Does it dry up like a raisin in the sun?*

WE ARE GOING TO CHANGE THE SOURCE CODE OF CULTURE

So this summer, at the 10th Outrageous Love Festival, there are two things happening. One is, we are actually getting together as da Vinci, taking our seat at the table, in this moment which demands a new Renaissance. And we are saying:

Our hearts are big enough to take it all in.

We are going to breathe in the joy, and we are going to breathe in the suffering, we are not going to look away, and we are going to actually evolve the source code.

> *We are going to change the source code of culture, which means we are going to tell a new Story of Value, which is the only way to change the vector of imminent dystopia—which is precisely what Leonardo da Vinci did in the Renaissance.*

As the old world order of the traditional world (pre-modernity) was breaking down and the new world order hadn't yet emerged—as *the old story* of traditional world was breaking down, but *the new story* hadn't yet found its way and emerged, in this time between worlds—what da Vinci understood is that what he needed to do was: **he needed to begin the telling of the new story**.

And he told the new story.

It was a new story of what it means to be a woman, and about the relationship between men and women.

It was a new story about how to do science, the third-person method and empirical validation.

It was a new story about universal human rights.

114

It was a new story about the relationship between the infinite and the finite, between Goddess and God and the human being.

It was a new story about relationships between human beings.

He told a new story, and that raised all boats, and invoked the great dignities of modernity.

Now, as we have said many times:

To the precise extent that that storyline was good and accurate, and rooted in value, **it actually birthed the dignities of modernity.**

But to the precise extent that that storyline was awkward or warped, or corrupted, or missing key dimensions, **it began to generate the disasters of modernity, which led directly to this moment** of extraction models, and exponential growth curves, and exponential weaponized technologies held by rogue non-state actors, and the race to the bottom, and the tragedy of the commons, which generates, for example, systems of AI that shouldn't be generated, etc.

In other words, it generated the world of today, which is governed by a *success* story—which is the only story we have left, because da Vinci didn't get all of the story right.

And even the parts that he got right, others, who took over and hijacked the narrative, didn't get right. **The broken narrative is what has generated the moment in which we are living in this success story, which is rivalrous conflict governed by win/lose metrics.**

Tragic!

And so, we respond to that by telling this new Story of Value. **One of the things we're going to do at the Outrageous Love Festival is we are going to take this new Story of Value, we are going to recapitulate the last 10 years, and take it the next step in a huge way.** That's one.

SABBATH IS THE TECHNOLOGY OF LIVING THE DREAM

But there is a second thing happening at the Festival, and there is a second thing happening at every *One Mountain*. There is a second thing that needs to happen in the lives of all of us, as we cross over to be the new human, to be *Homo amor, the fulfilment of Homo sapiens*, to invoke the new human and the new humanity, which is: **you've got to live the dream *now*.**

> *You can't change the world unless you are willing to already live in the world that's already changed.*

I'm going to tell you something wild. **One of the primary technologies of the ancient lineages is exactly this, it's *living the dream*.** Does anyone have any idea what that technology is called? That technology is called *Sabbath*.

That's what Sabbath is. Sabbath means that for 24 hours, every seven days, *you live the dream*. For 24 hours, every seven days, there are no social hierarchies. Every man, woman, and child, every servant, rich or poor— socio-economic distinctions disappear.

We don't focus our creativity into shifting the external world. **We take that creativity, and we direct it inward, and we actually *create ourselves*.** We literally *re-soul* ourselves. *Shabbat va-yinafash*: you shall Sabbath and *re-soul yourself*—a sacred text.

So, **Sabbath is the technology of living the dream.**

I want to tell you something wild. Stay close, friends. Are we together, everyone's with us? This is wild! When I was in Dharamsala, I spent some really beautiful time with the Dalai Lama. It's a story I've told you at other times, how I got there, and how we met; we had an argument, and he invited me to come to Dharamsala, and we spent some really crazy beautiful time

116

together, both private time and public time. In the private moment, he said to me, *how did the Hebrew wisdom tradition survive the exile?*

Because, of course, the Tibetan exile today is very real. The Chinese have crushed Tibet, and there's this huge Tibetan exile. He's in Dharamsala in northern India, which is where I met him the second time; we met first time at the Pope's summer residence in Castel Gandolfo, but we met the second time in Dharamsala in his home.

He said, *the Hebrew wisdom tradition, how did they survive?*

I said to him, *Sabbath!*

What does Sabbath mean? When this tradition went into exile, instead of focusing all of the energy on the revolution, on *how are we going to liberate ourselves from the exile?*—although that happened, that was true, there was an enormous focus on *how can we liberate ourselves from the exile and actually reestablish this Hebrew wisdom vision?* There was an enormous emphasis on that—but at the same time, there was this notion of Sabbath, which meant that no matter where you were, no matter how brutal the exile, no matter how harsh the pain, no matter how outrageous the pain

Every seven days, you live in outrageous beauty. Every seven days, you live in Sabbath. And Sabbath is the liberated world. **Sabbath is to live the dream.**

Sabbath is the realization that you can't change the world unless you're already willing to live in a world that's already changed.

Wow, does everyone get how huge that is? It's huge!

LAUGHTER MATTERS

Homo amor has to be a revolutionary and *Homo amor* has to be an evolutionary. *Homo amor* has to be tilting against every windmill—but with strategic excellence, and being willing to engage in conversations of strategy, and being willing to step up, and go all the way in this lifetime.

And *Homo amor* needs to be already living the dream. Can everyone feel that? It's gorgeous.

I've mentioned it to you all before, and maybe we'll come back to this at the Festival. I want to just give you one last piece of it, and it is so beautiful.

It means that *laughter matters*.

It means that we should be *smiling*.

It means we should be *laughing*.

It means we should literally be in **a felt sense of joy**.

Umberto Eco wrote a very important book that I sometimes mention, and I hope to get back to it this summer, called *In the Name of the Rose*. It is a story about a medieval monastery in which the monks start dying, and people aren't sure why. This monk who is higher in the hierarchy comes to investigate. It is a long, dramatic story. But in the end, he reveals that all of the monks who died were poisoned, because each of them had gone to the library of the rectory and taken out Aristotle's book, *Nicomachean Ethics*. They would study it, and they'd be interested in laughter, and they'd turn to the page on laughter, joy, humor. But the assistant rector, the assistant friar, poisoned that page on laughter, so anyone in the monastery who went to learn about laughter and its importance, they would turn the page to that page on laughter, and they'd be poisoned—not because that monk began as an evil person who would poison people.

He began with the dream of a better world. He thought the world was lost, and he was utterly committed to bringing in a better world. But he didn't understand, *in this world of abject suffering, how can people be laughing? That's somehow a violation of Christ! It's a violation of the God-Force.* So he poisoned people who were laughing, in order to be able to heal the world. Does everyone get that?

Go back to Langston Hughes:

> *What happens to a dream deferred?*

118

Does it dry up like a raisin in the sun?

So, friends, let's laugh.

Let's laugh together.

Let's laugh insanely, and let's laugh sanely.

Let's celebrate.

Again—it's the most important sentence in the world:

We can't change the world unless we're willing to already live in the world that's already changed. *Live the dream!*

That's our introduction today. That's the couple of notes I wanted just to take us inside with, as we talk about celebration and existential risk in the same breath. My friend, several weeks ago, in a *Holy of Holies* sessions wrote me a note:

All I can feel all the time is existential risk, how can I celebrate?

It was such an important question, and this person spoke for so many people. I've gotten versions of that question from the best and the brightest and the deepest. I just think it was just so important that we get this and we feel it. Total celebration and pain, both at the same time. We laugh out of one side of our mouth, and we cry out of the other side.

EVOLUTIONARY LOVE CODE: CONFESSION OF GREATNESS

More than confessing their sins, every human being is obligated to *confess their greatness.*

Every human being is obligated to *live their greatness.*

Obligation, duty, honor, and nobility are not social constructions of Reality.

Obligation, duty, honor, and nobility are real.

Your greatness is your deepest heart's desire.

To confess your greatness is to confess your heart's desire.

And we must also confess our vulnerability.

To confess our greatness without our vulnerability is to lie to ourselves.

To confess our vulnerability without confessing our greatness is to deny God.

CONFESSION OF SIN BECAME A TOOL TO SUBJUGATE PEOPLE INTO SERVITUDE

Just feel that energy of celebration, *we are celebrating!*

That's what festival means; festival means *festivity*. That's what *Hallelujah* means. *Hallelujah* is *hallel*, which is ecstatic celebration; ecstatic celebration at the hardest times. We hold it together.

I want to talk to you a little bit about **confession of greatness** now. It's wildly exciting.

Then we're going to come together, and we are going to do prayer. **Because prayer is part of celebration, it's part of confession of greatness**, and we are going to not skip that this week. Last week we didn't, because we were deep in the *dharma* of moving beyond the Beyond Roe vs. Wade polarization. By the way, it was wildly important, maybe one of our most important weeks *ever* last week. If you really want to get a sense of what's going on with Roe vs. Wade, it is worth listening to the last week and what we need to do to create the new world, and to move beyond the polarization we are in. We are going to come back to that in the next couple of weeks.

Let's go to confession of greatness.

What does *confession of greatness* mean? Let's look again at the code. Let's see if we can capture this in the best way that we can.

Why do we need to confess, and what does confession mean?

Confession is this major idea, what do we identify confession with? Church.

What do you confess? You confess your sin.

And the word sin in Hebrew is *chet.*

It's one of the few things that the New Age actually got right. It is translated in a number of tracts which come from the New Age world, and they translate it accurately. It's a word from archery, the world of Zen, and the art of archery. ***Chet* means, quite literally, *to miss the mark.*** *You missed the mark, you blew it.*

In other words, *you got it wrong, you made a big mistake,* which was actually a big violation.

So you *confess your sin.*

Now, confession became, in the classical Christian liturgy, the very center of service. It's not that it's wrong. *To be able to recognize where I missed the mark requires enormous courage.*

Confession of sin, however, moved beyond that courage, and *confession of sin became a tool to subjugate people into a kind of servitude* because **the emphasis on the places that we are broken began to obfuscate or occlude those places that we are whole.**

And the sin, or the breakdown, or the missing of the mark. There's no person who doesn't sin every day. There's not one person in the world who doesn't sin every day, in one way or the other.

We don't even like the word sin; we don't like to use that word anymore. As Thomas Carlisle said, quoted by Matthew Arnold: *Socrates is terribly at ease in Zion.* Socrates is *Western thought, at ease in Zion,* Zion meaning a place where you are actually held accountable, where there's this notion of sin.

Actually, sin is not a bad idea. Sin happens when we violate certain things.

- For instance, when we are not kind, we don't just miss an opportunity for kindness, there is actually a violation of the nature of Cosmos.
- When we are not madly loving, it's not just we weren't madly loving, we are violating *the Universe: A Love Story*.

Sin means that there's an ontological violation of something that's real.

But as we all know, sin got hijacked. Sin became a tool of oppression. Sin became a tool of suppression, a tool of domination. And so, that notion of confession, in the courageous sense, got hijacked into something that demeaned our humanity. It degraded who we are.

THE NEW LOCUS OF CONFESSION HAS TO BE CONFESSION OF GREATNESS

In order to recover our identity, we don't need to leave confession behind. But as we begin to articulate a world religion, as we begin to articulate a world spirituality—a world religion which is a context for our diversity, a world spirituality which is a context for our diversity—**we need to reclaim confession.**

But to reclaim confession, we can't go directly to confession of my brokenness, which is confession of sin. We have to go to confession of greatness, and that's so critical. The new locus of confession has to be confession of greatness. But not as a spiritual bypass, not as a *pollyannish* idea. Actually, **confession of greatness is far harder than confession of sin.**

Here's where it starts to get wildly beautiful and insanely interesting beyond imagination.

Confession of greatness demands something of us that's exponentially more beautiful, true, and good, exponentially greater than confession of sin demands—because basically, if you are in violation all the time, **if you are sinning all the time, well, what does anyone expect from you?**

122

In other words, if you are a worm, if you're a fallen creature, if you're lost in sin—*well, that's just who I am. Why would you expect anything else from me?*

If you are a snake, well, then you are going to poison people.

There's an old Zen adage which my friend Diane Hamilton used to share with me all the time: *Trust people to be who they are.* Basically, if you tell people, *you are sinful*, and then they become sinful, then trust them to be in violation.

- ♦ If I am a worm, I'm just going to be a worm.
- ♦ If I am fallen, well, I'll just be fallen.
- ♦ If I am just a materialist, separate self, who is a product of a meaningless Cosmos which is utterly random, with no context of intimacy, and a higher sacred order, and a sense of ultimate meaning and ultimate value, well, then I will be an expression of that breakdown.

But that's actually not accurate.

That's not who I am.

It's not the nature of Reality.

I want to cite a text for you, with your permission. It is one of the insanely beautiful texts. It is a sacred text from the original text called *the Torah*, and it is in a book called *Deuteronomy*. It's in *Book of Deuteronomy, Chapter 26*. Everyone is familiar with it, even if you've never read it, because it's the place where we talk about pilgrims. It's where the idea of being a pilgrim comes from.

So, the pilgrim goes to the Temple. The pilgrim goes to Jerusalem, and when the pilgrim goes to Jerusalem, the pilgrim is a philanthropist, and the pilgrim offers what are called *tithes*, a 10th of the income—a tithe for the poor, a tithe for the educational institutions. There's a whole set of tithes, in which we share. (Unlike Google and Amazon which manage to pay no taxes, unlike techno-feudalists that pay no taxes, unlike a world in which we don't distribute taxation evenly. Actually, taxation needs to be distributed in a beautiful way. Taxation is a privilege: I get to participate in sustaining the evolutionary communion of pioneering souls. So I am giving my tithes).

The pilgrim goes to Jerusalem, he gives his tithes, and then there is a declaration that the pilgrim says. What does the pilgrim say?

I'll just give you four or five words of it. He goes to the different tithes, and he says, *a'si'ti ke'khol asher tzivitani*: I've done it all perfectly. Everything you asked for, I've done it all. Fantastic. Perfect. I got it. I hit the ball out of the park.

Then, the masters in the third century said that this text in which the pilgrim says, *I hit it out of the park, I did everything you asked from me and I did it perfectly—that's* **called confession**. It's a text in the second century actually, in a tractate called *Yoma, Chapter 3, Subsection 5*.

This text of *I've done it all perfectly* is called confession.

Why is it called confession? Because in this moment, you are confessing your greatness. **We are confessing our capacity.**

- I was commanded; there was a responsibility placed on me.
- I needed to support the evolutionary communion.
- I needed to step up and tithe—and I knew exactly how to do it. I did it courageously, and I did it generously. I did it fearlessly, and I did it perfectly.

That's my confession.

In other words, **my confession is my greatness.**

But stay close, friends. This is so deep, this is like the deepest of the deep.

The only thing that holds me accountable is my greatness.

You see, **if I have this capacity, well, then Reality demands it from me.**

I only count if I'm accountable, and I'm only accountable if I possess greatness.

CONFESSION OF GREATNESS IS ALWAYS UNIQUE

Here's the next stage. **Greatness is never generic.**

It's a very important sentence: there's no generic greatness.

For our European friends and our Chinese friends, the word *generic* means one-size-fits-all; the same for everyone. *Generic is the opposite of unique.* There's no generic greatness; there's no generic confession of greatness. **There's only Unique Self greatness.** My confession of greatness is unique.

My confession of greatness is my Unique Self confession. **It's always the confession of my unique greatness, because it's only my Unique Self that holds me accountable.**

You live the dream in your moments of greatness

Now stay with me for a second, we are going to put the two pieces of today together. You see,

even when I haven't transformed all the way (and no one's transformed all the way)

even when I am still a work in progress (and everyone's still a work in progress)

even when I am an imperfect vessel for the light (and everyone's an imperfect vessel for the light)

—I can still live the dream.

And I live the dream in my moment of greatness.

In other words, it's not just about the liberation of the world.

Celebration before the world is liberated is the first part of our talk today. You've got to actually live the dream; you've got to actually be willing to already live in the world that's already changed. But that's true not just about the public world; it's true about my personal world.

In other words, even before I am transformed—that would be a kind of secular word, a religious word would be even before I'm *redeemed*, and the Eastern traditions word would be even before I'm *liberated*, whichever word you like: *transformed, redeemed, liberated*—even before that happens, you've got to live the dream.

Live the dream means to identify your moment of greatness, and know that that's who you really are, and celebrate that moment of greatness.

The celebration of your moment of greatness is what it means to live the dream. I am willing to celebrate it, and not to succumb to the voices that say: "Oh, you did that great once, but that's not who you are. Oh, one time you really showed up, but look at all the times you didn't show up, look at all the times you failed."

95% OF THE GAME IS THE WILLINGNESS TO FAIL

We have promised each other these five Dharmic principles of baseball we haven't gotten to yet, but I will give you one of them in advance.

In baseball, you fail far more often than you get on base.

I was with my son a couple of weeks back, and we saw two games in a row at Oracle stadium. It was awesome, a lot of sun and a lot of sunburn. It was 18 innings. One game on a Tuesday evening, the next game on a Wednesday morning. We came two hours early each time to be there for batting practice, and we were watching baseball. Basically what happens is, *almost no one gets on base.* My son made me promise that I won't do anything else during the game, which I didn't, so I watched the game intently with him. We got these great seats, like 10 seats behind the dugout, and we're watching the game. **Most of the time, people struck out, or they popped the fly, so the ball was caught and they were out.**

I want you to get what this great American game of baseball is. We're Dutch patriots, and we're German patriots, and we're Swiss patriots, and we're Chinese patriots, everyone from around the world, South America, we're Estonian patriots. But today happens to be July 3rd, so it's the day before the Fourth of July, which is America's Independence Day, and America's great sport is baseball. So this is our honoring of the Fourth of July, the honoring of baseball. What's baseball? Baseball is actually the best of America, and it's the willingness to fail—what Zion and I basically watched is *men failing*. That's what happened. Most of the game was people failing, and only occasionally would someone get on base, only occasionally would someone get a hit. The scores were 2-1, 3-1.

So, 95% of the game is the willingness to fail, and then get up in the batter box again—not to fall into a depression, not to fall into self-loathing, not to fall into a collapse of self, but to know:

- I'm going to get up.
- I'm going to pick up that bat again.
- I'm going to get in the right position.
- I'm going to do everything in my power for the sake of the larger communion, as part of the Unique Self Symphony of my team, to have that bat connect with that high-speed ball, and sail out of the park.

Like, wow!

I keep failing, and failing, and failing—and I keep getting up in the batter's box, **knowing that at some point I'm going to come home.** Because that's what all of baseball is about. It's about getting home, *getting to home plate* is what it's called.

See, that's what confession of greatness is.

Confession of greatness means that *I keep failing, I keep falling, again and again.*

I am in the same pattern, and I've been there for 20 years or 30 years.

Then I've got this one moment when *Oh my God, I was there!*

My heart was open.

I was kinder than kind.

I was madly loving.

I was creative.

I was present.

I was audacious.

I was courageous.

That's actually who I am.

Kook, the great evolutionary mystic, writes, *amitat mahuti mit-galeh be'reʼga gad'lu'ti:* **the essence of who you are is revealed in your moment of greatness.**

That's actually who you are. All of the failures—that's part of the rules of the game.

The capacity to go up, and realize that you're up, that Reality is calling you, and the team needs you.

That you get over all the times when you struck out, and all the times when you popped the fly, and you're actually willing to do it.

Sometimes you even work together with other people, and you hit a ball up high. They catch the ball, but another runner steals a base. **And so sometimes you're getting yourself on base, and sometimes you're moving forward evolution itself.**

WHEN ALL OF REALITY CHEERS YOUR MOMENT OF GREATNESS

Confession of greatness means:

I'm playing baseball, I am up to bat. And *who I am* is who I am when that bat cracks the ball and the ball sails, and sails, and passes the lights, and—in San Francisco—goes into the bay. Bases are loaded, and it's a homerun. The entire stadium gets up and cheers at the top of their lungs, and I walk those bases. That's my moment of greatness. That's who I am.

In the world, those home runs are usually hit not in public, without an audience. Heroism takes place in private, in moments in which no one would know that I am actually called in that moment to my Unique Self. **The moment when I take my unique risk, I celebrate my greatness, I recover my Unique Self, I be the best that I can possibly be, and even more,**

And actually all of Reality cheers. All human beings that ever were, or will be, living in that Akashic field, as the Buddhist sutras say, beyond time, literally, all of them cheer…

when I take my unique risk,

when I live in that moment of greatness,

when that bat connects with that ball.

If there's any trust and love between us, and I hope there's a lot, I can promise you this:

If you would actually feel what's happening in Reality, and the symphony of Reality, you would realize that literally, **billions of people across space and time rise to their feet, ecstatic, cheering as you walk those bases.**

Knowing that that's who you are.

That's what it means to confess your greatness.

That's what it means to confess my greatness.

That's what it means to confess our greatness together.

We've got to begin this today.

We've got to talk about living the dream in the collective world, living the dream in the public square, living the dream in our personal lives and our collective lives.

We talked about celebration: being willing to live in the world that's already changed. Because we understood that you can't change the world unless you live in the world that's already changed. Meaning, **I go into Dream Time, I celebrate, and I live the dream. I don't** *defer* **the dream.**

But in my own life, the same thing is true.

Just like we need to create One Mountain, we need to create a festival in the public square. Meaning **we need to live the dream, even as we are madly committed to the evolution of the source code, and to addressing existential risk.**

To be *Homo amor*, to cross the other side, to face this moment between stories and between worlds, we need to be able to laugh at the same time; we need to be able to live the dream, we need to be able to not defer the dream. That's in the public square and the public space.

In our personal lives, even as we fail again and again, we have to realize that's actually *not* who we are. That **the essence of who you are is revealed in your moment of greatness.** That's the first Dharmic principle of baseball, that's the Fourth of July.

That's what liberation means at its best: I am willing to confess my greatness.

And it's only that confession of greatness that calls me home.

CHAPTER 6

BASEBALL PRINCIPLES—A HOME RUN INTO THE HEART OF HOMO AMOR

Episode 302 — July 24, 2022

THE META-CRISIS IS A RISK TO THE EXISTENCE OF THE FUTURE ITSELF—YET WE ARE FILLED WITH HOPE!

So who are we? What is One Mountain? What are we doing here together?

We're articulating a new Story of Value, in response to what we can only accurately call *the meta-crisis*.

The meta-crisis is a breakdown in the commons.

It's a breakdown in the *epistemic* commons, meaning in *a shared Story of Value*, which has caused what we would call a Global Intimacy Disorder, which is, itself, a root cause for what Nick Bostrom at Oxford called in the early 2000s, *existential risk*, that is, risk to our very existence as a species; *a risk to the existence of the future itself.*

And so, we are in this moment when, on the horizon of humanity, there is a potential catastrophic risk and existential risk, coupled with an unimaginable degree of suffering, *unnecessary suffering*, for so many people.

Some of it is physical; for example, billions of people without access to water. Some of it existential and emotional: a million suicides a year, 25 to 50 million attempted suicides minimally around the world, particularly in the most affluent of places, and depression as the fastest growing malaise in the world.

We live in a world of outrageous pain, and at the very same time, we live in a world of Outrageous Beauty and Outrageous Goodness, and there are billions of acts of goodness and kindness performed all the time.

Yet, there *is* a breakdown.

The breakdown is a breakdown in the very Story of Value in which we live. We are not living in a Story of Value anymore. In fact, postmodernity has declared that all stories are false, are fabrication, are *fictions* in one quotation, are *figments of our imagination* in a second quotation, are but *social constructions of Reality* in a third quotation.

Yet, the premodern traditions and the great old traditions, each one, still argues that it has some version of the exclusive truth.

We don't have a universal grammar of value.

We have *deconstructed* value.

We have deconstructed the notion that we are actually actors in the same shared story, with a shared vision, with a mutuality of purpose that's intrinsic to Cosmos itself.

We are not aligned with value.

We are not aligned with the Story of Value.

That breakdown is the root cause of existential risk.

Existential risk is ultimately rooted in our inability to live in a shared Story of Value, which is an expression of this global intimacy disorder.

Intimacy comes from a shared story.

The threat of existential risk:

from rogue Artificial Intelligence (AI), from hitting our planetary boundaries through an extraction model that's extracting from the earth what it took billions of years to manifest, to this huge growing gap between haves and have-nots which will make the caste system of India look like a liberal dance party at the most liberal summer camp.

In the caste system that the world's developing, for the first time in human history, the wealthy will actually be better than everyone else—because they'll be augmented, technologically and cognitively; and they will have access to longevity technologies, to health technologies, to aesthetic technologies. And none of this will be available to the rest of humanity (even if there's a basic monthly income which will pacify the masses).

In other words, **through new systems of augmentations and cognitive, medical, and aesthetic enhancements, and just through capacity to focus time and energy on ethical, intellectual and moral training**—time and capacity not available to most people—**the wealthy actually have the potential to become virtually a different species than the rest of the world.**

All of this together creates literally two humanities.

We are going to have this massive caste system which will make *The Hunger Games* movie look like a Sunday afternoon picnic.

So dystopia actually lurks on the horizon.

If Covid told us anything, it told us that there's a breakdown in information, that the information we are getting is not accurate on either side of the aisle. And it told us that the system is not too big to fail. That's what I have been calling, for the last 10 years, in various forms, *the second shock of existence*, what Bostrom calls *existential risk*.

And, not only we're *not hopeless*.

We're filled with hope.

133

We're filled with energy.

We're filled with a sense of possibility.

Because hope is a memory of the future.

That's what hope is, it's a memory of the future.

This memory of the future is a vision, a new emerging vision, of a new Story of Value.

The emergence of a new human and a new humanity: the transformation of *Homo sapien* into *Homo amor*.

That is the inexorable movement of Cosmos itself. Cosmos moves from matter (the physio-sphere, the **First Big Bang**), and all the levels of matter, into mind.

1. **Matter triumphs in life**, then all the levels of life, which is the biosphere.
2. And then **life triumphs in mind**, which is the noosphere, and all the levels of mind. Those are **the first three Big Bangs.**
3. Then, the human being, the depth of the self-reflective mind, what we call *Homo sapiens*, then triumphs… and **it is actually a new human and a new humanity**; a new possibility for humanity.

In our evolutionary meditation, which we did at Wisdom School for so many years, we would unpack this vision. We would actually meditate our way through the entire evolutionary process. Just like matter triumphs in life, and life triumphs in mind, but we don't *end* with the human self-reflective mind which stalemates itself. We actually *emerge*; **we emerge, and we become more.**

We become a new possibility of what it means to be a human being, to be *Homo amor*.

Homo amor who feels the story of the whole.

Homo amor who becomes conscious that evolution lives *in them, in us, in we*.

We become conscious together of the entire evolutionary process.

We realize the evolutionary process lives *in us*.

We realize that now, in this moment, we can actually shape the future.

We've moved into the Anthropocene, the world in which **humanity participates in the evolutionary story.** I become a conscious expression, in my body and my mind, of the evolutionary process.

I realize that I am a unique expression of that process, and that process is driven and animated by Eros, that Reality is held together by Eros, or allurement.

All of Reality is *allurement*; the allurement of different parts to each other that create larger wholes. The dance between allurement and autonomy is a fundamental and foundational principle of Cosmos that lives in us.

I am a Unique Self, meaning I am a unique set of allurements.

Value lives in me. I am allured to value, and I am repelled by the violation of value.

- ◆ When I see George Floyd brutally murdered, that's the repulsion I feel at the violation of value.
- ◆ When we see Ukraine, and we see Russia moving to crush Ukraine, even with all geopolitical complexities, we understand this is a violation of value—and we are allured to value and its fulfillment.

That's what we are here together for. What One Mountain is about, is that we've made this declaration, which is: we are not willing to look away from the meta-crisis, and we are also not willing (as many groups of people who call themselves Doomers), we are not willing to say, *it's over and there's nothing we can do.*

We are not willing to look away.

We are not willing to look down.

We reject the voices that say *Don't Look Up*.

We are actually doing what Robert K. Lifton, the great writer called 30 years ago, when he began to think about existential risk, we're *facing in*. He wrote a book called *Facing Apocalypse*. *We're facing in*.

Sometimes we step back, sometimes we step closer, but we refuse to ever look away. We are *facing in*.

We are identifying what are the root causes of existential risk.

We are realizing that those root causes themselves are rooted in this global intimacy disorder, which itself is caused by the failure to live in a shared Story of Value.

We are therefore engaging, after all the deconstruction, in the great reconstructive project.

STEP FORWARD AND PLAY

That's why this matters so much.

I really want to invite anyone who wants to step forward and play. If you're willing to play a larger game, if you're willing to participate in the evolution of culture and consciousness, if you're willing to participate, if we're willing to participate together in the evolution of culture and consciousness, which is the evolution of love... *then step in*.

I am going to say a strange sentence, which is going to make you feel crazy, and it makes me feel crazy. But I want to say it anyway. There's a moment in which we have to be superheroes.

And we need to be a league of superheroes. A superhero is someone who refuses to look away. When you refuse to look away, then you access your superpowers.

You begin to wake up

You begin to grow up

136

You begin to show up.

By *you*, I mean *we*, because it's always *we*. We wake up, we grow up, we show up—because we refuse to look away, and so we are animated. We're not interested here in commodifying Spirit and building some platform. That's not our game. That's a complete waste of time and energy at this moment in time. **We are interested in coming together as a Unique Self Symphony, in which everyone's got an instrument to play.**

---

*All of us—we are a league of
superheroes together.*

That's what we have to be, a band of superheroes that don't turn away.

Not because we are grandiose—because we are grand.

Psychology is afraid of human grandiosity, but it forgets to recognize human grandeur.

We're in the Anthropocene. This is ours to do. This is the time. This is the moment. And we are the people. We are the people we've been waiting for.

So I am madly delighted and excited, and it was worth every minute of driving 10 hours yesterday not to miss this moment with you.

We have a huge day coming up. We've got a huge code for this week.

Away we go, *oh my God*!

EVOLUTIONARY LOVE CODE: PLAYING A LARGER GAME

Reality is always asking you a question: are you ready to play a larger game?

Are you willing to play baseball?

Are you willing to play the largest game of baseball there is?

137

THE ERA OF PAX AMERICANA IS ENDING

Oh my God, so this is a big week, and we are going to play baseball. Let's knock this out of the ballpark.

I got a text from Tom Goddard Ronen, who's with us, just so you get how baseball finds its way. This is not planned; this is a text just from a couple of minutes ago. We are working on a book together, Tom and I, which is based on this Unique Self process that we did together for many years at our Wisdom School at Shalom Mountain. Tom is working on the last version of the draft. Tom writes to me, *I'm in the homestretch.*

What's the homestretch? The homestretch is from baseball.

So we're going to talk about baseball. Now, if you're European (there are lots of Europeans here), when you think baseball, think *soccer* (we are going to talk more about baseball at the Intensive in Europe, but think soccer).

I am not going to share any baseball clips today, but I just want to share with everyone a few baseball movies that are going to be in the backdrop (and there's also a bunch of soccer movies).

Now this doesn't work for football, it doesn't work for rugby. It works for baseball in the United States, and I'd say in Europe, it works best for soccer. So feel free to replace baseball with soccer as you're listening, if you are listening in a European mode.

We live in a global world. It can't be about just the United States anymore. The United States has actually played a leadership role in many, many ways, and continues to pour into Reality. And the United States is flawed like every place, and there are critiques that are valid and important about the World Bank (David Graeber has written important critiques about how the World Bank has created debt). There are shadows in the United States, that's absolutely true. And the United States is, in many ways, a very great country.

America bashing is not in fashion in my heart and soul, I'd rather recognize the intrinsic and gorgeous greatness of every country.

The United States, since World War II and since Bretton Woods (which was the new world order that's created peace for 70 years in much of the world), has been in large part facilitated by the United States. *And* **the era of *Pax Americana* is ending; we need to move into a new world.**

America electing Donald Trump, who is—whether you're a Republican or a Democrat—obviously not the right choice for President, who violates basic human values on a daily basis in the most brazen way, **signaled the end of *Pax Americana*.**

BASEBALL IS A PLACE WHICH IS HOLDING A MYSTERY

So when I talk about baseball, I'm not talking about baseball in the sense of *Pax Americana*, **I am talking about baseball in the sense of a place which is holding a mystery.** I want to talk about baseball today, and we've promised to talk about this for a bunch of weeks.

I'm talking about baseball, of course, in context of the new Story of Value.

I thought this would be a great last piece before we start with the incredible lineup, incredible batters in the batter's box, who are going to be with us for the next five or six weeks in One Mountain—a baseball analogy.

Here we go. Do we have a drumroll here? I am actually so excited to do baseball with you. I'm crazy excited to do baseball. Let me just tell you how I got to baseball.

I personally have never liked baseball. I've gone to a couple of games, and for me, when I was a kid, baseball has always looked or felt something like, *you're getting together to watch the paint dry.* Let's get together and watch the paint dry, it's very slow.

So, when I was young—eight, nine, and ten, I wasn't moved by baseball, never really paid much attention to it. Then my son, Zion (who is rockstar beautiful), I planned a father-son trip with him for June. We did this father-son trip, and it was a beautiful trip.

I did the trip for a lot of reasons. One is that his mom has actually been very sick, and I had the sense that he might need to come live with me. He's been raised by his fantastic mother, who's a great teacher and writer, Mariana Caplan. Mariana has gotten sick, and God willing, she's going to get better. So I wanted to do a father-son trip with Zion to talk about the future.

We agreed to get together in San Francisco, I picked him up and we got a hotel room right in the heart of San Francisco, and we spent quite a few days, just the two of us, I think it was four full days.

The agreement was: lots of baseball, and we get to eat whenever we want. So we found this little cafe next to our hotel, which was like this diner, open 24 hours a day, so we would have lunch at like 1am. We did everything just father and son, no rules, just that we have to go deep. The rule was, we had to go as deep as we could in everything. So we had this wild time.

We went to see *Harry Potter*. There's one Harry Potter play that JK Rowling wrote, it's called *Harry Potter and the Cursed Child*. We got second row seats in the play, and we went to see two baseball games.

The two baseball games, one was Tuesday evening, and the next one was Wednesday morning. To each baseball game, we came two or three hours early. For the second game on Wednesday morning, we basically opened the stadium; we were like the third person in the stadium.

Because Zion explained to me that there's *batters practice*, and at batters practice, you can actually get a ball. A couple of hundred people come early, and the players do batters practice, then you can catch a ball.

So I'm like, *I love my son madly, I don't like baseball honestly, but I promised to come to this baseball game.* The agreement we made was: no phone, no internet, no reading other books, no working on anything, we just have to watch every play together. And so, within 24 hours, I went to two baseball games. I got a major sunburn, because we got the tickets for like the sixth or seventh throw, right behind the dugout. It was the Kansas City Royals against the San Francisco team, the Giants, at Oracle stadium.

So we are watching baseball, watching every single scene.

And I just started thinking about baseball with Zion, **what *is* baseball?**

There's a whole bunch of baseball movies.

- *Field of Dreams* is one baseball movie, that's one big one, with Kevin Costner. It's an incredible movie.
- There's another movie called *The Natural*, which is another baseball movie.
- There's a baseball movie called *Bull Durham*. That's movie three that I want to just mention.
- There's another baseball movie called *A League of Their Own*, which is about how women's baseball started in the United States during World War II, a really important movie.
- Then there's another movie called *Sandlot*.

Here we go. So I'm not going to go through the movies, I'm going to just mention them as we go. This summer at our Intensive, I want to look at these movies more seriously, in relation to some soccer movies.

But what I want to try now to see with you and understand with you is: *why is baseball magic?*

BASEBALL IN RESPONSE TO THE META-CRISIS: WHY IS BASEBALL MAGIC?

Who has heard of Walt Whitman? Who knows that Walt Whitman was a baseball reporter? He was a baseball reporter. So Walt Whitman, the great poet writes: *"I see great things in baseball. It's our game, the American game."*

(Again, you could write the same thing about soccer in Europe). He says, "I see great things in baseball. It's our game, the American game." Now listen to this. *"It will repair our losses and be a blessing to us."* Isn't that amazing? That's wild.

By the way, we are in totally serious mode today.

We are going to be totally talking about the baseball vision of *Homo amor*, and baseball in response to the meta-crisis.

But we're also *playing*, because we've got to play. We are in mid-summer, so let's play.

In *Bull Durham* (which is by the way the all-time record-breaker of baseball movies, starring a young Kevin Costner, and Susan Sarandon), the opening line of the movie is where Susan Sarandon does this fantastic monologue. She says, and I'm ad-libbing her monologue:

"I've been to all the churches. I've tried Christianity and Judaism, and I've tried tarot and candles and meditation, and I've tried prayer. I've tried everything, none of the churches work for me.

There's only one church that's ever worked for me, which is the church of baseball."

So what's the church of baseball?

What's Walt Whitman talking about?

NEW GROUNDING OF THE COMMON-SENSE SACRED AXIOMS OF VALUE

I want to try and unpack baseball with you.

I want to try and unpack, if I can, what I want to call *the fourteen principles of baseball*, and how baseball actually represents something unbelievably important and wild in society, which has insane value, which is insanely important, and sacred, and all of that.

Here it is. I want to say it, and then I want to try and unpack it, but first, I want to say it.

Baseball represents value.

That's what baseball is, baseball is about value.

It's not about premodern value. It's not about the value the way the traditions thought about value: God gave my people value, our value is better than yours. It's not a premodern traditional ethnocentric vision of value.

Baseball represents *intrinsic value in Cosmos*, in the way that people intuitively understood that to be true before postmodernity came along and deconstructed value.

Now, I've called this notion of value, in serious writing (which has been published on the web, it's going to get published more seriously this coming year) I've called this *Common Sense Sacred Axioms of value.*

Modernity was defined by Common Sense Sacred Axioms of value.

Common Sense Sacred Axioms are things like:

- Choice matters.
- Effort is rewarded.
- Fairness is super-critical and you can't do without it, you've *got* to be fair.

So fairness, choice matters, effort... there are about 15 Common Sense Sacred Axioms of value. When the premodern world fell apart and modernity came into form, these Common Sense Sacred Axioms of value became *the shared grammar of value of much of modernity*—which the postmodern world came to deconstruct.

Now, the Common Sense Sacred Axioms of value are very, very important.

We can't go back to them. We can't ignore postmodernity. We have to respond to postmodernity's critiques (although I'm not going to do that here today in *One Mountain*).

But we need to *reclaim these Common Sense Sacred Axioms of value that are represented by baseball.*

But this time, we have to *ground* them.

Meaning, they were just *assumed* in modernity.

Everyone said, *we're going to borrow from the social capital of premodernity,* which assumed value through Revelation and through meditation. Everyone assumed value. They thought about who had the best value—but everyone assumed value.

That broke down, but *some* of the social capital or the spiritual capital of premodernity entered modernity—even though, philosophically, people like David Hume, and ultimately, Immanuel Kant, and then Neo-Darwinism and logical positivism, and existentialism, they all deconstructed value.

Nonetheless, **Common Sense Sacred Axioms of value remained**.

Then postmodernity came and deconstructed them, and **now we need a new reconstructive project that actually integrates the best of premodern, modern and postmodern understandings of value**, and we need a new vision of value. That's what we're doing at the Center, this new vision of value which is core to *Homo amor.*

But in this new vision of value, we need to reclaim these Common Sense Sacred Axioms of value. But not *unconsciously*, like modernity did.

We need to actually root them and ground them in Cosmos.

We call that new grounding of those Common Sense Sacred Axioms of value, *Evolving First Principles and First Values of Cosmos.*

That was a big sentence.

I'm not going to work out how that has solved the postmodern critique of the Common Sense Sacred Axioms of value. We are not going to solve that right now. We've talked about that at length in a bunch of *One Mountain* talks we did on First Principles and First Values, so I'm not going to talk about that now.

Now I just want to focus on the fact that **baseball is an expression of value, and it's an expression of Common-Sense Sacred Axioms of value.**

Meaning, no one has grounded them in great philosophy, *they're just a given*; we just *know* they're true, we just live in them. **That's what took us through modernity, until postmodernity came along and deconstructed that.**

Now we need to engage in a reconstructive project to take the best of premodern, modern, and postmodern into a new vision of value.

That's what we're calling *Evolving First Principles and First Values*, or what we call an *Evolving Perennialism*.

And our name for that is *the new Story of Value*.

And our name for that new Story of Value is *CosmoErotic Humanism*.

If you're new to *One Mountain*, don't worry about that. This is a big field; you don't need to swallow it all whole now. We are trying to articulate here an evolution of the source code, and today, we're just going to focus on baseball.

But first, I just want to take one movie. I'm going to go through 14 principles of baseball, and I'm going to do it pretty fast. But I want to just start, just to ground with you, this notion of baseball being about value. I'm not going to show you the clip now. I'm just going to tell you the story.

THE STORY OF FIELD OF DREAMS: "IF YOU BUILD IT THEY WILL COME"

In *Field of Dreams*, Kevin Costner hears a voice.

The voice says: "If you build it, *he* will come."

145

Then it says: "If you build it, *they* will come."

He's in this field, he has married this woman he doesn't quite know, they fell in love. They fell in love, and he winds up in a farm somewhere in Iowa, and he's in the field.

He's not much of a farmer, but he's in the field, and he hears this voice. The voice says, first: "If you build it, *he* will come." Then he hears: "If you build it, *they* will come."

He's not sure what to build, and then the next morning, he sees a vision of a baseball diamond, and he knows that somehow, he's meant to build this baseball diamond. So, he takes this big portion of his Iowa cornfield, which is a very bad economic idea, and he builds this baseball diamond.

Then this player shows up who was his dad's idol, and he has this broken relationship with his father. The name of the player is Shoeless Joe Jackson, one of the greatest players that ever lived. But Shoeless Joe Jackson was on, I think, a Chicago team, the White Sox, with eight other players, and they're thrown out of the league for cheating. But they actually *didn't* cheat.

So, they're thrown out of the league for a violation of value.

Common Sense Sacred Axiom: *don't cheat*.

It's not built on any big philosophical thing, just *don't cheat*; that's a Common Sense Sacred Axiom of modernity. They're thrown out of the league for cheating, which is a violation of value. But it actually didn't happen, they actually didn't cheat, which is even a *bigger* violation of value: they've been falsely accused.

To be falsely accused is to have value violated in your soul, and I actually know something about that. So these guys die. Shoeless Joe Jackson was his name, and these seven other players, they die. They're never able to play baseball again.

So he hears this voice: *"If you build it, he will come"*, and who shows up to this diamond?

Shoeless Joe Jackson.

Now, you understand: what's happening here is: **baseball is transcending death.**

In other words, this is a very, very spiritual, transcendent, metaphysical movie. It's a wild movie. The only place Shoeless Joe Jackson can exist out of the realm of eternity in this world is in the diamond.

They invite Shoeless Joe to come into the house, but he can't; he can't leave the baseball diamond, because **the baseball diamond itself participates in the field of eternity. The Field of Dreams itself is part of the field of eternity**.

That's beautiful.

It's a crazy, beautiful movie. Come to *One Mountain*'s sister, the Outrageous Love Festival, to our Summer Intensive, and we're going to look at a lot of clips here. It's wildly beautiful.

So Shoeless Joe Jackson comes, and then all the other players that were thrown out of the league come, and they start playing baseball in this field. But the only people that can see them playing are Kevin Costner, his wife, and their daughter. But his brother-in-law Ray, who represents the ordinary world, he can't see what's happening here. All they see is this crazy baseball diamond.

They're coming to foreclose on the property, because they've cut down too much of the crops so they can't turn a profit. He's about to lose the farm the next day.

Ray is saying: "You've got to sell the farm and I'm going to get you a good price. Sell it and get rid of this baseball diamond".

Kevin Costner is saying: "No, we're not going to sell".

Then his daughter at a certain point says: "Daddy, we don't have to sell the farm".

147

She has this almost kind of prophetic voice.

Ray, her uncle and Kevin's brother-in-law, says: "Karen, please".

Then she says: "People will come".

Then Kevin Costner turns to his daughter and says: "What people, sweetheart?"

She says: "From all over. They'll just decide to take a vacation, and they'll come to Iowa City. They'll think it's really boring, so they'll want to pay us, like buying a ticket".

Ray says to his brother-in-law: "Are you crazy, you're seriously listening to your daughter?"

He says: "Yes".

But wait a minute, why would anyone pay money to come here?

She says: "To watch the games. It will be just like when they were kids a long time ago, they'll watch the game and remember what it was like".

Ray says, the brother-in-law who wants to foreclose the property: "What the hell is she talking about?"

She says: ***"People will come!"***

Ray says: "Alright, this is fascinating, but you don't have the money to bring the mortgage up to date, so you're still going to have to sell".

Kevin Costner says: "I'm sorry, Ray, we got no choice. People will come, Ray, they'll come to Iowa for reasons they can't even fathom. They'll turn up in your driveway, not knowing for sure why they're doing it. They'll arrive at your door, as innocent as children longing for the past. Of course we won't mind if you look around you'll say, it's only X dollars per person. They'll pass over the money without even thinking about it, for it's money they have and peace they like."

Of course now the brother-in-law, who wants to foreclose, because Kevin Costner has got no money to pay his bills, because he's built this baseball stadium, thanks to this niece as Craig says, "Ray just signed the papers".

But the daughter keeps talking: "No, then they'll walk off to the bleachers and sit in their shirtsleeves on a perfect afternoon. They'll find they have reserved seats somewhere along one of the baselines, where they sat when they were children and cheered their heroes, and they'll watch the game. It will be as if they dip themselves in magic waters, the memories will be so thick! They'll have to brush them away, the memories from their faces".

Then Ray, the brother-in-law, just can't take this. He says *when the bank opens in the morning, they'll foreclose.*

But the daughter keeps talking: "People will come, Ray!"

Then Ray says: "You're broke, you sell now or you'll lose everything".

But she keeps talking.

She says, or Kevin Costner says: "The one constant through all the years, Ray, has been baseball. America has rolled by like an army of steamrollers. It's been a race like a blackbird rebuilt and erased again—and this is true about Europe—but baseball has marked the time. The field, this field, this game, it's part of our past. It's part of who we are. It reminds of all that once was good, and it could be good again. *People will come! People will most definitely come!*"

It's an amazing scene. It's easy to click out during that scene, but it's an amazing, amazing scene.

At some point, she falls and she gets hurt. One of the players who's actually a doctor, who had come from a different point in the Wheel of Time, actually steps out of the field to treat her and takes care of the daughter after she falls. They were sitting on the bleachers talking, she falls, and he takes care of her.

149

For the first time, **Ray can actually see the players**. So Ray completely does a 180-degree turn around, and he says to Kevin Costner, *you can't sell.*

So what's this scene about?

The scene is about the *Good*, it's the key scene in the *Field of Dreams*.

Baseball reminds me of the good in everything

Baseball incarnates value, and sport at its best, but baseball and soccer are the best incarnations of them. **Baseball incarnates value.**

FOURTEEN PRINCIPLES OF BASEBALL

Let's just take a look at fourteen principles of baseball.

- ◆ Number one, there's a cathedral, there's a temple, and the temple is the baseball stadium. When I came with Zion to Oracle Stadium on Wednesday morning in June, it was early in the morning, and we were like the third or fourth ones in the stadium; we got up really early to get there early. You see this gorgeous baseball diamond in this beautiful stadium, and you realize this is a temple. It's a temple, and people are coming to the temple like people have always come to temples. This is what Susan Sarandon calls at the beginning of Bull Durham, this is the church of baseball.

- ◆ Number two, baseball incarnates ritual. Baseball has a set of rituals that hold us. But it's more than that.

- ◆ Number three, baseball has principles. There's a set of principles, there's a set of laws in baseball, which are about how the game is played. Everyone subscribes to the same principles, and those principles are about eliciting greatness and excellence from the players. So those principles are about what? They're about eliciting excellence and greatness from the players, that's three.

150

- ◆ Four, the goal of baseball is to come home; a homerun. Tom wrote to me this morning, I'm in the homestretch, meaning I want to come home. The goal of baseball, like the goal of spirit and value, is to dream our way home, and to live those dreams, and to find our way home. That's what baseball is about, it's about getting home. But it's not just about getting home myself. Sometimes I sacrifice a fly so someone else can get home. It's about the whole team coming home. It's about driving other people home. But the movement in baseball, number four, is a movement towards home.

- ◆ Number five, baseball has saints, and it has heroes. (Of course baseball has holy men and holy women, when it's played by women. We'll talk about that movie, A League of Their Own, when baseball was played by women in the United States, beginning in World War II, from 1943 or 1944 till 1954. Incredible story.) But baseball has saints, and it has heroes. Just like any great system of spiritual transformation does, baseball has saints and heroes.

I want to say something about those saints and heroes. They're not like movie stars; movie stars are about *celebrities*. It's a superficial structure, or phenomenology of celebrity. Baseball heroes are different. **Baseball heroes are about incarnating value.**

That's why in *Field of Dreams*, when Shoeless Joe Jackson was accused of cheating and thrown out of baseball, it was so devastating. Shoeless Joe Jackson says to Kevin Costner, *it was like having my arm and my legs amputated.* Not just because he couldn't play baseball, but because **baseball is value**.

That's why building the stadium—*if you build it, he will come*—and fixing that false accusation, and restoring value, was this great mystical moment in *Field of Dreams*. So the heroes of baseball, the saints of baseball, are not just celebrities in that kind of superficial, shallow sense. But they're meant, in their ideal form, to incarnate value.

I remember, I grew up partly in Columbus, Ohio, which was near Cincinnati. It was a time when Sparky Anderson was the coach of the Cincinnati Reds, which was then called the Big Red Machine. Whoever remembers baseball this was the Big Red Machine, and it was Pete Rose, and Johnny Bench, and Dave Concepcion, and Tony Perez, this incredible team, and Sparky Anderson was the coach.

Then Pete Rose is accused of doing something unethical, which is this very small infraction. But it's a violation of value, and Pete Rose is now out of baseball, and everyone's devastated. Because the baseball hero, this is number five, is not a movie star. **It's a different quality of hero, at least in its ideal, if you will, platonic form.** So that's five.

Maybe I'll just say one more thing. There's this great scene, from the movie *Sandlot*, which is one of the five baseball movies. It's this movie about this ball which is signed by Babe Ruth. It's a growing up story of baseball, about two kids, actually a group of kids in this neighborhood. It's a fantastic baseball movie.

But there's this moment, twice in the movie, where they talk about Babe Ruth, and they say, *he's the Great Bambino*; they go through all the nicknames of Babe Ruth. It's a fantastic scene, and it appears twice in the movie, where you get the sense of who Babe Ruth was.

The second great scene from *Sandlot* is the opening of the movie, where the announcer says: "In 1932, the world changed. It was the World Series, it was the ninth inning, and Babe Ruth was up, and he nods to center field with his bat, saying, *I'm going to have a homerun into the stands there.* It had never been done before, and then he went and did it. Then a superhero was born, a super Titan! That's baseball. *I said I'm going to do it, so I'm going to do it.* **This Promethean human capacity to fulfill and to show up as value.** So that's number five.

- Number six, in baseball, everything and everyone is accountable. Just like in the great traditions, there's this Book of Life, because we count, we're accountable. In baseball, we count; we count homeruns, and we count stolen bases, and we count RBIs. In other words, everything counts. There's a public ledger in baseball, and all of the history of each player is public and available; there's no advertising, and there's no image, and there's no branding that can change that. That's actually the original blockchain is baseball, when it's immutable and it's there and it's for public witness. So that's number six.

- Number seven, when you're up in baseball, most of the time you fail. So baseball is the ritualized experience of failure. Seven out of 10 times, you don't get on base; you either fly out, you strike out. Basically, most of baseball, for the batter, is spent failing. If you have a 300 average in baseball, you're batting 300, that's unbelievable. You have a lifetime average of batting on 300, that's unbelievable; 350 is like insane. Because basically, most of the time, you're failing. So baseball is the ritualized human experience of failing again and again and again, and not losing heart. And holding, and being of brave heart, and getting up to the play again and again. And not falling into resignation, and working with it again and again. And then picking up that bat, and getting in the right form, and being willing to give it everything you have. To show up and to wake up, with all of your energy, and all of your passion, and all of your potency, and all of your power. It all begins again every time you come up for bat. So number seven is, baseball is about failure. How do you live in failure without losing heart? That's number seven.

- Then number eight is, it all begins again every time you come up to bat. In other words, every time you come up to bat, you can change your record. Every time you come up to bat, you can be a hero. Every time you come up to bat, you can lift that stadium to its feet, with ecstatic exultantly that will blow your heart and mind open. You can actually be cheered by all of Reality for showing up with everything you got. In other words, in baseball, yesterday doesn't determine today; every time you get to start again. That's number eight, and it's gorgeous.

- Number nine: who you are in baseball is not just your record, but there are these greatest moments. Remember that principle: The essence of who I am is revealed in my moment of greatness. So there's moments of greatness that are wildly valued. Gorgeous!
- Number ten is, the way you create greatness in baseball is both by how you hold failure and by connecting the dots of your moments of greatness.

When you connect the dots of your moments of greatness, then you get the story of your life.

One of the things we have in modern stadiums, is they will actually play you the game back in its moments of greatness at the end of the game, or they'll play yesterday's game. They don't play for you all of the empty space, but that's actually part of it; you can't get rid of it. All of the empty space— all of the staying in, all of the strikeouts, all of the staying in deep right field or deep left field, and not seeing a ball for five innings, but just staying there with steady presence—*hold, hold, hold,* you're holding the field, that steady presence then creates those moments. Then when you link those moments together and you connect the dots, you get the greatness of your life.

Life is about connecting the dots of your moments of greatness, which you only get to do if you hold the field in between those moments, and you don't collapse in them.

It's about moving beyond resignation, sitting in the emptiness, that's what fills up at those moments of greatness, and connecting those dots together which become the story of your life. That's 10, that's a big one.

- Number 11, baseball is unique because it's about autonomy and communion together. Basketball is a team too; there's a big team, the team moves together down the court, players stand out, so you've got some autonomy and communion as well. But in baseball, you have it in a much more extreme form. Because each player, all nine of them, are in their own position—whether it's the shortstop, or one of the base men, or deep in the outfield, or you're batting, or you're catching, or you're pitching—you're both in autonomy and in the communion of the team. We all need each other, and yet, you're also highly individuated in your place. It's really about you, and it's about you being in that lonely, singular, beautiful place in the context of a larger community. Because you realize, wow, there are people, people all over the world holding a piece. But you're holding your own piece. It's different from basketball; you don't get absorbed in the team. It's different from soccer even. There's a kind of singularity in baseball which is very unique. There's the extreme communion of the team, and there's this radical individuality happening at the same time.
- Number 12: the Field of Value, which is the Field of Dreams, lives beyond the individual expressions of it. This is a very big deal. In other words, every baseball player is a Unique Self and a unique expression of that Field of Value. But even when that baseball player is done playing, and they move on in their lives, or they may even move on from this world, the Field of Value remains; the Field of Dream remains. For example, the Yankees are still the Yankees, and the Dodgers

are still the Dodgers, and the Red Sox are still the Red Sox. There's an unchangingness to the Field of Value. Fenway Park has been there for a long time in Boston, and Yankee Stadium. In other words, there's this sense of rootedness in an evolving but eternal Field of Value. So the Yankees remain, even if all the Yankees have changed. The separate self of individual Yankees have disappeared, the Unique Self have left their mark, and they've had their continuity, but the Yankees, and the game, and the stadium, which are all expressions of this magical Field of Value, the Field of Value remains. That's number 12, the eternity of the Field of Value; the stadium, the name of the team. Often you hang up the uniform and the number of one player, because that number represents Unique Self. Number always represents Unique Self; we talk about that in the book Soul Prints in part four, where I talk about a number as Unique Self. So, you might hang up someone's number. But the uniforms, the fields, the diamond, the rules of the game, the ethos of the game, all of that remains. Okay, that's number 12.

- Number 13 is about the fact that you need constant practice—constant, rigorous, deep, beautiful practice—to do really simple things with elegance and grace.

That's a big sentence: **you need constant practice to do really simple things with beauty, elegance, and grace.** You can't always do them with beauty, elegance, and grace. You're going to strike out a lot of times. But actually, your life is connecting the dots of those moments of greatness when you did those *second simplicity* things with beauty, elegance, and grace.

And what do you do in baseball?

You hit.

You catch.

You throw.

You run. That's it, that's the whole game. You hit. You throw. You catch. You run. You wait. You deal with failure. You're part of the team. There's enormous practice to be able to catch that ball, to pitch that ball, to run the way you need, and to throw. There's this sense of enormous practice to get those moments of elegance and grace that are unlike anything else. That's number 13. I would call 13: **enormous constant practice to do simple things with elegance and grace.**

♦ Number 14 is, in baseball, we surface the idea of healthy competition. When we talk about one of the root causes of existential risk, we talk about Reality being constructed as a success story, where the story is a rivalrous conflict governed by win/lose metrics. But that doesn't mean that we get rid of competition. No, competition is important. But the competition can't be zero-sum competition: If you didn't make it, you die. In the marketplace we've created in the world today, if you can't self-commodify, you actually, quite literally, die. You're actually written out of society. And so, competition is important but it can't be a zero sum competition. It's got to be a rivalrous conflict, which is beautiful; competition is healthy and beautiful, we shouldn't get rid of merit. Baseball represents merit. It's not a kind of communist system which got rid of merit, and got rid of hierarchies of value, and got rid of appropriate competition. Baseball is rivalrous conflict. But it's not just governed by win/lose metrics, although it is in part. But it's also governed by a Field of Dreams and by a Field of Value. Baseball is a Field of Value, and sport, and delight, which is bigger than just the rivalrous conflict. The players are playing together in the shared Field of Value, and the shared Field of Value is much bigger, ultimately, than who wins the game. It's a competition. But it's healthy competition on a team with this dialectic between autonomy and communion, where the team is larger than any individual player, and there's a commitment to the larger Field of Value, the larger Field of Dreams, the field of baseball. There's an umpire, and the umpire makes calls, and those calls are binding. So it's not a kind of crony capitalism. It's a healthy, conscious Field of Value and Field of Dreams.

Now, I think you get a sense here of what we mean by this game being this sacred play.

I'm going to end with this piece and we're going to do a little baseball prayer. It's exciting!

Baseball incarnates value, and we have looked at 14 ways in which baseball incarnates value, and I want to just add two more pieces, we'll finish with these.

THE STORY OF THE MOVIE *THE NATURAL*

One of the ways you see how baseball incarnates values is, in this movie *Field of Dreams*, it says: "Baseball is good, and it can be good again." Good is value; good is *the Good, the True, and the Beautiful*.

Second, when you look at the movie *The Natural* with Robert Redford, it's a very subtle movie.

All five of these movies are worth watching, but *The Natural* is a very subtle movie about Robert Redford. He has a childhood sweetheart. He's a natural. In a very early scene in the movie, his father says to him: "You've got a gift, son, but you can't rely on the gift. You've got to practice. If people just rely on the gift, they fail".

His father, just a few minutes later, has a stroke and dies under an oak tree. The next day, or that night, there's this stormy night, and lightning hits the oak tree, and Robert Redford, who's a kid, goes down to the oak tree where his father just died, and he makes a bat out of that oak tree where

158

his father passed and where he practiced with his father. That bat is called *Wonderboy*.

In the early scene, you see this girl watching him when he's a little kid, practicing, and they grow up. Then right after his father dies, he gets drafted, and they're in love, and they're going to get married. He says, *I'll come back for you.*

Then he goes, and he's on his way to the big leagues, he's on a train, and he meets this woman. She kind of enchants him; she seduces him. He walks into her room, because she says *come meet me in my room.* So he walks into her room, like, *what's this about?* She puts a veil over her face, and she shoots him, and he disappears for 16 years.

The movie starts after those 16 years; we don't know what happened in the intervening time. He's now coming back 16 years later to reclaim that simple dream of baseball and value, and he explodes onto the scene at age 36, and then he loses it. Until there's the scene where he sees a woman stand up. He's been in a slump for a long time, and that woman is that original girl that he was in love with.

He can't quite see her, but he sees that she stood up, and you see actually **the Goddess rising**. They somehow align, even though he can't see or doesn't know who it is, and he hits it out of the park. He goes to find her and can't find her. **But in the end, they find each other, and when she's in the stadium, he can actually find himself.**

What the whole movie is about is these forces that go to rig baseball, to have players sell out for the sake of commodifying baseball, and they actually offer $20,000 to throw a game; this great violation of value. They threaten to blackmail him, because they have pictures of when this woman shot him. She was apparently killed afterwards, which had nothing to do with him, there was some terrible tragedy that happened there.

But they threatened to frame him. So he takes $20,000 because he has no choice, and then he realizes that he just can't do it. He says, *I won't do it, this is over, I'm going to go play baseball. I'm not throwing the game. I can't violate value,* essentially.

He goes to the game, and the game is hanging in the balance, and he can't quite find it. The woman who was his old beloved sends him a note because she has a son. He doesn't realize it's his son, when they made love right before he went on that train ride to the Majors. So she says to him, your son is in the stadium, and it's just like, *huh?!* He becomes the father, and he becomes the man.

There's this incredible scene. He shouldn't be playing the game, because that bullet that was lodged in him from that original shot has kind of wreaked havoc, and his whole system could collapse if he even plays one more game. But he has to play; he puts his life on the line for value. There's this last scene where he's up, and he just connects with the ball, and you just see value at play as that ball hits that bat and it soars out of the stadium. Then the last scene is him pitching back and forth with his son.

When I went on that baseball trip with Zion, there were four days together, and I had hurt my back quite badly. I was in some serious amount of pain. But at the end, Zion said: *Dad, let's throw the ball,* kind of like that scene at the end of the Redford movie, *The Natural.*

At the very end of the movie, he gets together with the woman of his childhood, and with his son, and they're throwing the ball back and forth. At the end of *Field of Dreams,* Kevin Costner with his father, they actually repair their relationship and they do a catch. It's just unbelievable!

So here I am with Zion, and Zion says: *Hey, let's do a catch.* But I don't have a mitt, so we go to a shop and we get this mitt, and it's not quite broken, so they oil it for us. Then Zion and I go out to this field, and my back is in wrenching pain, but the pain literally disappears, and we just spend half an hour just throwing the ball back and forth in that simple way.

Immeasurable value!

We both said that maybe our favorite part of the whole trip was just that half hour, throwing that ball back and forth.

When we enter the *Field of Dreams*, the field of Father and Son, the field of the immeasurable, the field of the non-commodifiable, the Field of Value, the field of transmission, that's baseball.

- Baseball is value.
- Baseball is the magic of value.
- Baseball is Common Sense Sacred Axioms that modernity knew.

Baseball and soccer, they both represent that same notion of value.

So, what we need to do is, after postmodernity deconstructed baseball and deconstructed value—we need to reclaim it. **We need to reclaim value at a higher level of consciousness.**

It can't be reclaimed as Common Sense Sacred Axioms; we can't go backwards.

We need to re-vision value.

We need to begin to talk about First Principles and First Values.

We need to explicate what value is based on.

We need to respond to the academic critiques, which are true but partial, and to actually re-vision value.

That's what we've been working on at the Center. Because to be able to re-vision value and articulate a universal grammar of value that's real is THE source code move that changes Reality.

It's bigger than Darwin.

It's bigger than Freud.

It's bigger than Einstein.

Because it's not about the exterior, it's about the interior sciences.

Imagine if we can articulate a shared grammar value; a baseball, a soccer, for humanity, in which we're all playing in that stadium, and we're all bound by a larger vision of value.

Yes, there's rivalrous conflict, but within the baseball diamond.

The baseball diamond which participates in eternity, which transcends death.

That's the invitation.

That's the possibility.

That's baseball.

Oh my God, that's what it means.

Homo amor is a baseball player, man or woman.

A LEAGUE OF THEIR OWN

In the movie, *A League of Their Own*, the last movie we mentioned, it's about women in World War II.

Women in World War II, for the first time, were released from the home, because men were on the front, and they began to work in the factories, they began to work in offices. That actually seeded women's liberation 20 or 30 years ago, because women didn't want to go back to the old way.

There's this moment where they start this league, and it's supposed to be for entertainment. But the women take baseball seriously, and they play this league gorgeously and beautifully. It's like **women emerging in their power, finding the depth of their masculine and integrating it with their feminine, and this new feminine emerging, which is part of *Homo amor*.**

Of course, the point is that women playing baseball in this new way foreshadows the emergence of the new feminine. That's the same theme.

162

Homo amor is the best baseball player, the best soccer player, that there ever was.

That's what it is.

We're in the *Field of Dreams* together; we're in the Field of Value together.

PRAYING IN THE FIELD OF VALUE

It's in that field that we find each other, and it's in that field that we pray.

We're not going to do Leonard Cohen this week, the Holy and Broken *Hallelujah*.

By the way, Leonard Cohen loved baseball.

But I just want to ask if we can for a second, just to do a direct prayer.

Let's just do a direct prayer.

Let's just pray for everyone.

Let's pray for each other.

Let's pray for anyone who's sick.

Let's pray for any part of us that's split off.

Let's pray for the new human and the new humanity.

Let's pray for the emergence of *Homo amor*.

I'm going to, with permission—and maybe we just all do it together, just so we have a chant—I'm just going to offer a chant into the space as people write their prayers, and then we'll read the prayers.

So here's just a simple chant as people read their prayers, and it's a chant for everything that's possible.

Chant wherever you are in the world.

You don't need a good voice to chant, I'm evidence of that.

You chant like we play baseball, with all our hearts and souls.

Thank you, everyone.

It's so good to be together.

What a delight and an honor to be with you!

CHAPTER SEVEN

TO RESPOND TO THE META-CRISIS, WE NEED TO REVISION WHO WE ARE

Episode 314 — October 16, 2022

THERE IS NO *NOW* SEPARATE FROM THE PAST AND THE FUTURE

Welcome, everyone. Welcome. Welcome.

It is so fantastic to be together. I mean, completely gorgeous!

What are the demarcating characteristic of *enlightenment*, my friends?

And **by enlightenment, we mean the realization of my purpose as a human being**—when I become who I could be, who I was *meant* to be, when I am aligned with the cosmic purpose for my life. And of course, that begins with the realization that **there *is* a cosmic purpose for my life**. I've got to *realize* there is a purpose, and to *align* with that purpose.

And then there are certain what I would call *litmus tests* for enlightenment. **A litmus test for enlightenment is the ability to experience the full radical newness and importance of the moment**, as it's happening. Not to get caught in somehow going blind and deaf:

FROM POLARIZATION TO PARADOX

- Unable to see the significance and beauty of a moment
- Unable to hear the resonance of the moment
- Unable to smell the fragrance of the moment
- Unable to taste the moment
- Unable to touch the moment

Because all healing lives in the moment itself.

That's why in Hebrew, the word *ragua*—for deep, spacious opening, for relaxation, when we fall into the depths of who we are—is the same three-letter Hebrew root as *rega*, which means *the moment*. In other words, **in the moment is its own spaciousness.**

So, a litmus test for enlightenment is the capacity to *open the moment.*

Now, to open the moment, I cannot do an Eckhart Tolle kind of *Power of the Now* thing, or what my friend, Ram Dass, Richard Alpert—and we liked each other a lot, had a deep love for each other—called *Be Here Now.*

Be Here Now, the *Power of the Now*—the way it was expressed, and the way it is classically expressed—doesn't actually *get us there*, because it is about the Now moment which is *separate* from the past and *separate* from the future. And **there is no Now moment which is separate from the past and the future.**

In order to be in the Now moment, and engage in the essential process of enlightened living, **the basic action is Now-ing.** And it's a process that I've got to engage in—it's an action I have to engage in—literally in *every second.*

Now-ing, does that make sense? Now-ing, as a verb: **I step into the depth of the Now.**

But in the depth of the Now, I have history and I have future, I have past and future.

Past and future live together in the Now—

- ◆ I am aware of, I am deeply connected to history and tradition.
- ◆ I am also deeply connected to the uniqueness of my experience right here in the Now.
- ◆ And I feel the future actually available to me here in the present.

For example, I can hear the future generations turning to us in this moment, in this Now moment, and saying:

Are you going to lay your lives down? Are you going to give everything to make sure that we're going to be born?

Because we are not in any kind of place where we *know* that the future will be born.

The possibility of the future being unborn or being stillborn is what we call existential risk. **The meta-crisis—which is quite real in this moment in time—requires the fullness of our presence in the Now, and the fullness of our response.**

But it's got to be a Now that is not a short-term Now. We need a wider perspective. We need to get out of our temporal myopia. But we are so focused on Ram Dass' *Now* or Eckhart Tolle's *Now*—who are both sweet and lovely modern people, reformulating ideas of mystical enlightenment, which said *it's only in the Now.*

No, no, in the Now is the past and the future.

In this Now, in which we are bringing with us **the depths of wisdom of the past**—of all the great traditions and their validated insights, from pre-modernity and modernity and postmodernity, and with this deep, **deep reaching for the future**, and feeling what the future needs from us now—that's the quality of enlightenment.

And I have to re-experience that quality in every Now moment. In every Now moment, I've got to re-experience that.

That's the invitation.

"SOCIAL SELF" IS A DEGRADED VIEW OF WHO WE ARE

The entire Tech-Plex comes out, in a very real sense, from the world of liberal culture, where the human being is literally reduced to what I would call a *social self*—meaning the human being is the sum total of social interactions.

That is the dominant position of liberal culture that is actually forming the world of technology—**the immersive environments online**, in which virtually all of us have to live in order to function in the world to some real extent, and in which the next generation is completely immersed in.

So it's not a tool.

Technology is not a tool—that's a huge mistake.

Technology is an environment. It's an immersive environment, and that immersive environment has *its own set of values*.

The primary value of the tech plex, as it exists now, is a **particular narrative of human identity**, which is that human identity is social, that **the human being is a *social self*.**

That has been formalized at the MIT Media Lab, for example, in the United States, which is probably the single most powerful place in forming the structure of the Tech-Plex in the last 25 years. They have articulated this very, very clearly.

Alex Pentland, the Director of the Lab, wrote an article called *The Death of Individuality*, where he said that the notion of the Western enlightenment, in which there is a rational self who can make decisions based on value, is dead. (He doesn't use this word, but he describes it, if you read his writings. He's written many, many articles. And he's kind of a hidden figure in this whole emergence of what I call *TechnoFeudalism*.)

He's got a whole series of words—like *social network incentives*, or *social pressure*, or *social conditioning*, or *social norms*—which are basically referring to what his teacher, B. F. Skinner, called *positive reinforcers*.

We reinforce behavior through multiple exposures to other people in your social web. Through very careful collection of data, and very careful understanding of how you are motivated, we can expose you in different ways to particular groups of friends online, in a constant and repetitive way, so that these groups of friends will, in a statistically significant way, shape your behavior:

They might cause you **to buy**.

They might cause you **to move someplace**.

They might cause you **to vote in a particular way**.

We can actually use the technology to *nudge* people (Cass Sunstein's term) into what the powers that be think is *right behavior*.

That's the social self. And it is a degraded view of self, because **it says that the human being is fully exhausted by their social structure**.

And what we are saying is—and this is what *One Mountain, Many Paths* is about—we are saying, no, no. What we need to do is, we need to re-vision who we are. In order to respond to the meta-crisis, we need to re-understand. We need to articulate a genuine new story of who we are, and who we are is not the social self of the liberal world.

TRADITIONAL VIEW OF THE SELF GENERATES META-CRISIS

My friend Dennis Prager created *Prager University*, which is a good example of conservative thinking all over the world that gets billions of views. They articulate a much more traditional, biblical view of the Self, who responds to Revelation, and who is—in a positive way—fulfilling the values that the Creator God imposed on the world. There is some truth in that, just like there is some truth on the left—**but both of them are pallid, weak versions of who we are.**

- The notion that there is a Creator God who is outside, completely outside, of the world, who gives us value—and our job is to hear that God's revelation and then to fulfill that value—is weak. It's not exactly like that.
- The notion that actually there is *no* Source that articulates value in the world, that suffuses the world with value, that we are merely *social selves*, responding to *social patterns*—the basic view of the left, the basic view of postmodernity—is also tragic.

Today in our culture, we've got places like Prager University, who are essentially expressing a **premodern**, biblical view of the world—and they are fighting with places like the MIT Media Lab, who are pretty much expressing a **postmodern** view of the world.

On the one hand, it is the social self of the MIT Media Lab Tech-Plex. People like Mark Zuckerberg and Larry Page are all deeply influenced by the MIT Media Lab, and they believe that the basic human being is a social self, and that we can heal existential risk and heal the meta-crisis by actually *organizing* the world:

- People will have identity markers.
- We will be able to track people and monitor people.
- We will be able to influence behavior.
- We will be able to shape elections.
- We can control the world through the invisible controls of a kind of *soft totalitarianism*, mediated through the Tech-Plex.

That's one view.

And then the other view, which I am going to call *the Prager University view*, the traditional view is that the human being actually can respond to value, that there is a Source of value in the world—but that that Source of value is ultimately outside of the world; that the world itself is neutral, but there is the Source of value from outside the world that commands us, and it's our job not to follow our instincts, but to follow those commanded values and to respond to them—**which is also a hugely weak view of the world.**

Both of those views of the world lead to the meta-crisis. In other words, the Prager University view is: I am a Separate Self, I should follow the dictates of the external commands.

But **this traditional view flies in the face of lots of fragrances and senses of how evolutionary science works, and how we actually understand value**—and that is not going to take the world. Since it is not going to take the world, it is going to wind up causing rivalrous conflict; rivalrous conflict, win/lose metrics.

Rivalrous conflict governed by win/lose metrics, in which everyone is claiming that they are hearing *their* version of the commanded voice, is one of the core and primary sources of the meta-crisis. Wow!

The meta-crisis is extraction models, exponential growth curves, polarization, that are all driven by win/lose metrics—and the win/lose metrics comes from this traditional view, where, ultimately, all the different systems are clashing with each other, and we've got to see which system is going to win. *That's* what the premodern world was. **If we stay in that traditional story, then we are going to stay in rivalrous conflict governed by win/lose metrics, which directly generates all of the dimensions of the meta-crisis.**

Because once you have polarization, then you cannot create a shared grammar of value, you cannot create global resonance, you cannot create a global coordination that we need to respond to the meta-crisis—because everybody is fighting, everyone thinks they are right, and everyone thinks that they need to triumph, and that their view of the world is the correct view of the world, and it excludes the other views, and it's only the triumph of my view that will actually get us home.

This kind of rivalrous conflict that doesn't actually fulfill the human being.

The human being doesn't have a sense of their own Eros, of their own expression of value—so there is a sense of emptiness. And then **emptiness creates that failure of Eros.**

That failure of my fullness creates all sorts of pseudo-eros. And pseudo-eros needs to be filled—we need to cover the emptiness of pseudo-eros. And all forms of addiction and acting out, all forms of excessive consumption, which also drive the meta-crisis, are the results of that pseudo-eros.

THE NOTION OF SOCIAL SELF GENERATES SOFT TOTALITARIANISM

On the other hand, when we look at the left side of the aisle, when we look at the Tech-Plex in all of its forms—this is going to generate a kind of *soft totalitarianism*. Not the old totalitarianism—where we got dragged away to Siberia—but **a *soft* totalitarianism, in which we engender a kind of invisible police state.**

It is a kind of thought police.

In very, very short order, everyone will have identity numbers, and those identity numbers will enact some form of what China calls *social credit system*—it will be enacted, in some version or another, in the United States as well.

For example, if you oppose the vaccine—which was a complex issue, but there were certainly good reasons to oppose the vaccine—if you oppose the vaccine, you lose your job, even though there is quite a bit of medical information that challenges vaccines. (Vaccines are a very complex issue, on both sides. I've tried to bring both sides together to sit in a room and talk about this face-to-face, and I've been unsuccessful.) But if you actually opposed the vaccine and the mandate to get a vaccine, you can be fired from your job.

My good friend, Dr. Venu Julapalli, who is a brilliant doctor, with his brother Vinay, down in Houston, neither of them got vaccinated. They didn't get vaccinated, because one of them was part of a health study, and the other actually opposed the vaccine in principle—not the vaccine itself, but that the hospital administration would *mandate* doctors to take the vaccine and give the vaccine. He felt, correctly, that this was a health decision that needed to be made by doctors—and when the hospital administration hijacks the autonomy of the doctor in making a health decision, then they are violating the basic relationship between doctor and patient. Venu is dutifully filing a lawsuit against Houston Methodist. But Venu is just one example. People have gotten fired from their jobs all over the place because they didn't agree with a particular policy.

Travel is restricted, jobs are restricted—and what will begin to happen is access to loans will be restricted, education will be restricted.

It won't be just about the vaccine. If you take issue with the dominant policies and views of the culture, then you will somehow be blackballed by that culture. And because you are online, there is extensive information about what you're watching, and what your opinions are, and how you feel about things.

Because we now have even *emotion detectors* on the web; the field of *affective computing*—tracking your emotion as you engage on the web—has actually exploded out of MIT Media Lab in the last 10–15 years. Many of Alex Pentland's students are leading that thing called affective computing, which will allow us to track very, very carefully how you feel about things, and how you respond to particular images.

Let's say there is an argument about the environment, and let's say there is a particular position on the environment which has a particular understanding of how you should think about fossil fuels.

Fossil fuels are a far more complex issue than the way they are cast. It's not that fossil fuels are evil. Fossil fuels are *complex*. Fossil fuels have saved many lives. The environmental issues are complex. My friends, Sean

FROM POLARIZATION TO PARADOX

Hargens and Michael Zimmerman, wrote a book called *Integral Ecology*, which takes you through the much more complex set of issues that need to be considered in terms of the environment.

But if you don't agree with the dominant position on the environment that's expressed by the dominant fields of media, then you will be, in some sense ostracized and "canceled"—once there is a kind of almost voluntary social credit system, imposed not by the government, but by some sort of alliance between the formal agencies of structure.

For example, the Houston Methodist Hospital actually said to Venu, *you have to get a vaccine, if not, you cannot work here.* That will be extended. There will be many, many more areas in which the core notion of freedom—the freedom to think carefully, the freedom to dissent—will be lost.

Ronald Reagan was not wrong when he said, *you can lose freedom in one generation.* Ronald Reagan was wrong about a lot of things, but he was not wrong about this.

So, that notion of the Tech-Plex is also a dangerous, problematic notion, governed by a certain view of who the human being is. And **it leads to a kind of soft totalitarianism, to the death of our humanity.**

OUR NOTION OF SELF CREATES OUR SOCIETY

So, the Separate Self view of the human being—that the human being is a separate self, and human beings and systems of human thought are in rivalrous conflict governed by win/lose metrics—leads to **existential risk, the potential death of humanity, because rivalrous conflict governed by win/lose metrics is actually the primary block to our ability to do global coordination.**

- We can't do global coordination, as we've said many times, without **global resonance.**
- We can't do global resonance without **global intimacy.**
- We can't do global intimacy without **a shared Story of Value,**

which is *not* rivalrous conflict governed by win/lose metrics.
It is a shared Story of Value that **we all get onboard on.**

If we cannot get onboard on that, then **we get to potential existential risk: the death of humanity. That's on one side, that's on the right.**

And on the left, we get to the death of *our* humanity.

We get to a soft totalitarianism imposed by Tech-Plex around the world—both in western open societies and in closed societies, just different forms of this kind of totalitarianism—in which **you lose the ability to dissent, to think freely, to gather information, to draw conclusions based on evidence and information.** When there is a dominant narrative, motivated by whatever the series of motivations are—sometimes they are sinister, and sometimes they're very natural; they're for the sake of health, and they're for all sorts of good and noble purposes—but when **there is a dominant narrative, and you challenge that dominant narrative, then you are considered somehow aberrant, and you lose access to the goods of society.**

That's where we are headed on the left. That's a big deal. In order to respond to that, what do we need to do?

- ◆ We need to take the best of what the left understands: this sense of a social self, participating in the larger social structure.
- ◆ *And* the best of the Tech-Plex, which actually has enormous good to offer.
- ◆ *And* the best of the traditional world, the best of the Separate Self—and from there, articulate **a new shared narrative of identity**. That's a big deal.

Next week, **we are going to articulate a new narrative of identity that actually integrates the best of the right and the left, and offers us a way forward in response to the meta-crisis.** That's crazy exciting. So stay tuned.

CHAPTER EIGHT

THIS POIGNANT MOMENT OF NEURO-CULTURAL PLASTICITY: A TIME BETWEEN WORLDS AND A TIME BETWEEN STORIES

Episode 315 — October 23, 2022

THE FIRST PRACTICE OF CHANT: *WE ARE THE MUSIC*

It is fabulous and beautiful to be with you. It is great to be with everyone. What we are going to be doing in the live, weekly *Evolutionary Sensemaking* broadcasts, is we're going to begin fifteen minutes before the hour, every week.

We're going to come together and just:

- Find each other in presence
- Find each other in chant
- Find each other in practice

Before we get to the *dharma*—to the new vision of First Principles and First Values embedded in a story of value, which is the single most important response to the meta-crisis—every week, we will begin with *yoga*. And yoga means *practice*.

Just like there are First Principles and First Values, there are *First Practices*. And one of the core First Practices—in all of the great traditions of value, in the great interior sciences, one of the most important practices is chant. And we are actually *scientifically* made of music. **We are music ourselves.** We are *constituted* by music. I gave a talk about it this summer, so I won't unpack the science of it now.

Science tells us that music emerges with spacetime, and the intervals in spacetime that create music quite literally live in us. It's scientifically true to say that we, quite literally, are music—so when we chant, we find that dimension of ourselves that is music.

We are going to do a little chant in the beginning, just to get started. We're going to pick up the pace of it a little bit, so we can *feel the feeling* of chant. I am going to do it once, a little bit off-tune like I always do, and we will pick it up and open it up.

We are spontaneous, we are here, we are just delighted.

It's *Let The Way Of The Heart*—and it's got some energy to it:

> Let the way of the heart,
>
> let the way of the heart,
>
> let the way of the heart shine through.
>
> Love, upon love, upon love,
>
> all hearts are beating as one.
>
> Light, upon light, upon light,
>
> all appear as the one.

Try it, wherever you are in the world. Together, all around the world!

This is the practice of chant—and the actual lived realization that *there's a way of the heart.*

THE WAY OF THE HEART INCLUDES THE MIND AND THE INTELLECT

The way of the heart *includes* the mind, the intellect, and rigorous thinking—and often lots of footnotes. The heart is both the organ of *feeling* and—and, as we now know, with an enormous amount of research from the last twenty years—the heart is also part of our *cognitive function*, and you cannot split those two.

Our ability to think and our ability to feel are inseparable.

The Universe *feels*, and the Universe feels *Love*.

I will tell you a little secret:

- I have, never in my entire life ever, like, ever, ever, ever, ever, ever had a good idea. I've never had a good idea, *not once*.
- I've had a *feeling*. I've only had a *feeling* that arrested me, that engaged me, that I *listened to*.

Often, we cut our feelings off, we split our feelings off—or we have a feeling, and then we don't *feel the feeling through to completion*. And then the feeling gets *arrested*. It gets arrested in trauma, or it gets arrested in the golden shadow of our *unlived* self. It is an *unlived* feeling.

When you listen deeply, you realize that the world is not *only* a great thought, as the physicist James Jeans pointed out a bunch of years back: when you look at physics carefully, the world seems more like a great thought. **The world *is* a great thought, but it's not *just* a great thought**.

If you look a little more carefully at physics, **the world is a great *feeling*.**

The Universe *feels*—that's scientifically accurate. Reality is marked by *allurement*; cosmic allurement guides and *animates* Reality at every stage.

So the world is not just a great thought, my friends; the world is a great *feeling*. The Universe feels, and the Universe feels love. And that love is One Heart, and it's One Love, and it's One Breath

THE WAY OF THE HEART: REALITY IS EROS

Let the way of the heart means, feeling *the interior quality* of Cosmos, feeling the allurement that draws us *uniquely*, and that draws us *together* to create the most beautiful world that we know is possible. It's the knowing that *the heart is real*. The heart is not a superficial function; the heart is not extraneous to the real stuff.

The heart is the most real dimension of Cosmos.

Reality is, at its core, Eros. Reality is Eros. Reality is One Love and One Heart.

Our minds speak the languages of Eros. Our minds unpack the dazzling cacophonies and symphonies of elegant order, beauty, and truth, that are expressions of the feeling tone of Cosmos.

- **Cosmos is intimate**, it feels intimacy.
- And it *desires*. Alfred North Whitehead talks about the *appetite of Cosmos*. **Cosmos feels *hunger*.**
- **Cosmos is hungry for value**: for the Good, the True, the Beautiful, for love, for delight, for joy, for a heartbreak that becomes transformation.
- **Cosmos is evolution**, and evolution at its core is a series of transformations.

WE LIVE IN A TIME BETWEEN STORIES

Let us set intention on where we are:

Where are we?

Who are we?

What are we doing here?

This is not a place for casual therapy. It's not a feel-good place, and it's not a doomer place where we say, *Oh my God, the world is about to explode!*

180

Although, of course there *are* reasons to feel good, and there *are* reasons for therapy, and the world *is* about to explode.

We are doing something very specific though. **We've got a very specific intention**—and I want to set that intention very clearly because it's easy to lose. I'm going to try and set it in a new way, with your permission.

Okay, are we in? Are we ready? Here we go.

We live in this time between worlds; we live in this time between stories.

If you've been here before, that is the sentence you know well because we say some version of it every week. And we always point to the Renaissance, which was also, in its own way, a time between worlds and a time between stories. When the premodern story was breaking down, when pandemics were sweeping Europe and Asia, and people were dying on the street (almost half of Europe actually died), we understood then that **we couldn't use the old tools of premodernity, of the traditional world to** heal the fracture, to heal the break, to heal the destruction, to heal the breakdown.

In order to move from breakdown to breakthrough, we needed to articulate a new vision, to tell a new story—because it's only a new story, and a new story of *value*, that changes the trajectory of history.

So da Vinci and Ficino, whom I mention all the time, and about a thousand other people gathered in Florence, under the patronage of the Medici's, opposed by almost all the other families in Florence, and **they began to** *think* **and to** *feel*. They felt in art; they felt in science.

They felt and asked the following questions:

What is the feminine?

What is Eros?

What is sexuality?

What is a relationship?

How do we gather information?

What's the nature of the human being?

Who are you?

Who are we?

Where are we?

What's there to do?

Where are we going?

What do we really want?

The new Story of Value that emerged, as we have shared many times together, was the story of modernity.

- To the precise extent that the plotlines were accurate, modernity birthed what Habermas, probably the greatest critical philosopher of the twentieth century, called *the dignities of modernity.*
- To the precise extent that they got the storyline *wrong*, which they did in the Renaissance, in major ways, it birthed the *disasters* of modernity. And those disasters have brought us to this moment in which we are quite literally not just poised before *dystopia*—we are poised before a potential extinction, the death of humanity, or the dystopian death of *our* humanity.

But we are *also* poised before utopia. We have the potential to unfold a world of unimaginable beauty, unimaginable depth, unimaginable goodness, of ever-deeper and ever-wider truths, a world in which no one's left out of the circle, in which everyone can respond powerfully and accurately to the great questions: *who am I, who are we, where are we,* and *where are we going?*

But *not* in a way that occludes the uncertainty, *not* in a way which dissipates the Great Mystery. The Great Mystery is there, and we always live at the edge of mystery, reaching deeper and deeper into the mystery and unfolding it into the light. Even as we reach deeper, in the same moment, **the mystery itself deepens**.

We always hold uncertainty, and we always stand before the mystery.

WE HAVE THE CAPACITY TO CREATE A NEW SUPERSTRUCTURE WORLDVIEW TO CHANGE THE VECTOR OF HISTORY

And yet, we have the capacity to *integrate*, to *weave together* the validated insights from all the great stories of value, into a new source-code tapestry, into a new Story of Value, rooted in what postmodernity denied: First Principles and First Values.

We have come to the conclusion—after decades of study, practice, and research—that at this moment of meta-crisis, when everything is at stake, the *only* response that will change the vector of history is a ***superstructure*** change.

- An ***infrastructure*** response alone is insufficient. Infrastructure would mean: *let's create new sources of energy.* That's critically important; renewable energy is critically important but insufficient. *Let's find ways to check for waste in water to prevent a bioweapons attack*—critically important but insufficient.

- A ***social structure*** change won't do it. Social structure means: *let's revision how democracy works, let's revision laws that demand that X amount of data scientists don't work for the Big Tech world, but actually work for the government, in order to be able to appropriately bind or monitor what Big Tech is doing.* That would be a social structure change, a change in law. Those are also very important.

183

- **But the only response that will change the vector of history is a *superstructure* change.**

There's infrastructure, social structure, and superstructure—terms we are borrowing from the sociologist Marvin Harris—but the crucial insight is that **only a superstructure change can change the vector of history**, meaning only a change in the answers to the three great questions:

1. *Who* are you? Who am I? Who are we?
2. *Where* are we? Where am I? Where are we?
3. *What's there to do*, or where are we going, which is deeply related to *what do I really want to do*, and *what's my deepest desire*?

Those essential questions: *who, where, what*? Those are the questions, and our answers to them become the new story.

VALUE IS REAL, AND VALUE EVOLVES

We have to answer those questions based on First Principles and First Values that are *real*.

We have to move beyond the postmodern deconstruction of value. We have to realize that value *allures*, that *we are guided* by value, and that value *evolves*.

Modernity and postmodernity were wrong when they said *value is not real*.

Premodernity was wrong when it said *value doesn't evolve*.

Value is real, *and* value evolves—that's the *post*-postmodern understanding; that's the basis for the new Story of Value. Value is real. And so we're currently working together to articulate fifteen basic core First Values and First Principles, and to articulate the plotline of the story. And the story is a love story.

THE POTENTIAL FUTURE IS VAST—THERE'S SO MUCH MORE VALUE TO COME

Now, I want to try and say, *in a new way*, **why this insanely matters,** as part of setting our intention.

A thought experiment: **your actions taken now will affect all of your future lives.**

- Imagine for a second **that there are 100 billion people who have lived**—which is about accurate: there have been about 100 billion people in the world since the beginning of the species, around 300,000–400,000 years ago, when *Homo erectus* as it were, stood on the savanna of Africa and became some version of *Homo sapiens*. Now, from that moment till today, there's been about 100 billion humans.

- **Now imagine that in some sense, you are *every one* of those people.** Remember the chant we started with: *all hearts are beating as one.* And in some sense, you *are* every one of those people. We all share the same essential quality of consciousness, and we're all indivisibly part of each other in some fundamental way. But for now, let go of the ontology of it, let go of the reality of it. Just hold it as a thought experiment.

- **Let's say you live every single one of those lives consecutively, one life after the other.** And in some sense, you *are* all of those people (and Andy Weir, in a short story called *The Egg*, actually articulated some version of this thought experiment). Imagine 100 billion people, one after the other after the other after the other after the other—and you are *all* of those people—how long would it take for those people to go through their lives?

And so that means that...

You're an early hunter-gatherer,

and you're at the beginning of agriculture,

and you're a man,

and you're a woman,

and you're a slave,

and you're a boy,

and you're a victim,

and you're an apex predator,

and you're a murderer,

and you're the one who's murdered,

and so on...

Do you get that? You're everyone.

You're the rapist, and you're the one who is raped.

You're the one who's filled with joy and goodness, and you're the one who's filled with black melancholy, who can barely move.

Imagine that you are *everyone*. You are literally all of those people, and all of those people live in you—that's going to take about 4 trillion years. About *four trillion* years.

- **Now imagine, for a second, the future.** If the average mammalian species lives about a million years, that means that at this point, four trillion years in, you still have 99.5% of your life left to live—meaning, if you unfold all of the future, you've only hit 0.5% of humanity. It means **you have an enormous amount of life left to live**.
- Now imagine, friends—**imagine that human beings actually learned how to take care of themselves to at least survive**

in a way that earlier mammals are unable to do. And imagine we live *more* than a million years—we live two million, or three million, or four million, or we even live the fullness of the possibility of this earth and the star, until they burn themselves out—and we transmute into the next possibility. **Imagine you live *all of that*.**

Then, within the framework of that thought experiment, which is real and valid, we would be literally *taking our first breaths* outside of the womb; we'd have taken twenty or fifty breaths so far. **We're in the first seconds out of the womb right now.**

And to get a sense, my friends, the future is vast and large; **the potential future is vast and large.**

Trillions and trillions of people.

Trillions of boys and trillions of girls.

Trillions of babies and trillions of loves.

Trillions of pearls of laughter and trillions of holy tears.

Trillions of transformations and creative acts,

Trillions of unique expressions of Reality, each one more dazzlingly beautiful than the last, each one with infinite value.

There are trillions of new emergent, of self-evidently precious value—each of which matters immensely and enormously—yet to come. There are trillions of irreducibly unique expressions of infinite value left to come, of infinite divinity left to come.

Or we could say: *There's more God to come. There's more value to come.*

But *infinitely* more value to come, *infinitely* more God to come—not literally infinitely but virtually infinitely. Wow!

THE FUTURE DEPENDS ON WHAT WE DO NOW

Now, let's go to the next level of the thought experiment.

Now you realize that your actions taken now will affect all of your future lives.

Do you get that? What you do now will affect all of your future lives.

One possibility is that it will affect whether you even *have* a future life. In other words, you may behave in a foolhardy way now, which will ensure that you have no future life at all. Now, that's kind of a shocking notion.

Imagine you're a teenager, and there's lots of things you do as a teenager.

- ◆ You want to experiment, go deep inside, experience the pain and beauty of the world, and get new fields of knowledge.
- ◆ But you also have to be careful as a teenager *not* **to take risks that will prevent you from growing up.** And it's the job of society, your parents, and your own internal learned, trained discipline to prevent this. You don't want to take a risk whereby through some foolhardy act you actually die—you actually never grow up into the fullness of who you are. Wow!

And sometimes we don't even realize we're taking those risks.

I remember in Bexley, Ohio, where I grew up, we used to go jumping building from building, and it was intensely dangerous. And it didn't even occur to me it was dangerous; I was never hurt. But looking back on it, it's like, wow, *what was I thinking?* We could have fallen. Sometimes you do it unconsciously—and sometimes, we're actually aware that there's this immense risk in what we're doing, but we split off the risk.

Now, **we are not even close to the adolescence of our humanity.** And at this moment, what we do in the next ten, twenty, fifty, 100, 200 years from now, in this immediate period will directly affect the future—according to carefully articulated and hard-crunched numbers, and an entire set of

188

writings on existential risk, by people like Nick Bostrom, the student of Derek Parfit at Oxford who coined the term *existential risk*, along with quite a few other serious investigators. Some of Parfit's other students, Toby Ord and Will MacAskill, have also done very good work in this regard.

I think their work is deeply flawed in terms of *how to respond* to existential risk, but they did an excellent job in both coining the term, articulating the *possibility* of existential risk, and bringing it deep into consciousness.

So that's real. Existential risk is absolutely real. That's the death of humanity.

What we do in this period of time could actually prevent us from growing up. It could stop us from living all of those trillions of lives, in some fundamental sense.

Or it could also cause the death of *our* humanity. **And the death of *our* humanity means, we don't actually go extinct, but we enter into a dystopian future.**

NEURO-CULTURAL PLASTICITY

I want to take a look at what that means—because it's a very big deal.

Right now, we are in a moment—if I could coin a term that emerged in conversations last week—of what I would call neuro-cultural plasticity.

Plasticity is a term from biological systems research from the last fifty years. A brilliant brain researcher named Thomas Metzinger (who coined the term and whose material I've been reading for the last two to three years) talks about plasticity. Plasticity means that we used to think that the brain—very early on in infancy, or perhaps a little bit later—is essentially ossified, or frozen, and it doesn't ever change after that. The brain is a given, and this belief has had enormous implications. We now realize that that's not true, that **the brain is constantly rewiring itself.**

For example, after you have an accident, and you lose, for example, one part of the brain, the other hemisphere will often rewire some of the functions of the lost part. And that's true not only of the brain but of the entire body. The body is *plastic*. **The systems of the body, including the brain, are plastic, and they have the ability, at certain moments of crisis, to rewire themselves,** until they again get appropriately set in the mold or the pattern that they will be in.

That's called *plasticity*.

But **not only is there plasticity in the biological system. There's plasticity in the *cultural* system.**

MacAskill, in a book that called *What We Owe The Future*, gives a very good example of this. In the sixth century, the Xiao dynasty ended in China, and then there was a period of 400 years of what was called "The Hundred Schools of Thought," in which you have major schools competing with each other: Confucianism, Taoism, and what was later called, retrospectively, Legalism, and also Mohism. You've got these major four schools of thought battling for dominance—until about 400 years later, when Confucianism wins the day, and for about a 1,000 years Confucianism dominates China.

He uses that as an example of these moments that are *in between*. That's what we mean when we say, *we are at a time between worlds*. When we say we live at a time between worlds and a time between stories, what we mean is that **there is neuro-cultural plasticity in this moment.**

We are at a time between worlds, we are at a time between stories. This neuro-cultural plasticity means that in this moment, it's not set; in this moment, it could go many different ways.

That's generally not the case. Generally, we are *in* a world, *in* a story, and you can't really even think outside of that story. *You live inside of that story. That story lives in you. You can't even see the story. You can't make the subject into an object. You can't see the story. You're just in the story.*

We are at this unique moment when, at least at the leading-edge, there are many of us who have stepped *outside* of the old story:

- ◆ We realize that we are not just at a place where, after COVID we need to *get back to normal.*
- ◆ We realize, as I've been trying to say for a couple of decades, together with Barbara Marx Hubbard, our partner—with whom I founded One Mountain, Many Paths, and who was the co-chair of our Center for the last few years of her life— that in some deep sense this is a *phase shift moment.*

We are at a phase shift in human history, unlike any that we've ever been in, in which *everything* is at stake, where all the old systems are breaking down, but the new system hasn't yet emerged.

This space *in between* is a completely creative space. And in the space in between, the relationships between parts *can be reconfigured.* **This space *in between* is a *neuro-cultural plastic* space, in which what we do affects everything.**

That wasn't true 200 years ago, and it may well not be true 200 years from now. It may not be true 100 years from now; it wasn't quite true 100 years ago. This time between worlds, this time between stories, is this space *in between,* where:

- ◆ We are either going to do **a reset by telling a new Story of Value** rooted in First Principles and First Values.
- ◆ Or there's going to be **a tragic, dystopian value lock-in.**

VALUE ARE NOT MERELY PRAGMATIC

Here's where MacAskill, Ord, and Bostrom go wrong. They are essentially beautiful people, highly moral, highly principled in their own lives. And yet, despite the fact that they come out of a what I would call Derek Parfit's "moral realism," **they can't quite articulate a genuine theory of value.** Value, for them, is, in one sense or another, *consequentialist*: value is merely based on its *utilitarian* effect in the world.

Once you try and do *consequentialist ethics*, they always break down, as the critics of consequentialism have pointed out, and they can't ultimately *motivate* you—because we are only truly motivated by an intrinsic sense of responding to value that's *real*.

You cannot deconstruct value and say that value is a mere fiction. This is the way the circle of postmodernity talks about value: *value is a mere fiction, value is a figment of our imagination,* value is a story, and value is pragmatically consequentialist. No.

Value is real; value is an intrinsic structure of Cosmos.

So we need to actually create *not* a world in which you just keep open, competing values—which is what MacAskill suggests. **No, we instead have to download into Reality a vision of a set of First Principles and First Values that are *evolving*.**

One of the First Principles and First Values is that these values themselves are always evolving. These First Principles and First Values form a Universal Grammar of Value. That Universal Grammar of Value is **a context for our diversity.** It is a context for many plural, various, subtle, and nuanced understandings and applications of value.

But at the center, there has to be **a shared sense of Evolving First Principles and First Values that are rooted in a Story of Value.**

We need to know that *uniqueness* is a value, that *truth* is a value, and that *peace* is a value. But these are all *real* values, not *pragmatic* values; we did not just make them up because it seems to be good for our ability to have a good meal today.

No, we actually feel and know that *value lives in us:*

That justice is a real value. That kindness is a real value. That Eros is a real value. That sensuality is a real value. Sensuality means it's worth being sensual with someone, that it's valuable. That the exchange of pleasure is a value.

In other words: There's a set of First Principles and First Values that animate Cosmos, and that move all the way *up* the evolutionary chain and all the way *down* the evolutionary chain.

In matter, life, and mind, there are evolving expressions of the same Field of Value.

One of these values is *mystery*, meaning that it's not all worked out yet. One of the values is that part of mystery is *uncertainty*—but that these are *real*, and that what we do *matters* ultimately.

Our lives are part of the Field of Value, and our lives are not over when they're over.

We participate in the Field of Value, and value is *eternal*—not in the sense of unchanging, but in the sense of that which is *beneath* space and time. **We participate in the Field of Value which is beneath space and time. We need, in this moment of neuro-cultural plasticity, to download those values into Reality.**

Because the alternative is a value lock-in. That's what MacAskill talks about accurately. A value lock-in means that at this time between worlds and time between stories, at this moment of what I'm calling *neuro-cultural plasticity*, **if we don't download First Principles and First Values**—which are valid and true, and which integrate the best of premodern, modern, and postmodern insights into a new "Evolving Perennialism"—**the alternative is a tragic dystopian value lock-in.**

IN RESPONSE TO NIHILISM, YOU GET CLOSED SOCIETIES

If we don't articulate a Universal Grammar of Value, then the first country that achieves technological supremacy will dominate the world

This is a very big deal, so I want to try and articulate for you what that means. This is the key of everything we're talking about today.

Before people emerge in their fullest and most noble selves, they always go through certain stages. Often, people never get past going through what I'm about to describe before they die. Some people do transform. But it's not just people—**humanity as a whole goes through these same stages.**

These are stages in which there is **a seeking of dominance**: we want to dominate, and we want our vision of the world to dominate after we're gone:

+ Alexander the Great wanted Hellenism to last forever.
+ Hitler wanted there to be a thousand-year Reich.
+ Chinese emperors, who reigned only fifteen years, spent that time planning for their dynasty to last forever, which of course it never did.

But there is a sense that we want our vision of the world to last forever. That's a big deal because we are in a world today in which **there is an enormous battle between open societies and closed societies.**

This is the way MacAskill tells this story. Although he clearly comes from the open society side of the world, **he refuses (in his chapter on value) to say that one set of values is actually better than any other set** because he has no *ultimate basis* to say that, other than consequentialism, which doesn't give you a ground in intrinsic value. Over the long term of history, he claims, we are actually not sure what works better. China is making a case that ultimately, over generations and generations, *their* system is going to work better.

So MacAskill cannot actually create a hierarchy of values. *Nothing can ever be ultimately better than anything else,* although there is lip service paid to that kind of claim—and beautiful lip service. For example, read Derek Parfit, his teacher, who is stunning. I have all of his books, and I've been reading through them the last seven or eight weeks. They are gorgeous.

But ultimately, we need to be grounded in the Tao, and the Tao is a Field of Value.

194

Once we step out of the Tao, we step into *the abolition of man,* as C.S. Lewis said it. The Tao is the Field of Value. Once we step out of the Field of Value—even if we have a couple of generations of benevolent articulators of culture, like Parfit, Bostrom, the young MacAskill and Ord, and blessings to you guys—ultimately, it's not going to hold.

Once you step out of the Tao, out of the Field of Value, you are ultimately in the realm of nihilism. When you are in the realm of *not* standing for actual value, then the nihilism emerges. **And in response to nihilism, you have various forms of closed society.**

That's what China is. That's what Russia is trying to be. It's what Hungary is becoming. That's what the Philippines is becoming. It's where Brazil is going. It's where Sweden—strangely—is going. It's where Italy is going. And France has very strong movements in that direction. And the United States has strong movements in that direction—movements towards some version of closed society.

Now let's look at a closed society, for example, from the perspective of China. This is a big deal. A closed society responds to this breakdown of value, responds to the sense that the West is not standing for value, and says: no, no—we are going to **superimpose values from above, and those values are going to be totalitarian.**

- ◆ Those values are going to create concentration camps around China.

- ◆ Those values are going to create a total surveillance system, without First Values and First Principles, in which there is no value to the individual:
  - There is no value to unique human personhood, and there is no sense of Unique Self.
  - There is no sense of the intrinsic value of goodness, truth, and beauty.
  - There is no sense of human personhood.

- There is no ultimate sense of universal human rights, let alone governance through more advanced forms than top-down, totalitarian, brutal, and murderous dictatorship.

The Chinese Communist Party today is essentially a mafia, which engages in the most brutal tactics of murder and mayhem. Let me just say that clearly. Anyone who has studied and read seriously about what the Chinese Communist Party is, knows that it's a degraded expression of what humanity can and needs to be.

THE CURRENT TRAJECTORY IS TOWARDS THE DEATH OF OUR HUMANITY

Let's say we *do not* manage to articulate a universal grammar of value. Let's say we just go about our lives, and we do our little projects and our little New Age engagements, and we do our transformations—but we actually ignore the fact that we are at this moment of *neuro-cultural plasticity*. We fail to download a compelling vision—a vision that's compelling to the people of China, a vision that's compelling to Russia—that begins to emerge as a *universal* grammar of value.

What's going to happen is that **the first country to achieve technological supremacy,** for example, to realize AGI (Artificial General Intelligence)—according to multiple estimates, there's a significant possibility in the next twenty to fifty years that this could happen—will have a huge advantage. If that country is China, **what China will seek to do is to *lock in its values*.**

Artificial General Intelligence means not *local* artificial intelligence, in which you can do one particular action exponentially better than humans, but you can do *everything* better than humans. Right now you have an artificial intelligence that can do *one* thing. It's really good at playing chess and go, but it's not good at ordering groceries. You have very, very localized, exponentially developed, local artificial intelligence—but it's not *general*.

If you get to an artificial *general* intelligence, and that general intelligence is owned by a closed society or a totalitarian state, within six months to a year, two years, the AGI will exponentially increase the rate of productivity and military power achievable by that country and **make them the dominant force in the world, in a very, very narrow window of time.**

In other words, the country that achieves that will dominate the globe. And when I say *dominate the globe*, it's not an old world. It means they dominate the entire planetary stack, all of the computational infrastructure. **The planetary stack of Reality will be completely dominated by that country.** Wow!

And that country will then download *their* value structure into the whole world.

In order to get food, to get a job, to participate in any way in society, you actually need to be part of what China today calls the *Social Credit System.*

- ◆ You have to be part of that world infrastructure. If you are not part of the world infrastructure, essentially, you die.
- ◆ And you only are allowed into the survival *infrastructure* if you assent to the imposed *superstructure* (worldview, value structure).

So within a generation or two, that downgraded, dystopian value structure becomes the value structure of humanity.

Wow! That's what I mean by the death of *our* humanity.

So there are two possibilities:

There's **the death of humanity**: extinction.

Then there's this other dystopian possibility, which is a second form of existential risk, which we've been talking about together in our Unique Self Symphony. It's not the death of humanity, it's **the death of *our* humanity**.

UP TILL NOW, WE HAVE NOT PRESENTED A COHERENT SYSTEM OF VALUE IN THE WORLD

What we've been saying week after week—and it's sometimes easy to lose the meaning—is that we are at a time between worlds, a time between stories. We are at this moment of **maximal neuro-cultural plasticity, when what we do *can* affect the future**.

That's a *very* rare place to be in history. There is no generation that's ever been, in all of history, at this place, where what we do can affect the future in this way.

Imagine we've lived for four trillion years, 100 billion lives. But we're just at the first 0.5 percent, as we said earlier. If humanity lives, like most mammalian species, a million years, we are at the beginning of all our future lives. **And what we do now could lead us to suicide; we could have *no* future lives**, meaning we will have essentially left, *in non-existence*, essentially *murdered* trillions and trillions and trillions of gorgeous, irreducibly unique expressions of *LoveIntelligence* and *LoveBeauty*. Boys and girls, and babies, and old men and old women, and wise ones. All of it!

Or we can engage in this great project, this overwhelming moral imperative of this time, articulate a new Story of Value based on evolving First Principles and First Values, and have the audacity to say, we want to download this and engage the world. And we want to talk to China, Russia, and every closed society, and *invite them* into this possibility, so they see that we actually *are* standing for value.

- **We are *not* trapped in nihilism.** We are not in what Putin thinks is a kind of weak and broken postmodern West.
- **We are actually standing strong for value and aligned with value in a deep way.** It is an evolving and coherent system of value. And it's a Story of Value that we are willing to place everything on the line for.

Up till now, the West has not presented a coherent system of value in the world. We haven't. Putin, Xi, and Orban, have looked at the West in a kind of postmodern breakdown, no longer standing for value in any genuine sense.

There was a moment where the West came together around Ukraine, which was critically important, and we've talked about that here (and Elena has done a beautiful job of bringing those talks together, and we're going to share them shortly with the world)—but that's broken down in many ways.

We have to come together and stand for value. But we can't do that because we actually don't have a *theory* of value. We don't have a vision of First Values and First Principles. We are stuck in all the postmodern critiques of value, which are valid, but we haven't moved beyond them.

What we're here to do is to tell a new story, **to tell a new Story of Value, rooted in First Principles and First Values, at this time of neuro-cultural plasticity, is the single most compelling moral act, with most consequences.**

What we do at this moment of plasticity, what we do at this time between worlds and time between stories, will affect *everything*.

What we need to do is give *new answers*. But not declarations, not *made-up* answers—the deepest, most beautiful, most gorgeous, most grounded, most validated answers we can—to the great questions of:

- Who am I? Who are we?
- Where are we? What kind of world do we live in?
- What's there to do? What's our deepest heart's desire?
- What does it mean to be a man and a woman?
- What does it mean to be in a relationship?
- What does it mean to create an economy?
- What does it mean to create politics?

All of that depends on these basic questions: *who*, *where*, and *what*.

That's what we are going to be doing. We are in this revolution, and our question is, are we ready to play a larger game?

Are we ready to participate, at this moment of maximum neuro-cultural plasticity, in the Evolution of Love and be brave and courageous enough, to create a universal grammar of value, even a world religion—but a world religion as a context for our diversity? It's not *one* religion where we say, "we *own* truth, you don't," but a *universal* grammar of value as a context for our pluralism, as a context for our diversity.

Literally, the future of Reality depends on it. The suffering, catastrophic risk, existential risk, the death of humanity, or the death of our humanity— all depends on what we do at this moment in time.

PLACING OUR LIVES ON THE ALTAR OF HISTORY

The rare privilege of being those people, born at this time, to have that privilege—and of all the people on planet Earth, somehow, we, and colleagues of ours around the world, have been granted this privilege.

We have the capacity to be here together on Sunday, to be participating in evolutionary sensemaking projects, and in editing projects, and writing projects, and funding and resourcing, in order to make this true.

And we've got to take dramatic steps:

What does that *mean* for each of us? What are we doing to show up, to wake up?

So that we can actually light this moment up with our mad commitment, our mad joy, because we can *see* it.

I want to tell you something. There are days when I wake up, and I'd rather *not* see it; I'd rather be blind. Because if you don't see it, you can just engage your life. But once She opens your eyes, once you can see it---if you could see it today---that means you are in. That means you have a place at the table of history.

This system that we are in is not an old-style system. It's not somebody downloading *dogma*. We are together as a Unique Self Symphony, creating this new Story of Value, resourcing and visioning it. **We are placing our lives on the altar of history and saying, we are here!**

We are here to do this. Wow, that's a big deal.

We are going to step into articulating this grammar of value. And we want to weave it together in a way so that:

- It's going to land in China.
- It's going to land in Moscow.
- It's going to land all over Africa.
- It's going to land all over Asia.
- It's going to land all over Europe.
- It's going to land all over the Americas.
- It's going to land in Greenland.
- It's going to land in Iceland.
- It's going to land in Australia.
- It's going to land in Africa.
- And I missed a continent, Antarctica.

We want to articulate an evolving shared grammar of value that calls us to the best of who we are.

Not to our lowest common denominator, which is how the web is architectured (the web-plex appeals to the lowest common denominator of human being). Instead:

We want to call forth **our nobility**.

We want to call forth **our beauty**.

We want to call forth the capacity for the fullness and gorgeousness of what a human being is, **a *Homo sapiens* who's becoming *Homo amor*.**

Homo amor, meaning the fulfillment of *Homo sapiens*.

Homo amor, who is omni-considerate for the sake of the whole.

Homo amor, who is an irreducibly unique expression of the *LoveIntelligence* and *LoveBeauty*, who is giving his or her unique gift, who participates in a planetary awakening in love through Unique Self Symphonies.

That's what we're here for.

TURNING TO THE DIVINE TO PARTNER WITH US

I cannot say *thank you* enough. We are going to finish today with a prayer, like we always do. And just thank you madly for being with us. We are going to finish with a prayer from Leonard Cohen.

Prayer is not an *old* idea. It's *not* a premodern idea. **Prayer itself is a First Principle and First Value of Cosmos, and it's the First Principle and First Value of *second person*—**

- ◆ There is not just *first person*, my experience with myself.
- ◆ There is not just *third person*, me *observing* Reality, looking at *it*.
- ◆ But there is *second person*: there's the space in between us. And that second-person is relationship.

There are very serious writers in quantum physics who understand that **Reality itself, at its core, is *relationship*.** Reality is relationship;, that's what it is. And it's relationships *between us*. There is a relationship between me and myself, but there is also a relationship between me and you. There are I-Thou relationships. But our relationships are *reflective*; they participate in the larger field of relationship.

Reality is not *just* third-person, objective fact. And it is not *just* my own internal experience. Reality is personal. There's an infinite Field of *Personhood*. Reality has a personal face.

- ◆ There is not just God as an Infinity of *Power*, all of the dazzling complexity and energies and forces of Cosmos.

- ◆ There is a second quality of Cosmos, which is a First Principle and First Value, which is *personhood*. There's a personal face to Cosmos that knows my name. We call that by many names—the Gods and the Goddesses of every tradition were an attempt, sometimes primitive—but it was a valid, correct intuition, that *there is a personhood to Cosmos that knows my name, that's holding me in every second.*

Leonard Cohen's song, "Hallelujah," has more covers than any other song because it speaks to that intuition. Leonard Cohen stands before the Lord of Song, the personal face of Cosmos, and says, *Hold me! Hold my holy and broken Hallelujah.* Because I know that, *There's a blaze of light in every word, it doesn't matter which you heard, the holy or the broken Hallelujah.*

So we turn to the Divine, and we say, *partner* with us.

- ◆ You live *in us*, as us, and *through us*.
- ◆ But you also *hold* us, and you are also *manifested in us.*

Those are somehow both true, paradoxically, so—

Partner with us. Hold us in our holy and broken Hallelujah, and hear our prayer. Hear our prayer, even as we human beings hear *your* Divine prayer.

Because in the great lineages, **humans respond to the prayer of the Divine**. And God says:

I need your partnership.

I need you to hold my hand.

I need you to walk with me in history.

I need you to partner with me in creating the new world.

And we turn to the Divine, and we ask for everything.

- ◆ We ask for health, we ask for longevity, and we ask for energy.
- ◆ We ask for goodness; we ask for joy.

- We ask for ourselves, our neighbor, our family members, our children, our cousins, and then for people we've never met.
- We ask for the goodness of the whole thing; we are omni-considerate for the sake of the whole.
- We bring it all—nothing is left out. Every place we go, we fall into Her hands, into the hands of *She*, who hears every note of our holy and our broken Hallelujah.

We move into prayer, and as we hear Leonard Cohen, who's very loving. He comes to us, to *One Mountain*, every week, and we play this chant, this prayer.

It is a mad joy to be with you, with all of the urgency! The urgency is also lined with joy at the privilege. We feel infinite concern—and yet we *celebrate*, and yet we're alive. We are filled with joy in every second. And what a joy, what a delight, and for me at least, a great honor of my life to be with you.

CHAPTER NINE

HOMO AMOR, THE FULFILMENT OF HOMO SAPIENS, IS RADICALLY PRESENT WITH THE PAST, PRESENT AND FUTURE: JOIN US IN THE HOMO AMOR REVOLUTION

Episode 316 — October 30, 2022

EVOLVING WHO WE ARE

Welcome everyone! Huge, huge welcome.

We just came to Vermont, and we bought a Center where lots of people are going to be. Zak Stein will be here, I'll be here. To be clear, just to share with everyone, I hate the cold. I came here anyways, because **we feel so deeply the urgency of this moment and the ecstasy of this moment.** It almost brings tears to my eyes—not almost, it brings tears to my eyes, I'm in tears today—when you actually *get* what this moment of time is.

I want to welcome any new people, and I want to welcome everyone who's been here with us. Because we are together.

We are the band of Outrageous Lovers. We are the revolution.

And if you feel I'm talking a little bit haltingly today, it's because I'm just filled with feeling, with emotion, about how much this *matters*. I want to try and set, again, **our intention of *who we are***. I apologize—insincerely—for the waves of emotion moving through me.

I was dreaming all night, and very much up and thinking and feeling—

- ◆ About what this moment is,
- ◆ And how this moment works,
- ◆ And how it unfolds.

We have an insanely huge day—so welcome, everyone.

This is the hub of the revolution—and that's very much what we say to each other.

It's like freedom fighters have always done, in every period. They would meet each other in the marketplaces, hidden from the eyes of the powers that be, and they would say to each other, *revolution*. And they'd look at each other in the eye, and they'd say, *revolution, revolution*. And all through history, there were people who looked at each other in the eye, because they felt that *something more* was possible—that there was more goodness, and more truth, and more beauty, and more depth, and more justice, and more integrity that was possible.

And **those people were not *separate* from evolution. They were *incarnations* of evolution.**

Because evolution is not a theory that lives *out there*.

Evolution is the pulsating throb of Cosmos, quite literally, that lives *in us, as us*, and *through us*.

We are evolution—quite literally.

Scientifically, all of evolution—quite literally—lives inside of us.

206

And that pulsing throb of evolution, poured through the lips of these men and women, the heroes. They would look each other in the eye, just like we're doing right now, and they would say, *revolution*.

There is a fist in revolution, because there is something that needs to be smashed. That's why Abraham (Ibrahim), this major figure in the three great traditions, is called the *iconoclast*. You know the other word iconoclast? It's one who *clasts* icons. And icons are the false idols. **Icons are the broken structures of thought and the broken structures of value that—we begin to realize—are degrading and defacing to human dignity.**

Because evolution is ready to move the next step. **Evolution is ready to evolve.**

Love is ready to evolve.

Value is ready to evolve.

Now, let us feel this together.

We are at this moment, unlike any other moment in history, and we've called it a time between worlds and a time between stories. The essence of what we talked about last week is to try and understand **what this moment of time *is*.**

I want to re-approach it now, and see if we can restate it and clarify it.

We are at a time between worlds, we are at a time between stories.

A decade ago, I was privileged to share with many of you that we need to shift our focus, that **we need to look very directly at existential risk.** I asked everyone to read a book by Ramez Naam called *The Infinite Resource*, which was a hard sober look at existential risk (at least in part of the book). And I understood that, and my partner, Barbara Marx Hubbard, my evolutionary partner who was with us last five, six years of her life, and co-founded *One Mountain Many Paths* with me. And *One Mountain Many Paths* is now co-founded by all of us. *One Mountain Many Paths* is this place where the Unique Self Symphony gathers to make the revolution.

So we had this realization a decade ago, that **we need to shift our focus to the meta-crisis, to existential risk, to the possibility of catastrophic risk.** We understood that in order to address the meta-crisis, we can't just address *infrastructure*—which means new technologies, which will avert existential or catastrophic risk without changing anything essential in ourselves.

This is the basic move of techno-optimism: *infrastructure* **changes.** And we *need* to look at every infrastructure change, infrastructure changes are wildly important. We would have actually endured a terrible famine in the last 20 years if a particular scientist from Mexico—he won the Nobel Prize for it—hadn't developed an infrastructure change: a new way of doing agriculture. **Infrastructure changes absolutely** *matter*. **But they're going to be** *insufficient* **to actually meet the meta-crisis.**

And *social structure* changes, new laws that restructure the way governments work and the way resources are allocated, may be important in critical ways. But that's also insufficient. It's not going to take us home.

We understood that we need a superstructure change, which means a change and evolution in *who we are.*

That's so big, my friends! And it seems so impossible—but it's not, because **it's part of the actual arc of the evolutionary impulse.**

THE FOURTH BIG BANG IN THE NARRATIVE ARC OF EVOLUTION

The evolutionary impulse explodes in the First Big Bang. And for many years, at *Shalom Mountain*, I would do a long meditation on what the stages of what we call these Big Bangs are.

- ◆ The First Big Bang is this explosion from *no-thing* into the world of *matter*, and we go through all the stages of the world of matter. The First Big Bang: cosmological evolution.

- And then matter triumphs in life, the Second Big Bang, the second momentous leap forward.

And although physics and mathematics can explain *something* of the world of matter, mathematics, as Stuart Kaufman points out, is insufficient to explain *biology*. Wow, physics can't explain biology, physics can't even *touch* biology. There's this new Big Bang, this new momentous leap, this emergence, and that is of **the world of *life***. That's **biological evolution**. And then we go through all the levels of biological evolution.

- And then life itself triumphs in a new emergence, which is **the depth of the self-reflective human mind**. An explosion of something new, **cultural evolution**.

In each of the levels of cosmological evolution—and then from cosmological to biological, and from biological to cultural evolution—there are both *continuity* and *discontinuity* (which is why we call it a *Big Bang*). In the move from matter to life, there's discontinuity. It's a new Big Bang, it's a momentous leap forward. In the move from biology, biological life, biological evolution, to the self-reflective human, there is *continuity* and there is *discontinuity*.

And this is not minor. Every piece that we are saying here, that we are actually putting forth—we've spent a decade on it—is what I think is **the most accurate understanding of Reality we have today**, that hasn't yet made it into the science books and in the history books. And we are now writing it up in a Great Library.

Every sentence is critical, because we are handling an enormous amount of challenges to thought here, and articulating it through this *second simplicity* formulation. By *second simplicity*, I mean the simplicity that comes *after* complexity.

- It's not **first simplicity**, it's not sloganeering. It's not a default simple understanding.
- It takes into account, after first simplicity, **all the complexity**: level two.

- Then level three is **second simplicity**.

I am speaking the language of second simplicity, but *all the pieces matter*.

What I am describing here is what I would call *a narrative arc to history*.

And that itself is a huge idea—that history *has* a narrative arc, that **history is a story**. That Reality is, from the very beginning, *a story*. That story is not just a human creation, but **the structure of Reality is a story**.

And it's what the lineages meant, in their own languages—in Sanskrit, and particularly in Hebrew, Aramaic—when they said, *God loves stories*. What that means is, that **the code for Reality is structured as a story**. There's a narrative arc.

- Reality is not just a series of facts, as science says.
- And Reality is not just—as religions have generally said— Reality is not just a vestibule, a pastoral room, in order to get to the real world.

No. This world is absolutely real, it ultimately *matters*. And **there is a story being told here, there is a narrative arc. History is going somewhere**. And we are actors, we are players in that story. And our stories are chapter and verse in that larger story. Wow!

And so, we get to this third level:

- Matter triumphs in life.
- Life triumphs in the depth of the self-reflective human mind.
- We get to the third level of evolution, which is cultural evolution.

Then we go through all the stages of human development. Life has triumphed in the depth of the self-reflective human mind, in the human being. Now, **is that the end of evolution?**

Is that the end?

Is it three Big Bangs—and we are done?

210

No, that's not the nature of the narrative arc.

There is what I called a number of years ago, a Fourth Big Bang.

This is at the very core of CosmoErotic Humanism. CosmoErotic Humanism is the name of the new Story of Value that we're telling, which is rooted in First Values, in Evolving First Values and First Principles. And at the core is this notion that we have articulated—together with Barbara Marx Hubbard, together with Zachary Stein, and other people around the world—and I call it *the Fourth Big Bang*. We are calling it together, in this Unique Self Symphony, the Fourth Big Bang.

The Fourth Big Bang means that the inherent narrative arc of evolution is that there is something more, there's more to come: there's more **value** to come, there's more **Eros** to come, there's more **love** to come, there's more of **our humanity** to come.

We don't triumph in the movement from biology to the self-reflective human mind, and the movement from what we might call *the biosphere*, to what the Russian early thinkers of the early 20th century called *the noosphere*, the worlds of self-reflective human mind and culture—**the noosphere is *not* the end of it.** There is something even deeper.

That deeper place is when there is an unfolding, an evolution of both the universe story and the story about who we are. There is an evolution of two stories: evolution of the nature of our identity, the identity story, and evolution of the universe story.

And that brings with it two other evolutions:

- One is the evolution of how we understand power, an evolution in **the narrative of power.**
- And there is an evolution in **the narrative of desire**; how we understand desire.

There is this major evolution, this movement from *Homo sapiens* to *Homo amor*.

That is not a fanciful movement, that is not a conjecture, that is not a wild idea—**that is actually the inherent logic of evolution itself**. That is the inherent logic of evolution itself.

WE ARE THE PEOPLE WE'VE BEEN WAITING FOR

We are at this moment, in this time between worlds, in this time between stories, in which *everything* is at stake. There is a meta-crisis.

***All* civilizations have fallen.**

We haven't solved the factors of the multifactorial issues and vectors that cause their failure.

We now have a global civilization—but now we have, for the first time, not only a global civilization, but exponential technologies which have the capacity to destroy the global civilization, in a way in which it will either be the end of humanity, **an extinction event**, or the emergence of **the collapse of structures of humanity as we know it at its best.**

What will emerge in its stead is a dystopian future, in which dystopian versions of closed society dominate Reality, in which there is a radical breakdown—in the movements towards **freedom**,

and the movements towards **deeper love**, and the movements towards **democratization of greatness**, and the movements towards **participation**, in which every human being knows that I have a Unique Self and I have an instrument to play in Unique Self Symphony.

Instead, we are going to move in an entirely different direction of **closed societies of an essentially a caste system**—in which we have an elite and everyone else, in which ecosystems break down, in which there's a hoarding of resources that creates a catastrophic view of the future.

And there *is* a capacity to respond to that.

What I want to do with you, is to listen, as a meditation, to Bono's song, which talks about *We're The People We've Been Waiting For*. And then I want to recapitulate what this moment is, with a thought experiment, with a meditation, so we can actually *see* this moment more clearly, and set the tune, set the tone for what's possible.

We are going to go into a meditation now, and we're going to do **this meditation through a song**. And then we are going to *respond* to that meditation.

To become *intimate* with this moment of time is huge.

Part of becoming *Homo amor* is to become intimate with this moment of time. I want to do, with your permission, **this huge *Homo amor* meditation that actually changes us and changes the source code.** Because we want to *download* this meditation, this study that we are going to do, into the source code itself—but we do that by *becoming it ourselves*.

Let's stay inside. We have the ability to focus, to put our attention. In Hebrew, the word for attention is *simat lev*: Let us place our heart, and **the placing of the heart is intention.**

We are now the band of Outrageous Lovers.

We are in the revolution.

We are at the heart of the revolution.

We are in this time between worlds and this time between stories.

And it's up to us, quite literally: we are evolution hanging in the balance, for real.

Just like that group of revolutionaries was in the Renaissance, led by da Vinci and his cohorts, who had to tell that new Story of Value, who had to shape the future in a new way, with radical audacity.

We *are* those people.

This is our moment, and this is going to be more real than we can even possibly imagine.

This is for real. For *realsies*, as a friend of mine once said.

Let's walk into this meditation, and then we come back together. All the way in! Ready, everyone? Here we go.

It's so big, I want to just make a prayer that we can get this right.

We are in this time between worlds.

We are in this time between stories.

So what does that mean?

We are at a time in which evolution is desperate to birth its new emergence. *Homo sapiens* is desperate to be fulfilled as *Homo amor*. And as is the nature of the Intimate Universe, **it's only that emergence of *Homo amor*, of the new human and the new humanity, that can respond to the meta-crisis.**

HOMO AMOR CONSCIOUSNESS IS: I AM EVERYONE, AND EVERYONE IS ME

What is the consciousness of *Homo amor*?

So let's go several steps here.

Step one. Imagine all the people that have lived in the world up till now. And on some deep level, **we realize that we are all those people.**

I have a friend, one of my dearest friends, Terry Nelson, who has led seminars all over the world for tens and tens of thousands of people. And one of the practices he does is that when someone would come late, let's say they'd come ten minutes late to a session, he would say this strange thing to the group. He would say, *we all came late.* And people would say, *that's strange, what does he mean, we all came late?* Terry tried to communicate

214

something—which was, I think even in Terry's mind, not logical, but his body knew its truth—which was, he would say to people, we're *all* that person; **there is no split between us and them.** Of course, on some level, there *is* a split; there's human responsibility, there's distinction, there's uniqueness. We are all Unique Selves, and that's absolutely true, of course.

And there is a deeper level of realization, which we understand that **we are also all part of the same True Self.**

And True Self means that there is a Field of one consciousness and one desire.

There's one heart, and there's one love, and there's one breath.

We are all irreducibly unique expressions of the Field, yes—and yet, we are also all inseparable from the Field. And the Field transcends space and time, in the sense of this limited moment in the spacetime continuum.

There is some true dimension—if you can access this—and this true dimension is available in physics through certain mathematical vectors, and this true dimension is available in the interior sciences. **There is some real dimension in which** *we are everyone.*

We are everyone that's ever lived. We are not actually separate from the Field.

- We are all of the lovers and we are all of the beloveds.
- And we are all of the murderers—and all of the murdered.
- And we are all of those who danced in joy—and we are all of those were madly heartbroken, tortured in tears.
- We are man, and we are woman, and we're every version of transgender that ever was, is, or will be.
- We are white and black and yellow.
- And we are deformed—and we are strong, and healthy, and sick, and frail, and fragile.
- We are wealthy elite—and we are destitute and poor.

We are all of it.

Imagine, for a second, being *all of it*. Imagine that actual consciousness.

You don't hold it in every second of every day, we hold Unique Self consciousness most of the time. But we have to have access to it—and the background of our foreground consciousness of Unique Self is *Homo amor* consciousness.

And *Homo amor* consciousness is: I am everyone, and everyone is me.

And there is a truth to that, there is a Reality to that, there is an ontology to that.

Imagine for a second, all of the people that ever lived—approximately 100 billion people. And if you stretch out those 100 billion people, as we said last week, one after the other, and you actually live each life consecutively, you will have lived for about four trillion years.

I am repeating this not as *information*; we are not in the realm of information now.

We are in the realm of *evocation*: we are evoking a consciousness inside of us. We are evoking a consciousness in humanity. **We literally are, in this moment, the leading edge of evolution, articulating its own nature!** And it is happening now, and we are happening now.

- Because we are it, and it is us.
- There is no leading-edge of evolution someplace else.
- It's ours.
- It's ours to *do*.
- It's ours to *be*.
- It's ours to *incarnate*.

This leading edge of evolution wants to incarnate now, together.

Imagine 100 billion people stretched out life after life. You've lived each life. You were all of the people.

And you were there at the dawn of civilization.

And you were in the earliest clans.

And you were a hunter gatherer, as woman and man.

And you were an early farmer, and you went through all the stages of farming.

And you were a serf, and you were a vassal.

And you were in the Chinese administrative bureaucracy, and you were one of the great Russian thinkers.

You were there everyplace.

You were in the Industrial Revolution.

You were all through every stage of Industrial Revolution.

You were Engels and Marx, and you were the factory worker in Manchester.

Wow! And this is actually where the great Russian thinkers would appear in the vector of history. You were among those great, brilliant, stunning Russian thinkers who wrote in the mid-19th century. For about 100 years, maybe 150 years from 1800, till somewhere around the middle of the 20th century, there was this explosion of Russian thought that's unimaginably beautiful.

- And you were the best of China, the depth and gorgeousness of China.
- And you were the best of the aboriginals in Australia.
- You were the best of it all.
- You've lived all of those lives; they stretch out to four trillion years.

Wow!

HOMO AMOR INTEGRATES ALL OF THE PAST, NOW, AND ALL OF THE FUTURE

But if you have any sense of what the future holds, if we don't extinct ourselves, and we live even the average life of what a mammalian species probably lived—and I won't go through all the calculations here—but you can imagine that we have lived, at this point, approximately 0.5% of our lives.

And if in fact we live longer than average mammalian species (because if we don't extinct ourselves, we might assume that we've learned something about self-care that an average mammalian species hasn't learned), then at this moment in time, we are literally *at the first breath*.

We are just a few breaths, a few seconds out of the womb.

The future is big, it is vast.

It's why the name of the Divine, in one of the great traditions of interior sciences, is *Yod-Hei-Vav-Hei*. Names of God in the great traditions are the source code structure of Reality; they are the DNA of Reality—that's what a name of God is, it's the DNA of Reality. And in this particular great tradition, which shaped the Renaissance, and shaped, in many ways—or intersected with—the Eastern thought, *Yod-Hei-Vav-Hei* is a four-letter name of the Divine.

- And the *Yod*, the first letter, is the future. *Yod* is the future.
- And then *Hei-Vav-Hei*, the next three letters, is the present.

So **the name of God is the impossible conjugation of the future and the present.**

People often cite, from the canon of Western Civilization, *The Book of Exodus*. They cite the statement by Infinity, *I Am that I Am*. But that statement doesn't exist, it's not in the original text. The original text is *Ehye Asher Ehye*: ***I Will Be What I Will Be***, which is the sense of the future.

Homo amor, the consciousness of Homo amor, is that I am all of the past. I'm actually aware, I *feel* all of the past: all of the past lives and all of the past epics, and all of the past histories, and all of the past cultures, and all of the unfinished business of the past, and all of the traumas of the past.

Both collectively and individually, as we go back in our own individual stories and we clarify the trauma, we find the deep space of radically awake and alive value that lives underneath the trauma, in which Reality is luminous and shining.

So we bring together all of the past; *Homo amor* receives all of the past.

And Homo amor lives in the depth of the present; Homo amor is the Now.

And one of the verbs of *Homo amor*-ing is *Now-ing*: the capacity to come back to the full presence of the present, and be available to the moment, and let the moment *love me open* and to love this moment open.

The only true decision we have from the perspective of the Now is, will this moment be open or closed? Is this *Now* open or closed? And so, in the name of God, there's *HVH*: the Now. *Hei-Vav-Hei*: the present, the Now the presence of the present.

And all healing is available in the Now.

All healing needed in this moment is available in this moment.

If I leave the moment, I cannot heal the moment.

If I am lost in the trauma, or in a strange techno-optimist future, which is willing to deface the present, I cannot heal the moment.

That is the Now-ing.

And yet there is a third dimension to the consciousness of Homo amor, which is the future, which is my willingness to be intimate with the future:

I feel the joy and suffering of the past.

I feel the joy and suffering of the present intimately.

It lives in me.

I am madly filled with joy. I am a little girl and a little boy. I am girl and boy, and we are dancing in the joy of the naked present.

And yet I suffer. I suffer all of the un-righted wrongs of the past, all of the injustice and all of the pain, and all of the joy, and the glory, and the triumphs of the past.

And I suffer *now*, and I am in mad joy *now*.

And I feel the future.

And the future is vast.

***Homo amor* is willing, *Homo amor* has the capacity, to incarnate the evolutionary impulse which reaches for the future, to become the name of God that is the future, and to feel the future—to literally feel the future, to be intimate with the future.**

We are developing a series of equations in the interior sciences, in this new Story of Value of CosmoErotic Humanism that we are articulating and formulating together.

There is an intimacy equation, it is one of the fifteen equations, and the intimacy equation begins, **intimacy equals shared identity**: we have shared identity with the past, we have shared identity with the present all over the world, and we have shared identity with the future.

So the trillions and trillions and trillions and trillions and trillions and trillions and trillions of unborn people, and unborn children, and unborn babies, and unborn men and women, and unborn creativity, and unborn beauty, and unborn poignancy, and unborn depth, and unborn meaning, and unborn value, and unborn divinity.

GOD PLUS HUMANITY EQUALS MORE GOD

The great paradox of the interior sciences (and there are traces of it in the exterior sciences and mathematical equations) is this paradox of the infinite and the finite.

Infinity births the finite, which makes more infinity.

That's one of the great realizations of the interior sciences: Infinity *plus* finitude.

Finitude means the Now, us: history, past and present. The Reality, the manifest world, all of our stories, all of our holy and broken *Hallelujahs*.

The human being is struggling for, reaching for, for Divinity. The human being reaching to become *Homo amor*. The human being reaching to become the Good, the True, and the Beautiful incarnate.

All of that. Can you feel that, friends? All of that. All of that is what we call *the finitude*. That's finitude.

Infinity plus finitude equals more infinity. **The future is more infinity**.

Let me say it differently:

God plus humanity equals more God.

Can you feel that? God plus humanity equals more God, which means the fundamental equation of realization is that **there is more God to come**.

Can you say that without crying tears of ecstasy and tears of pain at the possibility—that we would murder God? that we would murder the future? that we would be unable to intimately feel the cry of the future, whose only voice is through the tear ducts in our eyes?

The only way the future can cry its tears, its tears of ecstasy and its tears of longing to be born, is *through us*.

221

We are at this moment in history, in which we *need* to feel the future, in which *Homo amor* consciousness *needs* to be born.

And I want to add something to this. The implication of this equation is that this moment is *contingent*. The word *contingent* can be used in many ways, but the way we're using it here is, *contingent* means ***it depends on us***.

If we don't do it, it might inevitably get there in some way somehow—but the level of suffering, the level of pain, the level of breakdown, could be unimaginably greater.

It is not like Spirit moves, and we are just puppets being tested in some simulation, or tested in some religious view of the world which says this world is just a testing ground. And by the way, that notion expressed by people like Nick Bostrom in Oxford—that Reality is a simulation (the simulation hypothesis)—and that notion of religion that says this world is this testing ground, those are actually very similar notions.

But that's not the deepest realization of Reality.

The deepest realization of Reality is that what we do here *matters*, that Reality is contingent.

That is, what we do, and how we come together, and whether we step into the fullness of who we are or we don't, actually matters *infinitely*. Because we are the face of Infinite; we are the face of the Divine. And God plus us equals more God. **God plus me equals more God.**

You cannot actually get up in the morning and be intimate with yourself unless you understand:

- God plus *me* equals more God,
- God plus *you* equals more God,
- God plus *we* equals more God.

That's actually true, wow! Do we begin to feel this?

THE CIVILIZATION WILL CRASH UNLESS WE EVOLVE THE SOURCE CODE

Now let's go another step.

Let us look at this moment, friends.

Let us become intimate with this moment.

In this moment in history, in what we called—in the beginning of our inquiry or meditation—a time between worlds and a time between stories. And a time between worlds and a time between stories means that **there are two qualities of plasticity**.

Plasticity is a term that was coined by William James. He talks about plasticity as an *emotional* plasticity, which is **the moment where you can shift your field of feeling**. Generally, our feelings are locked in, we cannot change our feeling tone. But there are moments we can shift and actually transform our interior experience of feeling.

Then we learned about **brain plasticity**. Merzenich taught us, with other researchers, that the brain—which we thought was absolutely fixed and unchanging—that the brain was actually plastic. And *plastic* means that at moments of crisis, we can—through profound practice—rewire the actual neural circuits of the brain. That's brain plasticity (and there are important works in the last 25 years written about brain plasticity).

Neuro-cultural plasticity means there are moments when culture is *plastic*.

- There are moments when culture is absolutely locked in; it doesn't shift. It can't be changed, it's fixed.
- And there are moments, there are times, which we might call *neuro-temporal* plasticity (*temporal* means *time*), which is why in Ecclesiastes, Solomon said: *There's a time for everything under the sun*. And what he meant was not just a kind of moralistic idea, he meant that *there is an invitation*, that time is a particular kind of invitation. The Hebrew word

223

for time is *zaman*, and *zaman* means invitation. There is an invitation in time. There is a neuro-temporal plasticity.

And that's the nature of this time:

This is a time between worlds.

It's a time between stories.

It's a time of neuro-temporal plasticity.

It's a time when we get off the desktop into the source code, and we have to both deal with our individual and personal lives, and whatever our traumas might be (and everyone suffers, and everyone suffers uniquely)—and take our seat at the table.

Right, dear friend? We actually need you, and we need the fullness of your presence with everything you can bring to the table. Because we are at a time between worlds, at a time between stories, where there's neuro-temporal plasticity. It means we can change it *now*.

There is neuro-cultural plasticity; **culture itself can be changed.**

Let's meditate on it.

Let's go back to the 6ᵗʰ century (and I thank William McCaskill for this reference). The 6ᵗʰ The Zhou Dynasty has just fallen, we are in China. And what emerges for the next 400 years is these Hundred Schools of Thought competing with each other. There's Taoism, and there's Confucianism, and there's Mohism, and there's what was retroactively later called legalism: each one of these is a vision of Reality, and they are fighting with each other to actually become the source code of China. For four hundred years, there is plasticity, there is possibility. And then at some point, four hundred years later, it locks into place.

There is a values lock-in, and Confucianism wins the day, and for a thousand years, Confucianism reigns in China.

But it is so much bigger than that. That's a unique moment in history, which you can feel, but that's just a model for what history actually is. It has long periods that are unchanging, and then there are unique windows of plasticity.

We are at a window of such plasticity, but this might be the last window. Because all civilizations will fail, and there has only been so far one *global* civilization, which is ours. And all global civilizations *must* fail if we haven't actually healed the source code.

Because all previous civilizations, as Joseph Tainter points out, failed, collapsed—because they operated based on simple first rules and first principles that weren't aligned with the ultimate nature of Reality (and Tainter doesn't say that, but we are adding that to Tainter). **We haven't solved all of the breakdowns and the causes of breakdown, the generator functions of breakdown, that crashed every single civilization.**

- Rome is gone.
- Persia is gone.
- Greece is gone.
- The Byzantine Empire is gone.
- The great American Empire is gone.
- The great Russian Empire is gone.
- The great Chinese Empire is gone.

And yet, we are operating according to many of *the same flawed first principles and first values*. But now we are a global civilization with exponential technologies—and that civilization *must* crash, unless we actually evolve the source code. We move from the desktop into the source code, which we can do *now* because there's a moment of plasticity.

That's where we are, we are in this moment of neuro-cultural plasticity in which we can actually change the whole thing. It's a plastic moment.

225

A NEW STORY OF VALUE IS POSSIBLE BECAUSE THERE IS NO VALUE LOCK-IN

Crisis is an evolutionary driver. Our crisis is a birth.

When there is a crisis in the brain, the brain doesn't turn off. The brain generates the possibility of plasticity, of rewiring the neural circuits.

There is a nervous system to the planet, and units of thought, units of dharma, units of superstructure, units of insight and understanding, units of value are the neurons of the nervous system of the planet.

And in this moment, no values are *locked in*.

We live at this time of enormous struggle, enormous polarization, in which most of the world has stepped out of the Field of Value. Value has become *identity*, and a vast system of identity politics have taken over the world.

Not just the United States—all over the world.

People have conflated the value they are standing for with their identity, but they are not really *in the Field of Value*. There is no sense of *intrinsic* value. We've stepped out of the Tao; we've stepped out of the Field of Value. But of course, you can't really step out. But we *think* we've stepped out.

We have transposed the value that we've chosen—

- whether it's the pro-life people in America who say, *life is our value,*
- the pro-choice, choice is our value,
- the Chinese have a particular set of values, they're saying *these* are the values that count, and no other values do.

And so does Russia. Putin, in a hidden way, is standing for what he thinks are a couple of values. But they are not really in the Field of Value; he has taken them out of the Field of Value. They have become absolutes, they have become his identity, and therefore all other values disappear and allow for atrocities of the worst kind in the battlefield.

226

In every system in the world today, *that's* where polarization comes from: everyone stepped out of the Field of Value and said, *my value is my identity, and I'm going to fight for my value.*

What we need to do is realize: **Wow, we need to re-step into the Field of Value together, and to begin to synergize and articulate a cogent new Story of Value.**

But that is possible today because there is no values lock-in.

That's possible, because, in fact, there *is* this polarization, like there was for 400 years in China, there are these competing schools of thought all over the world.

But what's going to happen?

What's going to happen is, is that in a relatively short amount of time, this time between worlds, this time between stories, this window of possibility, in which we're a global civilization, will be over.

We are threatened with an imminent collapse, either catastrophic risk or existential risks. There's a meta-crisis. We can't look away, we can't bypass it.

And yet, there's possibility of unimaginable kind. **Because evolution is the possibility of possibility, and all of the energy of evolution that was there at the moment of the Big Bang literally lives in us on this call right now.**

It lives in Reality now, and we can generate a new future if we just become intimate with the future and we hear *Her* call.

WE NEED TO REANIMATE OPEN SOCIETIES

So, on the one hand, there is meta-crisis. On the other hand, it's a neuro-culturally plastic moment, it's a neuro-temporally plastic moment. We can actually *do* something. We can actually shift.

And what do we need to shift?

What do we need to do?

What's the actual demand and invitation of this moment?

There are two things we need to do.

One, we need to reanimate open societies. Open societies need to understand what they stand for.

Open societies need to move beyond the postmodern moment, in which value was collapsed, deconstructed. Modernity began the deconstruction of value, and postmodernity—which is really modernity on steroids, as Habermas points out—completed the deconstruction of value. We need to step back into the Field of Value, and we need to *animate*:

- The value of freedom
- The value of liberty
- The value of uniqueness
- The value of choice
- The Good, the True, and the Beautiful

As Reality is in Cosmos, and not materialist constructs in which we vie for power because there is no Field of Value, which is how Foucault, at least early Foucault, understood Reality.

We need to reanimate open societies. In this great battle with closed societies, we need emerge triumphant. Open societies need to emerge triumphant in this moment of time. **We actually need to save the best of Western civilization. We need to know that that needs to happen.**

Because if that doesn't happen, here's what will happen. I'll just give you one vector, just one scenario. There are multiple scenarios; there are utopian scenarios and dystopian scenarios—but I am going to give you one very serious scenario that has a significant and real possibility. You wouldn't cross a bridge if there's a 30% chance it is going to collapse, and you and your family are going to collapse on it. *Those* are the percentages we're talking, possibly significantly greater.

At some point, we are going to reach AGI, some version of Artificial General Intelligence. That's one of the imminent existential risks, and it's going to be sometime in the next twenty years, maybe faster, maybe forty or fifty years. The vectors are unclear, but it's real. We don't exactly know *how* it's going to happen, it might look differently than we think. But one very real scenario is, we will reach Artificial General Intelligence.

One country, let's say a closed society, let's say China, achieves Artificial General Intelligence. That will allow them, in a year or two years, to exponentialize their military and to exponentialize their economy, and they will quite quickly dominate the planet. They will own the planet.

But they are going to own the planet not in the way that you would have a thousand years ago. They are going to own as it were the entire computational planetary stack. Because everything moves through that computational—algorithmic, machine intelligence—stack. An ultimate Internet of Things, in which **affective computing has sense detectors everyplace, actuated eyes and ears everyplace, knowing what you think and what you feel.**

That's exactly where affective computing (*affective* means *emotional*) is headed, coming out of the MIT Media Lab in the last 20 years, headed by Rosalind Picard, tone of the students of Alex Pentland.

Affective computing allows computers to know what you feel. And if you feel something which defies the powers that be, let's say in China (in this scenario), you are actually knocked off the grid: you can't get food, you can't get a job, your family can't get health insurance.

Just like WeChat in China is a one-stop shopping for everything, there is going to be a one-stop shopping. Through a biometric signature, you're going to get access to the web. And if you feel against what you're *supposed* to feel, you are knocked out of the system, you are frozen out. We are going to go back to the place of the early clans, in which if you didn't identify with the clan, you were left outside and died.

We are actually moving quite rapidly to that possibility, in which a closed society achieves AGI and they impose a values lock-in. There is a values lock-in that takes place, and that value lock-in is a values lock-in of dystopian value. And that lock-in is mediated not like Confucianism was. Confucianism, the values lock-in of Confucianism was mediated by multiple factors, including the technology of *writing*. The Chinese administrative state deployed writing to lock in the values of Confucianism. But **in this moment, a new Chinese state could deploy Artificial General Intelligence to lock-in values. And they could lock them in for a million years.**

Can you hear that?

So what's the challenge of this moment?

There is actually a twofold challenge.

One is, we have to reanimate open societies with value, so that open societies actually *understand* what is the fight that we are in. And most of the young generation has no idea, and most of the old generation has no idea, although there is a faint memory in the older generations of the fragrances of value.

But if you look at the studies now of how millennials around the world relate to democracy, they don't even understand why it's a value. If you look at the studies on how many people are having sex in the world, sex is going way down in the world, because people have lost the *value* of sexuality. It's an actual value. It's a First Value and First Principle of Cosmos. The value of irreducible uniqueness, the values of irreducible personhood—those are all getting lost.

We need to actually reanimate, friends, open societies.

WE NEED TO WEAVE TOGETHER THE UNIQUE VALUES OF ALL CIVILIZATIONS

But now here is the momentous leap. We have to do something even deeper. We have to go to the best of Russian literature, the best of Chinese literature, to the best of Asian literature, and **we have to tell a new Story of Value that actually is so compelling that we overcome the polarization between open and closed societies, that we *all* come onboard in a new Universal Grammar of Value as a context for our diversity.**

We don't want to be homogenized.

We don't need a totalitarian sameness.

But we *need* to articulate a new Story of Value, in which actually everybody can come onboard.

Because Xi and Putin—I don't mean them specifically, or their circles of advisers, I don't even mean *them* specifically, but that movement that's driving those kinds of totalitarian closed systems—**they look at the West and they think the West is a postmodern wasteland that's not standing for anything.** That there is no sense of alignment with nobility, and with noble sacrifice, and with grand vision.

And Putin and Xi have a sense moving in them, perhaps in corrupted and distorted and degraded ways on multiple vectors, but also in sacred ways, at least sparks of the sacred.

- ◆ Xi, brother, if you are watching, I cannot get onboard with the million people in your concentration camps.
- ◆ Putin, brother, I get why you feel like NATO is encroaching upon you, and that's real. And I also saw Oliver Stone's movie about Ukraine burning in 2014, so I get your point of view— but that doesn't give you a right to do those atrocities in the battlefield. **Because there is a Field of Value that you are in, and power is *not* the only value.**

Now I think, you think, brother Putin, that value is not real. I get it, brother. **But value *is* real, and we have to re-articulate value theory, and to articulate a vision of value.**

We've got to articulate a vision of value, and **that vision of value needs to hold the deepest insights of every great tradition, the deepest insights of every culture. Every culture has to confess its weakness, and confess its greatness.** Whether it's Christianity or Islam, whether it's the Aboriginal systems. We cannot do a kind of New Age valorization of the aboriginals, or a New Age valorization of the Incas and the Aztecs. No, every culture had its tragedies, we have to confess the tragedies of our culture, and confess our greatness.

We need to weave together the unique value of every civilization, based on the unique epistemological methods, the unique ways of knowing, and weave that together into a new Story of Value.

And that takes resources, and that takes time, that takes energy.

I've spent the last 10 years—together with friends—working out how to do this. We can do this. We need to resource it, but we *can* do this.

We need to tell a new Story of Value, which is more compelling and more powerful than the most enticing, most intoxicating movie.

It's the drama of Reality.

It's the drama of the Fourth Big Bang.

It's the drama of *Homo sapiens* becoming *Homo amor*.

It's the drama of *Homo amor*, who embraces all of the past, which means

- I bring onboard, I integrate the best and truest and deepest validated insights of **all of the great cultures**, and I confess their *weaknesses* and I confess their *greatnesses*. I = We.
- And we weave together the best of **the present**.
- And then we weave it together, animated by the voices of **the**

future that live in us, and we create something **new**.

We are the new name of God.

We are the impossible conjugation of past, present, and future.

We are at this time between worlds.

We are at this time between stories.

We are at this moment before a potential values lock-in, in which it's *open*.

And we need to articulate a universal grammar of value as a context for our diversity.

Wow! Can you hear that, friends? Can you feel that?

That's actually possible. You might tell me it never changes. Friends, it *always* changes. **The one unchanging law of history is it always changes.**

And what causes the change?

What causes the change is always a new Story of Value.

But at this moment, we need to put together not a *declared* story, but a *validated* new Story of Value that integrates the deepest validated insights of *everyone*. Everyone, friends, has a seat at the table!

This won't be possible after X amount of time passes.

TELLING A NEW STORY OF VALUE—IT CAN BE DONE!

I know, friends, I *get* that we've got to pay attention to everything in our personal lives. And we have to pay attention to health. And if we are working in our nuclear family, we have to work in our nuclear family.

233

And if we're working in our traumatized systems, we need to work in the traumatized systems.

Yes, yes—on all those commitments. *All* of our holy and broken *Hallelujahs* need to be at the table.

And, they don't exhaust us, and they can't.

- ◆ We need to step up, and get out of our own way, and take our seat at the table of history, which is the telling of this new Story of Value.

And practically, at the Center, we need to hire three people to do key pieces of research on this. So we need to fund that, we need to resource that. Yes, yes!

We don't need to pay me a salary. I don't take a salary. I want to get *that* out of the way, no ego here. Let's get it out of the way—No salary, no drama, no egoic building of organizational structures, no win/lose metrics: *which organization is building bigger*? None of that, let's get it all out of the way. That's why I don't take a salary.

But what do we need to do? We need to hire a bunch of researchers— Chinese, Russian, great traditions. We need to resource and up-level in order to articulate a Story of Value.

I want to tell you something—shuddering as I tell you: *This can be done! This is actually doable.*

Together with Barbara, together with Zak Stein, together with my friend Daniel, together with *She*, I spent the last 10 years thinking about this day and night. **This can be done!**

We actually *can* tell this new Story of Value, it's fully possible.

It is a New Universe Story.

It is a new story of identity.

And it is one that—when Russia looks at it, tens and tens of millions of people in Russia, hundreds of millions of people in China, they read the story and they say: Oh my God, yes, we are *in* this story, we're not *out* of the story!

Across the Americas, South and North.

Across Antarctica, and let the penguins come onboard.

Across Africa, across Asia, every place, in Australia.

WE ARE SPEAKING IT INTO EXISTENCE

Can you take one more leap with me? Who is up for taking one more leap?

I completely get that there is genuine evil taking place in the world today, in different vectors in the world. I know that there is evil taking place, and I want to just name it clearly. And I apologize, Mr. Xi, and I apologize, Mr. Putin—but you guys are responsible for the perpetration of atrocity.

That's evil.

And *evil* is the opposite of *live*. It spells *live* backwards. It's the opposite of aliveness.

I know that there is also corruption and degradation that's lost millions of lives, that's taken place through the medical industrial complex in the West. Now, I am not arguing for a moral equivalency. I'm saying that evil has many facets, and many faces, and many forms. **And I know that all of us need to atone for what we need to atone. But we need to move forward together.**

And if it is going to be a clash of open and closed societies, let us gird up as open societies and articulate a Universal Grammar of Value—so we *know* what we're fighting for. And at the same time, let's vision a possibility *beyond* even that polarization. Let's vision a shared grammar of value, in which *everyone* can come onboard. And it can be done. It can be done! Wow!

I want to just ask everyone, *who trusts that it can be done?*

I trust that it can be done. *I trust*, I've got to start there.

It's very easy to say *No*—I challenge you to say *Yes*.

I know how to say no, it's very easy to say no.

I challenge you to say Yes, to have *the courage* to say Yes.

It can be done. It can be done. It can be done.

Do you have—I ask every one of you here—do *we* have the courage to say *Yes*?

Yeah, we might have gotten something wrong here.

You can focus on: *Oh right, this is what they got wrong, Marc got this wrong, Marc got that wrong.*

I challenge you to move beyond that contraction, because that's a *contraction in you.*

I acknowledge, let's say I got 20 things wrong. Take that as a given, *I got 20 things wrong.*

But *feel the possibility*.

If you don't feel the possibility, then you can't feel Homo amor, and you actually don't understand evolution.

I'm challenging you here, whoever the *you* is, I'm challenging you here.

Evolution means the possibility of possibility. And the possibility of possibility is that quarks become culture, that mud becomes Mozart, that bacteria becomes Bach, that slime become Shakespeare.

I am not swearing by every detail of what we said. I'm saying, *Oh my God, fire spreads.*

236

It can be done!

We are visioning it.

We are feeling it.

And by feeling it, by visioning it, by articulating it, by speaking it, **we are speaking it into existence.**

Vayomer Elohim: and the Divine spoke. And the speech itself, **the speech enactment creates Reality.** And remember, **God plus we equals more God.** So we—our story, our coming together here on *One Mountain*, this revolution, this *One Mountain Many Paths*—we can do this.

It's not that *someone else is going to do it.*

And people will do what they do around the world, and we'll join hands with anyone that's actually deep in the story.

But we are not waiting.

It is not *someone else.*

IF THIS MAKES SENSE TO YOU—THAT MEANS THAT IT'S YOURS TO DO!

I am going to do this last step.

- ◆ Do you want to know if it's *your* responsibility?
- ◆ Do you want to know if it's *your* joy?
- ◆ Do you want to know if you and I have a seat at this table?

I'll tell you how to know. Here's how you know.

Is there *any* part of you that *got* any of this? If there is any part of you that got any of this, if this made any sense to you at all, that means that it's *yours.*

Because if you didn't have the consciousness that it made sense to you, you wouldn't be here. You wouldn't be in the circle.

237

To the overwhelming majority of the world today, this would make absolutely no sense. Do you get this? But if you felt this in any way, if you felt this in any way—

Okay, I got this wrong, take it as a given. You don't like my shirt. You don't like me. You don't like my glasses. I got ten things wrong. Take that as a given. Let that go. Did you get *any* of it? Did any of it *speak* to you? **Could you feel the possibility of possibility alive and moving and pulsing and throbbing in you, for even a split second?** Even if you didn't feel it pulsing and throbbing, did you get a sense of it for a second?

If you got it even for a second, then it's yours.

If you got it for a second—I'm going to ask everyone—just say: *it's mine to do.*

Who can say that? It's mine to do. It's mine to do.

Before it's *ours*, first, it's *mine*. It's mine to do.

In my life, in my personal life and the trajectory of my *being* and *becoming*, it's mine to do. I was born for this; my consciousness understands this. I live in a place in time, and with a possibility that I can actually be here, and this is not a coincidence.

There is an intimacy in our meeting, and there's a vector in which we come together as a Unique Self Symphony. It's mine to do. *It's mine to do.* I am the Chosen One.

THE FOURTH BIG BANG NEEDS TO HAPPEN THROUGH US

Let us see if we can take this up one level, Unique Self Symphony: **it's *ours* to do**. It is ours to do.

We are a Unique Self Symphony. It is ours to do!

We are in this moment, birthing the next level and the next possibility of Unique Self Symphony. It's ours to do. This is a moment of neuro-cultural plasticity and neuro-temporal plasticity, we are at a time between worlds, we're at a time between stories, and **the Fourth Big Bang needs to happen through us.**

Because who are we?

We are evolution.

We are the personal face of the evolutionary impulse.

And the next level of intimacy in the world is *evolutionary intimacy*.

And *Homo amor* is demarcated by this new quality of evolutionary intimacy.

Because **Reality is the progressive deepening of intimacies**—and this is one of the core structures in the plotlines of the new Story of Value that we are validating now in a thousand footnotes. And we need to resource those footnotes, because we need to resource the research to validate all those footnotes—but here's the sentence. Here's the sentence, we've spent the last five years on this, day and night, on this one sentence.

Reality is not just the progression of simplicity to complexity. Reality is the progressive deepening of intimacies.

Can you get that in your body?

Reality is the evolution of intimacy.

And the new intimacy is evolutionary intimacy.

And evolutionary intimacy means I'm intimate with past and present and future. Can you feel that? I'm intimate with past and present and future.

I can feel all of the future generations, because I am *all* of the future generations.

And, Terry, this is what you were saying when you taught those seminars all over the world, implicitly. All of those future people are me. I am all of those future people, quite literally, at some deep level of Reality, validated by the frequencies of mathematical equations in physics, and validated—more profoundly even—by the deepest calculus of the interior sciences. I am all of the future.

Imagine you are a teenager, and you've got this huge life to live. Do you suicide? Do you take risks that suicide you, that prevent you from living that life? You can't. You can't.

It's ours to do, friends.

We are the Unique Self Symphony.

We can live all those future lives.

And the way we need to do it is to realize our radical intimacy with the nature of this moment.

That's what we did today.

We did a *Homo amor* meditation.

And in this *Homo amor* meditation, all of us have a place, and everything has a place.

Friends, our suffering has a place, and I want you to understand that. This is not a notion which says, let's sweep away the personal suffering, and only work as the revolutionary, and ignore family. Don't ignore family; family is infinitely valuable and matters. **But don't let yourself be exhausted by the story of the personal, even if it's exhausting.**

I promise you friends, I know a little bit about suffering. And at least some verticals of suffering, I've suffered exponentially. I've lost nights and nights and nights crying in different vectors of personal pain. I know something

240

about personal pain. Most of my family was gassed, go back a generation. It didn't go well. My mother was buried alive, quite literally, by the Gestapo at age four. Literally buried alive in a grave, quite literally. I know something about suffering. I know something about trauma. But you've got to bracket the trauma, holy brothers and sisters. Let's deal with the trauma and bracket the trauma.

And one of the ways I bracket the trauma is: **I feel the call of the future**. I feel the possibility of possibility living inside of me.

- Yes, we take **the present** seriously.
- Yes, we need to recover memories of a **better past**, in our personal life and in our collective lives. We need to receive the baton of the past, and reanimate, and liberate the sparks from the broken vessels of the past, and engage the present.
- But we're called forward by **the future**. Our vitality, our life, we are filled with the full power of the name of God. *Yod-Hei-Vav-Hei*. The impossible conjugation of the *Yod*: the future with *HVH* (*Hei-Vav-Hei*): the present. And the future calls us; we are called by our future selves.

Wow, what a crazy delight to be with you!

THE NEW NAME OF GOD IS THE INFINITE INTIMATE

What we are going to do now is, we are going to pray.

I am sure not everybody made us through the hour, because I know we're after the hour. I know we're longer than the hour. So, thank you everyone who stayed in, and totally honor that people felt they had to leave. Total honor and blessings, of course. But thank you for being with us. Let us bring now all of us to the table, and let's pray.

We are not praying to the God who doesn't exist.

And the God you don't believe in, that caricatured God, doesn't exist.

We're not praying to the God who's outside the world entirely, and who commands us to a kind of emasculating obedience.

No, we are praying to the God who's the Infinity of Intimacy. The Infinite Intimate.

The new name of God is the Infinite Intimate, that is Infinity desiring Intimacy, that lives in us, as us, and through us—even as She holds us.

And we bring before the Infinite Intimate everything, our holy and our broken *Hallelujah*.

And we're going to play our hymn, the holy and broken *Hallelujah*, by my brother, Leonard Cohen. And as we play it, I want to invite everyone just to pray. Just to pray.

And ask for everything. Ask for yourself. Ask for real, ask for everything.

Ask for your son, for your brother, your sister, your mother.

Ask for your uncle, your first cousin.

Ask for the women of Iran.

Ask for the feminine that's degraded and the masculine that's degraded.

Ask for all the men who are being raped in prisons in the United States.

Ask for all the people who died unnecessarily in the last two years from COVID.

Ask for everybody. Ask everything for everyone.

The holy and the broken *Hallelujah*.

Remember how we started? We look at each other in the eye and what do we say? Revolution! Revolution! This is the moment. Evolution! Revolution!

The holy and the broken *Hallelujah*.

CHAPTER TEN

FROM META-CRISIS TO THE CROSSING: FROM HOMO SAPIENS TO HOMO AMOR

Episode 319 — November 20, 2022

EVOLUTIONARY LOVE CODE: THE CROSSING

We are at the time of the crossing. The time of the crossing is a time between worlds and a time between stories. Unlike any time we have ever been in before, the crossing is a pivoting point in history. Unlike any time we have ever been in before.

The Crossing takes place as we are poised between utopia and dystopia. It's the moment that Abraham stood in, when he heard the call to cross to the other side. It's the moment that the slaves stood in, when they needed to decide whether to return to Egypt or to cross the Red Sea to the other side.

This is the great moment of The Crossing. All the wisdom traditions in the world—premodern, modern, and postmodern—knew that this moment would come. We are at a phase transition which will either mean the

collapse of human history or the birth of the most beautiful world we can imagine. **We will either birth a new human and a new humanity, *Homo sapiens* will fulfill itself and become *Homo amor*, or we will experience collapse, stagnation or extinction.**

This is the moment where every human being and humanity as a whole is asked one question:

Am I ready, am I willing to play a larger game, to participate in the Evolution of love?

Am I willing to be the new human and the new humanity?

What a beautiful code!

Let's just talk about it for a second, The Crossing.

Where does *The Crossing* come from?

It comes from one of the great epic moments in history, that precedes *this* moment but is deeply related to it, in which Ibrahim—Ibrahim who births Islam, and who births Hebrew wisdom, and who births Christ consciousness, the three great traditions of monotheism—is before this pivotal moment. And he has to make a decision, *who is he going to be?*

In the language of the text, the entire world, the mainstream is on one side (*Mi'iver achad*, and the word Hebrew, *Ivri* means side). The whole world is on one side—and yet there are those who can see around the corner.

There are those **who can feel possibility.**

There are those who understand in their bodies that evolution is the possibility of possibility—and they see another way. **They see a better way.**

They see **an evolution of value.**

They see **the human being transforming to something more noble, more good, more beautiful, more alive** than anyone at that time dreamed was possible.

And Abraham crosses to the other side. Literally, he crosses from one side of the Euphrates River to the other side. In the language of the interior sciences, *that's* the moment of the crossing.

THIS MOMENT IS BUILT INTO THE VERY STRUCTURE OF REALITY

Every wisdom tradition, whether premodern (traditional), or modern, or postmodern, understood that **we are going to come towards *a crossing moment.*** A crossing moment—just so you can get a sense of it, a feel for it— it is not something we are *making up.* It's not something we are *contriving.*

- It is not just that I've spent the last ten years together with the fellows of the Think Tank and colleagues around the world, reading, in the deepest way we know how, economics and politics and governance and sociology and anthropology and the great traditions.
- It is not just that it's clear, from the context of the presence, that we are in this time between worlds, we are in this time between stories.
- It is not just clear that it's *not* going to just return to normal, that the system is not too big to fail, that we are poised before stagnation, collapse, or extinction, in a very real way. That those are actually real.

It's not just that, and we've talked about that in depth in the past.

It is that **if you look at the deep structural intuitions of history, there was this deep understanding that humanity is not just going to go on**. That if humanity just goes on, humanity will implode upon itself.

All civilizations have fallen. All great civilizations—every single one has fallen. We haven't solved *any* of the core issues that caused the fall of all the great civilizations. And Joseph Tainter, in his book on the rise and fall of great civilizations, talks about this in some depth, and it's worth reading.

But today, we have a global civilization, with exponential technologies available to rogue actors. The thought that this global civilization will survive—when we haven't solved *any* of the generator functions that caused the failure of all the other previous generations—simply makes no sense. It's actually *not* what's going to happen.

But here's the gorgeousness of it:

This is not a surprise. This is actually built into the very structure of Reality.

It's why the ancient traditions saw that there were two possibilities. And in their language—which is not our language, it's not the language of Festival 2.0—what they talked about was *Messiah*, the end of days, some great, beautiful, Messianic positive explosion, or they talked about *Armageddon*, which is some form of collapse, some form of complete breakdown. They actually *understood*—and **every single great wisdom tradition had its version of a breakdown or a breakthrough story**. Meaning, James and Marc aren't making this up. **This is baked into the very source code of culture and consciousness.**

Now, the words that we are going to give to this, at this pivoting point in history, the words are: Existential risk, catastrophic risk, breakdown. Or the emergence of a new human and a new humanity, breakthrough.

Wow! All of a sudden, you begin to understand the old language of *Messiah*, which was often xenophobic and homophobic and was all about one religion, and it was about obedience and a kind of giving up of self—no, we are not having that conversation. But **the intuition that a new human and a new humanity will be birthed, that was real, *that* was important.**

We call that new human and that new humanity *Homo amor*. The fulfillment of *Homo sapiens* in *Homo amor*.

The emergence of a new human and a new humanity, which lives within the context of a universal grammar of value. A universal grammar of value as a context for our diversity. *That* is the great invitation!

HOMO SAPIENS HAS COME TO THE END OF HER POSSIBILITY

Every single dimension of collapse, every generator function of existential risk, in the end—as we've talked about in great length at the Festivals for the last 10 years—is rooted in a global intimacy disorder. And **to heal the global intimacy disorder, we need to emerge a new level of intimacy.**

Just check between any two people in a couple, in a friendship, or whatever kind of couple it is—**when there is a collapse in intimacy, you need to generate a new order of intimacy.** And a new order of intimacy means that—

There is a new *self*, there's a new *identity*. There is *a deeper part of me* that I'm willing to put on the table. I've got to actually *transform* in order to transform intimacy.

We are at this moment in which *Homo sapiens* has come to the end of his or her possibility.

- ◆ *Homo sapiens*—in her glory—has generated all **the great dignities of modernity.**
- ◆ But in her pathologies, she has generated the cultural pathologies, which are what Habermas called **the disasters of modernity.**

All of our progress has brought us literally to the precipice. And at this precipice, **we have a choice: we collapse, or we understand** *The Crossing*— that we can actually cross over to the other side, we can become the new human, and we can become the new humanity. *Homo sapiens* can become *Homo amor*.

But it's not that we are going to *preach* it to the world, we don't preach. We *be*!

We are going to be *Homo amor*.

We are going to become *Homo amor.*

We are going to embody this new consciousness.

We are going to try and identify and understand, what are the qualities of *Homo amor?*

What does it feel like to be *Homo amor?*

What are the economics of *Homo amor?*

What are the relationships of *Homo amor?*

How does *Homo amor* play in politics?

How does *Homo amor* play in business?

How does *Homo amor* play in every dimension of Reality?

We are not just going to *write* a Great Library together, we are going to *be* a Great Library.

We're going to be *Homo amor.*

And we are going to, with the grace of *She,* invite everyone who is ready.

Anyone who can hear the call, who is ready to answer the call, who is ready to say: I don't just want to be successful in the win/lose metrics, in the rivalrous conflict governed by win/lose metrics—in which I am successful and then I die. I want to answer the call at this moment of history and cross to the other side. I want to become *Homo sapiens* becoming *Homo amor.*

And that's the great invitation.

We've got to get this right.

We've got to hit it exactly right.

We need *Her* grace.

We need each other.

Maybe the last sentence: **to say *I love you* is to say *I need you*.** So, we are loving each other, we are needing each other, in the deepest and most beautiful way.

We are ready to play a larger game.

We are ready, quite literally, to participate in the evolution of love.

PRAYER IS THE REALIZATION: WE ARE NOT ALONE IN COSMOS

What we are going to do now is, I just want to just take a moment, and actually offer prayer—offer prayer and step into prayer now, *the holy and the broken Hallelujah.* Now, I just want to say a word with permission, everybody, about prayer.

Because prayer is huge. Prayer is not the prayer to a cosmic vending machine God, who demands obedience and wants to make sure you are not self-pleasuring too often, because that's sinful. No, not exactly.

When we talk about prayer, we are talking about **the realization that we are not alone in Cosmos,** the realization that we are all *held*, the realization that, in the end, Cosmos is *personal.* The political is personal and the personal is political—but it all begins and ends with the personal.

Cosmos is a field of personhood.

Cosmos is a field of intimacy.

And what the great traditions called *God* and identified as the Infinity of Power, which is outside the Cosmos, was just part of the story.

That infinite power, that God power, that infinite Divinity, both *holds* Cosmos and *is* Cosmos, both *holds us* and *is us.*

It is not only the *Infinity of Power*, but the *Infinity of Intimacy* that knows our name.

Did you ever wonder, friends, why Leonard Cohen's song *Hallelujah* had more covers made about it than any other single song? Because it's speaking to something.

It's speaking to *the holy and broken Hallelujah*, which is the depth of our personal stories. Our breakdowns and our breakthroughs, our pain, and our depression, our hope and our anguish, our agony and our ecstasy—it's all there.

But that holy and broken Hallelujah is not *irrelevant*.

It's not that we live it *alone*.

It's not that we are lost in lives of quiet desperation.

It's that that personal story is chapter and verse in The Universe: A Love Story.

That personal story is encrypted in the heart, mind, body of Reality.

Your personal story—and my personal story—is kissed by the lips of the Divine, it is infinitely valuable, it *matters*. And *there is a blaze of light in every word, it doesn't matter which you heard, the holy or the broken Hallelujah.*

So, with quivering tenderness, we come together. This is a time to step up, to step in. And just follow the words of the chant as prayer. And as the words of the chant move through and waft through our space, we are going to offer our prayers in the chatbox.

As we are listening to Leonard Cohen, we actually write:

> I'm praying for my Uncle Morris who's about to have an operation,

> I'm praying to have enough resources to keep the Center for Integral Wisdom going, which has now become the Center for World Philosophy and Religion.

> I'm praying to cross over to the other side.

I'm praying that at this moment of The Crossing, it can all become real.

I'm praying that we can begin to write the constitution of the new world; the constitution of *Homo amor*, the constitution of the new human and the new humanity.

I'm praying that all politicians know that the political needs to be personal, that all of us know that we cannot abandon the politics, and that the personal needs to be political.

That we can literally cross over to the other side.

So are you ready, friends?

Are we ready for The Crossing?

Are we ready to cross over to the other side?

Are we ready to participate in the evolution of love?

If we are, let's turn to the Infinity of Intimacy that knows our name.

And this is different than an ordinary podcast.

We're not afraid to turn in prayer.

We don't think, *oh my God, we're going to turn in prayer, they're going to say we are regressive fundamentalists.*

We are not abandoning prayer to fundamentalism.

We are *liberating* prayer from the grips of a regressive fundamentalism, and reclaiming the realization that Cosmos is personal.

- Cosmos is first person: the first person Divine in Eros that moves in me.
- Cosmos is third person: all of the sciences, third-person analysis of Reality.
- And Cosmos is second person: Cosmos is a great love affair. It's a great CosmoErotic Universe.

251

Cosmos is defined by a CosmoEroticism that turns to the human being and says, *partner with me.*

We call that CosmoErotic Humanism, the great new Story of Value. It's exciting. It's wild. It's ecstatically urgent.

CHAPTER ELEVEN

WHAT WE NEED FOR THE ATTENTION REBELLION TO SUCCEED

Episode 382 — February 4, 2024

A NEW STORY GENERATES NEW REALITY

We are here in this time between worlds, we are here in this time between stories, responding to the meta-crisis, and knowing that crisis is an evolutionary driver, that our crisis is a birth, that as things fall apart, they also can fall together, that emergency can generate emergence, that when the vessels *break*, in the language of the lineage of Solomon, there is a new possibility.

The original Hebrew word for breaking is *shever*. It means breaking, and it means nourishment. There is promise, there is nourishment, there is possibility. When the breaking happens it's either going to be a *breakdown*, or something will open in our hearts, and we'll be able to see more clearly than we ever have before, and it will become not a breakdown, but a *breakthrough*.

That's the feeling of *ein shalem m'lev shivura*. **There is nothing more whole than a broken heart**.

In this moment of meta-crisis, we don't move to denial, and we don't move to a doomer position. But we move to *respond*—to respond by telling a new Story of Value

We tell a new Story of Value because we know that **a new story allows us to generate a new Reality**.

The meta-crisis emerges from the broken plotlines, the broken structures of the old Reality. To the precise extent that the story told in modernity was accurate and beautiful, it birthed the dignities of modernity. But there were plotlines missing or broken—for example, the plotline of value.

The plotline of value got lost. We lost the thread of the Story of Value. **We thought we could *assume* value even as we *denied* it**. We thought we could make intrinsic value—the Good, the True and the Beautiful—an axiom even if we would undercut their roots and claim (*wink-wink*) that they're really just made up.

We thought we'd get away with that. And we did, in modernity. But postmodernity called the lie out and said, "No, no, no, you are making these stories up. There is no Story of Value."

And once there is no Story of Value, then all that's left is separate selves lost in rivalrous conflict governed by win/lose metrics, generating fragile, complicated systems without inherent allurement between the parts— because there *is* no inherent allurement between parts. *It's all contrived. It's all random. It's all a reductive, materialist, random Cosmos without telos, without purpose, without direction.*

And of course, that's not the case. Of course, that defies the inherent nature of science, but that became the dogma. That dogma was invested in the apparatuses of power and generated all the fragilities of modernity, and all the fifteen vectors of the meta-crisis that threaten us with either the death of humanity or the death of our humanity.

So, what do we need to do?

- We need to reweave the plotline.
- We need to retell the story.
- We need to reclaim the thread.
- We need to revalue value itself.

What I want to do today, my friends, is something which I think is wildly important.

It's a change that actually does, quite literally, change everything. It adds a new dimension to the Story of Value that really opens everything up in a new way.

Our topic today is going to be *attention*.

EVOLUTIONARY LOVE CODE: EROS IS THE PLACING OF ATTENTION

Eros is the placing of attention.

The placing of attention generates Reality.

The placing of attention is the ultimate creative act.

The placing of attention is the ultimate moral act.

Reality emerges from the Infinite placing attention on finitude.

Attention and devotion are joined at the hip. To be the receiver of well-placed attention, and to place attention well, makes life self-evidently Good, True, and Beautiful.

Placing attention is a First Principle and First Value of Cosmos.

Evolution evolves through differentiation and integration, which is the placing of attention.

Evolution is the evolution of attention, which is the Evolution of Love.

THE INTERNET IS DESIGNED TO SCATTER ATTENTION

We are at this new moment in society, in which **the act of attention hijacking is the primary movement of the new robber barons**—of the new oligarchs, of the new techno-totalitarians.

The theft of attention—stolen attention, *stolen focus* as Johann Hari calls it in his book by that name—is the basic movement of the mainstream structures of society. It has enfolded, enwrapped, engulfed society. Not by providing it with *tools*—the internet is not a set of tools. That's a mistake. The internet is an *immersive environment*, in which the next generation is being raised, which is based on the radical *scattering of attention*, to borrow a term from Nicholas Carr in his 2011 book, *The Shallows*.

There has been this entire leading-edge literature, and Nicholas Carr began the conversation, in his book *The Shallows*. And then he wrote another book called *The Glass Cage*. Then he wrote another book, which is a collection of his blog posts. His blog is called *Rough Type*. He collected his blog posts, and he put them in a book called *Utopia Is Creepy*. He is describing, essentially, the hijacking of attention.

Our colleagues, Tristan and Aza, at the Center for Humane Technology, have placed their attention on the robbing of attention. Much has been written about BJ Fogg and his Persuasive Technology Laboratory, which has taught generations of app designers how to hijack attention. The words used are *how to maximize engagement*, but engagement is a euphemism. (Euphemism is one of the core strategies of techno-totalitarianism.)

Engagement is a euphemism for addiction.

Addiction is the consistent and obsessive hijacking of attention from the discomfort or the emptiness of ordinary life. One doesn't have—or loses—the capacity to sit through it until it gets to *fullness*.

We can't hold our attention on the actual experience of life in order to access its depth, and its pleasure, and its potency, and its potentiality, and its possibility.

We get discomfited by its pain, and so we *turn away* our attention. And the consistent turning away of attention is called addiction.

The internet is designed to scatter attention.

It is designed to interrupt plotlines.

It is designed with multiple links in every sentence that don't allow you to enter into the placing of attention, and the depth that emerges from the artistic act of *true* engagement.

That disruption of attention generates the shallows. The shallows is the opposite of depth.

Carr has written about it. And Shoshana Zuboff's book, *The Age of Surveillance Capitalism*, addresses it in a different way. A book by Brett Frischmann, *Re-Engineering Humanity* (2018), addresses the same issue. Doug Rushkoff has talked about it in multiple ways. There is a veritable literature on this distraction of attention.

But if you notice, the tech plex is not paying any attention to the literature accusing it of hijacking attention. Why? Because **the literature that accuses the tech plex of hijacking attention has not given any compelling reason *why* attention shouldn't be hijacked.**

It is not against the law. Advertisers have always sought to attract attention. True, this is an immersive environment, and true, it's micro-targeting—as opposed to the old broadband advertising of television, and to that which emerged from the printing press, which is generalized writing. When writing becomes advertising, it is generalized broadband advertising.

It is different from the micro-targeted advertising that emerges out of the tech plex, which uses machine intelligence to develop a personality profile, a voodoo doll of you. It crafts and sculpts this voodoo doll by mining your data. It turns your *dark data*—all the ways that you unconsciously place your attention—into a personality profile in order to micro-target you.

It is true that it's not the same as the old advertising, but essentially the tech plex says, "So what? Technology advances, and ways of attracting attention advance, and it's a free market."

Nir Eyal, a favorite son of the tech plex, a student of BJ Fogg's at the Persuasive Technology Laboratory wrote a book called *Hooked*. *Hooked* means that the purpose of the technology is to addict you. He wrote another book called something like *Indistractable*, meaning, *just turn it off.*

Nir Eyal says, *What's the problem? We're trying to hook you and attract your attention. You have free autonomy as an end user, turn it off.*

What's the problem, says the tech plex, with stealing attention?

They shrug it off. Writers like Hari say, "We have to value attention." But why? You see, neither Zuboff, nor Hari, nor Rushkoff, nor Carr, nor Harari —and I could go through the list of people who discuss this issue—**none of them assert what needs to be asserted in order to be morally outraged and astonished by the hijacking of attention**.

And what is that? We have to actually affirm that **attention is a First Principle and First Value**. Before anything else, attention is a First Principle and First Value of Cosmos.

If attention is *not* a First Principle and First Value—not a part of the very value proposition that suffuses all of Cosmos—then the hijacking of attention is not a problem.

A BRIEF HISTORY OF ATTENTION

Let's start with attention at the human level, in the premodern world.

There is a writer named Kreiner who just wrote a book called *The Wandering Mind*, which is one of those books that critiques the modern loss of attention and compares it to the medieval period where the monks, for example, were very careful to guard their attention.

But why were the monks careful to guard their attention?

What were they using their attention *for*?

Why did the monks, and the priests, and the imams, and the different religious practitioners—why did everyone basically take attention to be a great value?

Because it was through attention that you placed your mind on the mind of God.

It was through attention that you discerned the will of God.

It was the elite who were tasked with merging with the Divine, with disclosing the will of the Divine, and with sharing that will with the masses. What they were supposed to do was to practice, to meditate, to pray, to fast, to dance, to whirling dervish, to place their full attention on the Divine in order to access the nature of Reality.

Premodernity was all about attention. It was that placing attention on the Divine in order to be obedient, in order to appropriately surrender, in order to know the Divine will, in order to hear the Divine voice, in order to interpret sacred texts, in order to achieve *unio mystica*, mystical union with the Divine.

What happens then? Then we go to modernity.

What happens in modernity?

Attention turns away from God. God is still invited to the party, but **there is a turning of attention from heaven to earth, from God to the human being**.

When you look at Michelangelo's creation scene, and you see the image of God, and you see the hands meeting—Adam is not *surrendering*.

Adam is filled with Eros.

He is filled with aliveness.

He is filled with dignity.

He is gorgeously formed.

We naturally place attention on his beauty, on his power and his potential.

There is a turning of attention to nature, to the natural world, to the third-person perspective—in art, and in science, and in moral philosophy. We begin to look from the third-person perspective, and we generate universal human rights, and we generate the scientific method. We generate new forms of measurement (Kepler and Galileo), which are new forms of *paying attention.*

It's an active attention, which generates new gnosis.

That's the movement of attention in modernity. **The importance of attention is taken as a given because it generates science.**

We turn to the human being, and we move to psychology. We look at our own inner workings and how they operate. Freud begins to dissect the human being much like one would a steam engine.

But something gets lost because **interior technologies begin to break down**:

- As modernity progresses
- As science progresses
- As the exterior placings of attention and methodologies for placing of attention get ever more sophisticated

Value gets lost as a plotline in Cosmos.

Attention becomes but a methodology.

And along comes postmodernity, and postmodernity says, *actually, all of these stories, including the story of science, including the stories of the Western enlightenment, including the stories of universal human rights, are really just stories. They are really just contrived. Even facts are really contrived values. Actually, the world is without a plotline. There are no First Values and First Principles, which means there is no telos, which means there is no plotline, which means there is no thread to follow.*

In essence, what postmodernity is saying is that **there's really nothing to pay attention to.**

YOU CAN ONLY PAY ATTENTION WHEN IT MATTERS

That incipient sense of *there is nothing to pay attention* to is exactly what Camus talks about in that famous first line in his existentialist novel, *The Stranger*, which I often point out. "Forget about psychology. Strangers are we, errants at the gates of our own psyche," writes George Steiner. Camus' opening line is, "Mother died today, or was it yesterday?"

Mother dying *should* grab my attention. It should *arrest* my attention. Mother died, but that can't arrest my attention—because it doesn't ultimately matter. **You only pay attention when it *matters*.** And when the world is said to no longer be constructed from *what matters*—it is reduced to *matter*—then nothing matters.

Then there's nothing to pay attention to.

Wow!

And so, the internet emerges—the first iterations in the '70s, and in the '80s, the '90s, it really begins to emerge. It literally *parallels* postmodernity.

The internet is the exteriorization, the exterior expression of the postmodern mind.

The postmodern mind says, "There is no plotline."

The postmodern mind would never do what Hawthorne describes in *Sleepy Hollow*. You'd never lean back against a tree and get lost in the depth of a plotline of reading, get lost in the inward space of meaning, create flow states of attention in order to disclose the depths of Reality—because there is no depth of Reality to be disclosed.

And plotlines don't matter, and authors don't matter, and unique forms of attention don't matter, which is why Kelly writes that we don't need *authorship* anymore. Let's just have all the *information*. It's all exterior information.

The internet is about the scattering of attention. It's about the interrupting of attention because there is nothing to place attention on.

The conceivers of the internet are the techno-totalitarians who speak in liberal slogans, but who are actually techno-authoritarian. That is to say, they are imposing a reductionist materialist dogma. Without having been elected, without actually having been *chosen* to teach, they are *encoding* the immersive environment with the premise that there are no plotlines, and that your attention can be stolen in every second.

Your iPhone is built to steal your attention.

Have you ever noticed that if someone is texting you, the little three dots come up? When you're on WhatsApp, you see someone's texting you. Why?

To steal your attention.

And it shows up as red or not red, lights up in blue or not blue, whether it's your text message or whether it's WhatsApp—in order to *demand* that you return the message.

When you get on LinkedIn, it tells you what your circle of following is. We have *likes* and we have *views*.

The entire internet is constructed to appeal not to the *depth* placing of attention, but to the *surface* vying for pseudo-erotic attention—because there is no genuine experience of the depth of attention.

- ◆ Eros, or the erotic universe, is the genuine placing of attention.

- ◆ The pornographic universe is the hijacking of attention, and social media is an expression of the pornographic universe.

The reason the techno-feudalists governing the attention economy ignore the objections of this new cadre of writers who are screaming, *You are attention thieves!* is because they don't see anything wrong with stealing attention. **You can only arouse moral astonishment and outrage if there's been a violation of value.**

When we see value violated, when we see George Floyd killed, we're outraged at the violation of value and we storm into the street. If there hasn't been an actual violation of value, we're not moved.

For example, Johann Hari calls for an attention rebellion, and everyone yawns—because Johann Hari, nowhere in his entire book about the stealing of attention, ever tells us what *value*, what intrinsic value of Cosmos expressed at the human level is being violated by the stealing of attention. He *does* say we have to value attention. He says it time and time again, but he refuses to declare attention *as a value.*

Unless I actually affirm that attention is a First Principle and First Value of Cosmos, there is no conversation. The conversation doesn't get off the ground.

TO BE IN LOVE IS TO PLACE ATTENTION

Let's do it right now, together.

Let's now affirm, in this moment, that **attention is a First Principle and First Value of Cosmos.**

That's what it is.

The God you don't believe in doesn't exist. God is mystery. God can't be named. But we actually try and *name* the force *that's beyond and that moves through you*, upon which, as Henry Miller said, you have to place all of your energy—and only that is the real business of living.

263

Those forces beyond that move within, that larger movement that lives in us—that's where we have to place our attention.

That quality of placing attention is the quality of the Infinite turning to finitude.

It's what William Blake meant when he said, *Eternity is in love with the productions of time.*

See, **to be in love is to place attention**. That's what it means to be in love. It's so beautiful. **To be in love means I'm willing to bracket myself and place attention on you.**

When I place attention on you, I am in devotion. My attention expresses itself as devotion.

I am turning towards you.

I am bracketing the self.

I am powerful.

I am not turning towards you because I have a utilitarian need, or an instrumental *telos*, or a superficial goal. **I am turning towards you in love.**

Isaak Luria, the interior scientist who incepted the Renaissance through the Lurianic mystery schools that live on the periphery of the Renaissance (and read Moshe Idel's book *Kabbalah in Italy*, which alludes to this, although it doesn't name it specifically), talks about this Divine act.

I am going to call Divine the Infinite Intimate. The name of God in CosmoErotic Humanism, our new Story of Value, is the Infinite Intimate. The Infinite Intimate steps back and brackets Herself in order to turn towards finitude.

That's what love means.

The parent brackets herself to turn towards her child.

The lover brackets himself/herself to turn towards his friend, her friend, his beloved, her beloved.

The bracketing of self to place attention on other is the primary act of Eros.

It is only when you place attention, that *gnosis*—knowing—emerges. Every form of knowing comes from the placing of attention.

SEEING WITH NEW EYES IS THE ESSENTIAL QUALITY OF EROTIC UNIVERSE

I was reading last night this book by D. H. Lawrence, *Sketches of Etruscan Places and other Italian Essays*. It's a collection of essays by D. H. Lawrence. He writes here, "Everything depends on the amount of true, sincere religious concentration you can bring to bear."

D. H. Lawrence is not known for his religion—and yet he says, "An act of pure attention, if you are capable of it, will bring its own answer."

Everything is about the placing of attention.

Attention is the realization that something other than me is real and is worthy of my concentrated attention, of the placing of my heart.

The original Hebrew word for attention is *sim lev*—the placing of the heart, which is the placing of attention.

When we say the sexual models the erotic (which is a core principle in one of the core works of CosmoErotic Humanism, *A Return to Eros*), what we mean is that sex *discloses* the nature of Eros. But of course, there have been twelve billion years of Eros before there is any sex. Sex encapsulates, models, incarnates Eros. But we want to live erotically in every dimension of life—and **to live erotically is to place attention.**

To live pornographically is to have attention hijacked. The pornographic universe is about the *hijacking* of attention, while the erotic universe is about the *placing* of attention. When we say the sexual models the erotic—what *is* sex if not the placing of attention? That's what it is.

Now, the pseudo-erotic placing of attention is when my attention is stolen by newness—by novelty.

Novelty attracts my attention.

That's the beginning.

That's an original erotic moment. But then Eros deepens, Eros discloses Her true face.

When I bring my attention to bear, it's not the new breast, or the new belly, or the new posterior, or the new shoulder, or the new bare legs that capture my attention because I've never seen them before (and so it's a shiny new object). That's the pseudo-eros of novelty.

No, no, no.

Erotic attention is when I can see with new eyes, not when I see new things.

To see something new and to constantly have that newness replaced by something else new is the demarcating characteristic of the pornographic universe. But to see with new eyes, that's the essential quality of the erotic universe.

I see you for the very first time, even though I've seen you a thousand times. And each time I place my attention on you, you are different. You're physiologically different. You are neurologically different. But you're also different from the perspective of your depth interior.

You are new.

You are emergent.

When I see you, I allow myself to fall into the rapture of radical amazement again and again, and I fall in love with you, again and again. That's how the sexual models the erotic.

Sex is a model—not of pornography, aka the pornographic universe—but the erotic universe.

If in-depth reading is erotic, social media is pornographic.

To liberate attention is to liberate the quality of Eros, which moves towards intimacy—which is my nature.

THE ATTENTION OF THE INFINITE DIFFERENTIATES UNIQUELY THROUGH ME

Attention is not generic. Attention is always unique.

In the new book, *First Principles and First Values* (written by David J. Temple, who's a pseudo-anonymous author), there is a set of interior science equations. These interior science equations took me about twenty years. There are eighteen interior science equations, which express the evolving First Principles and First Values of Cosmos.

One of the equations is about uniqueness. I am not going to read you the entire equation, but **uniqueness is the unique capacity to *allure* attention and the unique capacity to *place* attention**. In other words, I am a unique quality of attention.

I am a unique capacity of attention, which means that Infinity sees uniquely through me.

To be a Unique Self means that the attention of the Infinite differentiates uniquely through me. That's what it means to be a Unique Self.

I am Divinity's unique prism of attention, which means that Infinity, the Infinite Intimate can only see a dimension of Reality through me.

There is all this discussion about loving God, "Who loves God?"

Let's get real. Why would you love God? What does it mean to love God?

To love God means to let God see through your eyes.

And to be a lover is to clarify your own attention, which is to clarify your Eros, to clarify your desire, because desire is where I place my attention. Desire is the focus. That's what desire is. Desire equals that which I value, upon which I place my attention. **When I clarify my desire, I clarify my attention.** To be a lover is to see with God's eyes, meaning with clarified attention.

It's even more. Let's go deeper. One last step.

When I love you, for example, when I place my attention on you, a unique dimension of me shows up to you and to me that doesn't show up with anyone else.

When I am in love with my friend, with my beloved of any kind—it's because I see you, I placed my attention on you. Love is a perception.

I see you, number one.

But number two, **I'm in love with you because you evoke—through the quality of attention you evoke for me—a dimension of me that doesn't appear in any other way.**

Isn't that gorgeous?

Infinity generates the multiplicities of finitude, which are multiplicities of uniquenesses—meaning billions of Unique Selves, because infinity, Divinity, Infinite Divinity experiences shocking self-recognition *through you.*

When Infinity feels your placing of attention on Him/Her, Infinity appears in a new way that She doesn't appear in any other way.

Reality is the Infinite placing attention on finitude, and finitude placing attention on Infinity—and both mutually generate each other.

Wow! Both create each other. It's not *a creator creates creation*. **Creator creates creation and creation creates creator,** which is why the *Zohar*, the *Zohar*, the thirteenth-century *Book of Radiance*, begins by saying *bereshit bara Elohim*. In the beginning God created—but the *Zohar* rereads that as *bereshit bara Elohim* 'in the beginning we create God'.

We generate—through our attention—the disclosure, the revelation of the Infinite that appears in a way it couldn't appear in any other way.

That's attention.

WE ARE RECLAIMING ATTENTION

Attention begins with subatomic particles placing attention on each other, and it goes all through the world of matter. Attention goes through the intra-attention mechanisms of the biosphere until attention breaks out at the human level, and unique levels of human attention.

Evolution is the evolution of attention, and the evolution of attention is the Evolution of Love.

We go through all the stages of human experience until we get to postmodernity, in which we lose the thread of the plotline. We lose the thread of the evolution of attention because of the exterior technologies, with their ability to place artificial attention, surveillance, tracking, eyes on you all the time. Superficial attention, which is the opposite of a loving providence. The actual storyline of the inherent value of Reality breaks down, and the win/lose metrics takes over, and attention is stolen and hijacked.

Writers call vainly for an attention rebellion. They say we should value attention, and they scream till they're hoarse. We should value attention, but they refuse to proclaim attention as a First Value and First Principle.

We are here to articulate the new Story of Value.

We are here to pay attention to attention, to place our attention on attention, which means to love attention, which means to affirm that attention is an expression of my personal, which is an expression of my desire.

Attention is the natural incarnation of my Eros.

Attention is my right. It can't be stolen.

Wow!

We are reclaiming attention.

We are placing our heart.

CHAPTER TWLEVE

"AMERICA FOR AMERICANS?" VS. "THERE ARE NO STRANGERS IN THE FIELD OF VALUE: THERE IS ONLY FAMILY"

Episode 421 — November 3, 2024

YOU CANNOT TALK ABOUT IMMIGRATION WITHOUT FIRST PRINCIPLES AND FIRST VALUES

There was a recent rally in Madison Square Garden, which I hadn't tracked closely. I heard there were some bad jokes about Puerto Rico, and then some bad responses from the president. I am not going to address garbage jokes and garbage responses. That was a major issue in America, but I hadn't tracked the rally; a dear friend of mine sent me a part of the text of the speech of one of the players of the rally, Stephen Miller. The theme of the speech, and the direct quote, was, "America is for Americans."

I want to—tenderly and fiercely—address that from the perspective of the Field of Value—as we engage the meta-crisis, and understand that the only possible way to engage the meta-crisis is through a new Story of Value

that is real. I want to make this vision real by taking this one issue—the issue of immigration—and seeing how we approach it.

Immigration is a huge issue in the world—every place and everywhere in the world. It has obviously become a huge issue in the United States, and, obviously, it's a central issue in this election.

But the utter confusion around the issue is so shocking, and so tragic, that it basically doesn't allow for the issue to be engaged, transformed, and evolved in any meaningful way. **You literally cannot talk about immigration without First Principles and First Values.**

What's at play here?

As I walked around New York yesterday, I was just blown away, my heart just insanely delighted by hearing so many languages. New York is a city of immigrants. People from all over the world. And I've always been madly in love with Manhattan. I lived in New York for about 12 years, from age 14 to 26, with a stint in Israel in the middle of it, and I was always madly in love with Manhattan.

I fell in love again yesterday, just hearing all the languages and seeing all the people—and I was just so proud to be American. I am Israeli and American—and, of course, Palestinian, and of course, Indian, and I am also, by the way, Chinese, and Russian, and Ukrainian, of course. I've got many nationalities, but I hold passports with the United States and Israel. And walking around New York, I just wanted to sing the *Star Spangled Banner*. America, oh, beautiful! Just gorgeous.

Who are the Americans?

Are we talking about my parents, who immigrated from Poland after World War II?

Are we talking about the Russians, or the Ukrainians, or the Chinese, or the Indians, who have immigrated and who participate in America? What does "America for Americans" mean?

"America is for Americans" gets thrown into the public space.

What does that mean?

How does the Field of Value relate to that?

I would like to do a really deep dive here—go all the way in, all the way in, all the way in. We're done with the easy listening and easy reading.

You can't discuss the issue of immigration, in any sense, shape or form, without having a profound understanding of what we mean by *value* and what we mean by *the Field of Value*. Without that, the conversation cannot begin. I want to go through about ten points—different questions and dimensions of the issue of immigration—and think these through in a deep way.

WHAT ARE THE ISSUES AT STAKE FOR THE HOST COUNTRY?

First, **what do we do in this new world, in which strangers meet each other?**

We now have a world in which there are flights all the time between different principalities, between different countries, between different nationalities. The possibility of movement is essential to the 19th century, and then, in a much more dramatic way, to the 20th and the 21st century. We can move. It used to be that we didn't move. When we were confronted with a crisis in one place, we had to work it out in that place. Now, we have this new possibility that we can move around.

We start meeting each other.

What happens when you have one population that wants to leave where they are and go someplace else—they want to immigrate? **Is there an obligation on a host country to accept immigrants?** That's a big question. Is there an obligation?

Let me say it differently. Is there a value "we need to accept immigrants" or is the host country fundamentally doing a favor, and we can make whatever immigration policy we want to our country? We get to do whatever we want, and there is no higher standard? There is no obligation? There is no value that makes this demand?

From the perspective of the host country, that's the first issue:

Is there an obligation, or are we doing a favor?

If you read the literature, you'll see that there are these two different assumptions at play. There is an entire host of legal articles, and policy articles, and political articles, and economic articles, and social articles, but it was very clear in everything I read that you had these two perspectives: is immigration an obligation, or is it a favor?

Secondly, if I say it's an obligation, is that because it's a moral norm?

Is this obligation a real value, a value in the Field of Value? Is it a value that's backed by the Universe, part of the inherent value structure of Reality?

Is that what we mean?

Or do we mean it's a value the way Harari talks about value, a subjective made-up social construction that the country decides to take upon itself, but it's not backed by the universe. It's not an inherent value.

In other words, there are two questions. First, is immigration a value, a moral norm, an obligation, or is it a favor that the country's doing to the immigrants? Second, what do we mean by *value*? Is it a real value, or is it a Harari value—a postmodern social construction? That's enormously important.

Try not to answer the questions. Try and see if you can get to that place where you can open up, heart and mind and body, and let's just see the field together.

Third, there is an issue of **circumstances**. Are the immigrants wanting to immigrate because of starvation, or threat of death, as Jews fleeing Nazi Europe, or Syrian refugees who want to come to Germany, who are fleeing a despotic and horrific situation? Jews who wanted to enter during World War II were turned away. Most of the American quotas were not filled in the last years of World War II.

Does the question of obligation change based on the circumstance of the immigrants? Here are two extremes:

- We are fleeing for our lives.
- We want a better life. Our life's okay, but we want a better life.

The in-between possibility is:

- We are desperate. We are not being killed tomorrow. It's not Syrian refugees or Jewish refugees from Nazi Europe, but, for example, we are in Honduras, and cartels rule, and rape is happening horrifically, and people are beat up, and people are murdered, and there is no chance of living a good life in many parts of Honduras today.

I just heard a story last night of a young Honduras woman and her daughter, who went through unimaginable pain and an unimaginable suffering, and saw people die all around them as they crossed bodies of water and went through an immigration story of pure horror because they were desperate to get out of Honduras and get to the United States.

So, there are three possibilities in terms of circumstance:

1. I am fleeing for my life, one way or the other
2. I just want a better life.
3. Desperation.

This issue could intersect with the dimension of obligation *versus* favor.

- I could take a position saying that allowing immigration is always a favor, because it's our country. Even if people are fleeing for their life, doesn't matter, this is our country, our borders.

- Or one could say that if you are fleeing for your life, then we do have an obligation.
- Or one could say that we have an obligation to help anyone; I open my borders whenever I can in any way. Even if people basically have a good life someplace else, but they can have a better life here, we have to open our borders. We have to invite people in, to be part of our story, beautiful.
- Or one could say that if people's life is basically okay, we don't want to take people in because that will have adverse effect on our country, but if people are desperate, then we are going to take them in.

We are related to other people's desperation. The issue of obligation intersects with the issue of circumstance.

There is another position that comes up in literature, which says that **we have to protect our country**. We are obligated to protect the boundaries of our country. (I am simplifying, but I am simplifying accurately; I am intentionally trying to use a super clear language.)

This position is: we've got to protect our country from invasion, and invasion can be foreign soldiers, or invasion can be immigrants. We have to protect our country from immigrants.

Well, then the question would be *why* I want to protect my country. There could be three different reasons:

1. Xenophobic: I just want people who are like me. I have no actual, grounded reason—other than I don't like other people who are not like me. That's one reason I would protect my borders. Not a very good one, but that's one reason.
2. I want to protect my **national identity**. I am in Ireland, and I have a sense of the Irish way of living, and I don't want Ireland

to be flooded with non-Irish, so much that the Irish don't have a place to live. Or, to give you a second example, I was just in Portugal recently with KK; many Portuguese told us that wealthy immigrants were destroying Portugal because Portuguese couldn't buy a home, Portuguese culture was collapsing, and Portuguese couldn't afford to live in Portugal, and other forms of culture were overtaking Portugal, and they felt they were basically losing their country. So, I want to protect the national identity, whatever that is.

3. I might want to protect **its values**. There might be the American way—not the American way in a xenophobic sense, but the American way in the sense of the Constitution, and the Bill of Rights—*we hold these truths to be self-evident*—and universal human rights. We might want to protect the values of the country. It is completely different from the issue of national identity: *will people who would come into the country violate the value structure of the country*?

WHAT ARE THE IMMIGRANTS' OBLIGATIONS TO THE COUNTRY?

Now, let's look at it from the perspective of the immigrants coming to the country.

When the immigrants come to the country, in order for them to be received into the country, do they have to give something up? Is there something that they have to give up?

Do they have to give up something of their own customs?

Do they have to give up something of their own norms?

Or, said differently, **is there something that they have to adopt?** Do they have to adopt something of national identity?

It would mean, for example, you'd want people to learn the local language as best as they can. That's important. That used to happen all the time, by the way. It happens less and less because of Skype and Zoom calls. People can keep in touch with their native land more effectively. And there are many, many more older people who come to new countries and don't actually step in. But you could say that we actually *do* need to step in, and that there is a process in which you adopt—you swear allegiance—to the new set of values. That's a big deal.

There is a process of immigration that's mandated by law. But law, in this case, incarnates value (which is what law is supposed to do). Law is not supposed to be a legal imposition. When law works, that law incarnates value. I come to this country, I need to give up something of my old allegiances, something of my old norms, something of my old values, and I need to adopt something of national identity. **But not just the national identity—something of the value structure of the new country.**

We have these two questions at play:

- What's the relationship of the absorbing country to immigrants? Do they have an obligation? Is it a value or is it a favor? If it is an obligation value, is it a real value or just a socially constructed value? What's the circumstance of the immigrants? That's one set of issues.
- The second set of issues, what are the obligations of the immigrants to the country? What do they have to give up? And what do they have to adopt?

It's very clear that, on this spectrum of issues, people take different positions.

For example, you have people who take a very strong position on the obligation of the absorbing country, and then a very weak position on the obligation of immigrants to adopt the values.

Now, I want to be clear. There are formal immigration processes, in which you become an immigrant and you formally adopt the values of the country. The question is, is that a real process or not? It used to be 50-60 years ago, let's say in the United States: when you came to America and you swore allegiance, it was a very big deal. But today, all over Europe, there are enormous populations coming from other cultures. They go through the technical legal process to become citizens, but as for swearing the allegiance, everyone knows that it is a joke. That's happening all over Europe today.

The third question is a question of **how long would it take for that process to happen.** Let's say my parents left Algiers, and they came to Paris, and that happened twenty five years ago. Now, I've grown up in Paris. How long was the process for me to be a full Parisian?

Does that happen immediately?

Did it already happen for my parents?

Or is there a historical process, over a period of time, that needs to play out?

That's a difficult question because there is a collective set of issues of countries coming together, and then there's the personal issue. The personal issue is: my parents came from Algiers twenty five years ago, I've grown up in Paris, I am Parisian.

THERE ARE NO STRANGERS IN THE FIELD OF VALUE

Now, with all of that in mind, I want to begin our conversation.

None of this actually works. This conversation, these seven or eight issues I laid out (and I could have laid out ten more)—none of this appears in headlines. In headlines, you just get pro-immigration, anti-immigration. None of this actually works, honestly, unless we are in the Field of Value.

This is where it really matters—if I am in the Field of Value, and I actually recognize that value is real. This is why when Harari attempts to discuss immigration, it's almost laughable. And when you read the literature on immigration, it is thin, and the arguments are confused, and even the seven or eight issues I just laid out are completely confused, and everyone is making assumptions about different things that don't match any wider set of visions. Someone might say, I am pro-immigration, yet they haven't laid out what are the real issues at play. Or they're anti-immigration, but they haven't laid out what the real issues are at play either. You've got to get underneath this, and actually think about immigration in terms of the Field of Value.

- First, **uniqueness is a value**; the national character of Ireland is unique, so Ireland can say, we want to preserve it. That's true. But no value ever lives by itself.
- There is another value, Eros—the desire for deeper contact and greater wholeness.
- And there is another value called **intimacy**, when parts come together and create **a new shared identity**. In this shared identity, there is mutuality of recognition, and there is mutuality of pathos (we feel each other), and there is mutuality of value (we are in a shared Field of Value), and there is mutuality of purpose.
- There is another value called **evolution**: values evolve, they are not static; and there is another value called transformation. **Evolution is a series of transformations, and constant transformation is a value.**

These are all core values.

In a local world, when I only saw my own people, I only saw the grandeur and the tragedy of my own people. I only saw the suffering and the wonder of my own people, and I could only impact my own people. Clearly the immigration issue wasn't at play.

We live in a different world. We live in a world in which viruses travel across boundaries. We live in a world in which every single existential risk is not local—whether we are talking about dead zones in the oceans, whether we are talking about the biosphere, whether we are talking about artificial intelligence, whether we are talking about climate issues, whether we are talking about rogue, weaponized drone systems, whether we are talking about nuclear stockpiles, whether we are talking about digital dictatorship in all its possible forms—there is actually not a single serious threat that's local. There is not one serious threat that can be handled by a particular country. We actually don't live in a local world. We live in a world where everything is global.

That's the nature of Reality today.

That it's a global Reality in which we see each other—we know what's going on, we see, we feel each other—**that changes Reality in a fundamental way.** If I actually understand that value is real, if value is real, which it is, and First Principles and First Values are real, and we all live together in a Field of Value, and there is a shared Field of Value which is the context for our diversity, and we see each other, we know each other, we recognize each other, we feel each other, it's a global Reality—**then there are no strangers. The very notion of strangers disappears because we are all brothers and sisters in the Field of Eros and Intimacy, quite literally.**

And we realize that each one of us incarnates First Principles and First Values. We may live them in unique ways, but we are all part of the same plotline of Cosmos. We are all living in a Cosmos which is Eros, and the plotline of Cosmos is the evolution of love—so there are no strangers.

- It's not just that if you're about to die, I should care, and give you succor, and open my borders—which I should.
- And it's not just that—if you are desperate, I should feel your desperation. If you're in Honduras and you're desperate, then your desperation matters to me, because we're intimate with each other.

The very notion that we can split the world into ossified boundaries is exactly what we call the global intimacy disorder. That's what a global intimacy disorder means. It means there is no shared Field of Value—and since there is no shared Field of Value, we don't know how to be intimate with each other.

THE IMMIGRATION FIASCO IS AN EXPRESSION OF THE GLOBAL INTIMACY DISORDER

You can't engage immigration without dealing with the global intimacy disorder.

This list of eight points wasn't the point I wanted to make. I wanted just to lay it out, so you could see it and feel the sets of issues. And now, what I am saying is, it's all bullshit. You can't even have the conversation—there is no conversation to be had—unless we overcome the global intimacy disorder.

The immigration fiasco is an expression of the global intimacy disorder.

You can't solve the global intimacy disorder unless you realize that the failure of intimacy is rooted in a failure of shared value. **We are not in a shared Field of Value, therefore we are not intimate with each other; therefore, we are debating immigration.**

But if we *are* in a shared Field of Value, then we are not strangers to each other. Then the entire premise with which I began doesn't exist, because there are no strangers.

We are all already beloveds in the Field of Value. We are ever always already beloveds. That's who we are. There are no strangers. If we are in a shared Field of Value, then—of course!—the care for someone else who is desperate and who I can give succor to is a core value. It's a core obligation. Of course it is!

That doesn't mean that we've ended all issues in immigration. It means that **immigration is *not* about strangers taking over my country.**

The shadow aspect of 'my country' is pure xenophobia, which is what it is. Xenophobia is what it is, and people like to live with people that are like them. Okay, got that. And then they develop hatred of other people. Okay, we got that. I understand that. Wrong. Major violation of the Field of Value, but I understand where it comes from.

Let's go up: No, no, I want to actually preserve my country because I want to preserve national identity. Okay, that's a value. That's good. That's valid.

But the deeper issue is not that. The deeper issue is: **what is my obligation towards you as my brother and sister in the Field of Value?**

If you are my brother and sister in the Field of Value, then I have to invite you in when you are having a hard time.

I have to invite you in when you're desperate. I have to be ripped apart and feel you.

I've got to feel your joy, and I've got to feel your pain. I've got to feel your peril, and I've got to feel your unlived potentiality.

You are part of my dream, and I'm part of your dream. And potentials, and promises, and potencies, and poignancies are not limited by borders.

The notion of no boundary consciousness is that, ultimately, that which unites us has got to be so much greater than that which divides us. I've got to be intimate with you, which means that I feel you, and you feel me, and you feel me feeling you, and I feel you feeling me.

The very tenets of the conversation that takes place around immigration are expressions of the global intimacy disorder itself. **This is the global intimacy disorder—and the global intimacy disorder, as we've said a thousand times, is rooted in a collapse of a shared Field of Value. So, the first thing I need to do immediately, I need to re-enact the Field of**

Value. We need to get over the massive problems in value theory, which got destroyed.

INVITATION TO PARTICIPATE IN THE FIELD OF VALUE

The value theory got destroyed, and the assumption became—*a la* postmodernism and its popularizer Harari—that value is not real; value is just a made-up social contrivance, a fiction, an intersubjective convention, a figment of our imagination. If that's true—if value is a figment of my imagination—well, then we're going to have a global intimacy disorder. Of course we are. And of course, we're not going to trust each other. And of course, we are not going to trust immigrants. And of course, we cannot have a real conversation about immigration because there is no shared Field of Value.

How can we possibly have the conversation?

No, what I need to do is I need to say, "No, no, there is a Field of Value."

We need to reclaim and evolve value theory. We need to articulate a notion of First Principles and First Values.

That, by definition, solves—resolves, evolves, transforms—the global intimacy disorder, because what it says is there are no more strangers. We don't become *familiar—familia, family*—because we have exactly the same accents, or because we have the same color of skin. We are not interested in the color of our skin.

We are interested in the content of our character. It's about the content of our character, which is our participation in the Field of Value.

That's what I mean by *a world religion as a context for our diversity*. We need a world religion as a context for our diversity, and the world religion is a shared grammar of value in which we all participate, and a shared Story of Value whose plotlines run across all the meridians of the world.

The plotlines of the Field of Value cross all the borders of the world. America is a particular expression of the Field of Value, and we want to strengthen that Field of Value.

Now, is it true that any country that stands in the Field of Value should ask the people that come and join it to participate with them in the Field of Value? Well, of course they should, of course they should, of course.

The country also needs to protect itself from subversive immigration. For example, the FBI in the United States has done some very good work on this, and the security services in Belgium have done good work on this, and the security services in France have done work on this.

We know 100% that there is at least about 1,000 people on terrorist watch lists, who have been sent through borders to the United States with the intention of doing very real damage. Are there people who are sent to America by agents that want to undermine the United States, who actually should not be sent to America, who are deeply, deeply problematic? Yes, of course there are. Of course, that's true. But that's not a political partisan issue. That's an issue that any intelligent country needs to deal with appropriately. That's always true.

Obviously, open borders doesn't mean that you invite people in who are going to undermine the value structure of your country. That's idiocy. A process of illegal immigration, which undermines the law, which doesn't allow for any kind of oath of allegiance, of stepping into the Field of Value is obviously problematic, and no one party and no one group owns that problem, which needs to be dealt with. That's a given.

But that's not America for Americans.

When someone says "America for Americans" in a way which becomes xenophobic, in a way which becomes an ethnocentric battle cry, we are abandoning the Field of Value itself.

THE MYSTICAL FOUR-FOLD SONG OF ABRAHAM KOOK

I want to read you a text. This is a text that I translated. I added some things to the text in terms of the Field of Value, but it's a core text of the interior sciences written by Abraham Kook.

There is a one who sings the song of her soul.

And in her soul, she finds it all, full and complete satisfaction.

That's what I would call **egocentric**. Not in a bad way; it's not bad egocentric. No, it's: there is a one. Beautiful. I sing the song of my soul. It's me and my family. And that's my life. It's beautiful. That's one level of living. That's egocentric living in the best sense.

And then Kook goes on:

There is a one who sings the song of the tribe.

This is **ethnocentric**, and there can be a beautiful ethnocentric expression. The Irish can love Ireland, and Americans can love America uniquely. Beautiful.

There's a one who sings the song of the tribe.

She leaves the zone of her personal soul, which she doesn't find wide enough,

and she attaches herself with tender love to the totality of the congregation of her people.

And together she sings the songs of her tribe.

She suffers her pains.

She takes delight in her hope.

She ponders high and pure ideas about her past and her future.

286

That's ethnocentric. That's beautiful, but that's not enough. You can't end at egocentric or ethnocentric.

Kook goes on and he says,

And there is a one who widens her soul even further.

She widens her soul. She widens her Buddha nature. There is a set of texts in Buddhism, which clearly identified the notion of Buddha-nature with value—soul with value, Buddha-nature with value.

Let's feel this, let's hear this:

There is a one, she widens her soul even further,

until it expands and spreads beyond the boundary of tribe

to sing the song of humanity, which is the song of the Field of Value,

and her soul is continuously enlarged by the genius of humanity,

and the glory of the Divine image that lives in humanity.

And she aspires towards the human beings' universal purpose,

and anticipates the higher wholification of all of humanity,

and from this living source, does she draw eternity of her thoughts and explorations,

her aspirations and her visions.

That's **worldcentric**. Now, let's expand even farther. There is **cosmocentric**:

There is one who rises even further than this in expansion,

until she joins herself in the unity with all existence in all of its totality.

She feels Gaia, and the creatures in the world, and the oceans, and the elements, the chemical table of elements, and she gives forth song and she lives the life of the emergent world,

and she participates in the entire Field of Reality.

And then—

And there is a one who rises with all these songs,

together in one intimacy.

Meaning:

- I'm egocentric.
- I'm ethnocentric. Go America.
- And I'm worldcentric. I'm not stuck in ethnocentric. We feed the world. Every heart, every soul. No one's blood is redder than anyone else's.

There are no strangers in the Field of Value.

And that's the code.

EVOLUTIONARY LOVE CODE: THERE ARE NO STRANGERS IN THE FIELD OF VALUE

There are no strangers in the Field of Value.

In the Field of Value, we are already allured to each other.

We are already brothers and sisters.

Immigration doesn't exist. The entire notion of immigration disappears.

There are no strangers in the Field of Value. There are no immigrants on planet Earth.

There is only one field, and one value, and one Eros, and one love, and one heart. That's the whole point.

That's what it means to be *Homo amor*.

WE NEED TO PARTICIPATE IN THE EVOLUTION OF LOVE

What do you mean, "America for Americans"? What does that mean?

Are you talking about apple pie? Are you talking about xenophobia? No.

Are you talking about American values? Okay, now we're talking.

But **American values are unique, intimate expressions of a larger Field of Value.** We are not going to solve any vector of existential risk by having a war of words with China. Yes, we need to take China on—but then we need to get beneath taking China on, and begin to say, "Let's go beyond Maoism back to Taoism"—as China is trying to do.

How do we find ourselves together with China, and Russia, and Albania, and France, and England? Is that possible right now? Well, no, it's pretty hard right now.

But we've got to do the work.

The work hasn't been done. We haven't done it.

What we are doing in the think tank—for the first time—is we are saying, no, no, let's articulate a compelling set of First Principles and First Values, with appropriate deep-dive scientific essays, which are irrefutable, and beautiful, which do the chemistry right, and do the mathematics right, and do the topography right.

Let's do the real work. Let's articulate a set of evolving—eternal and evolving—First Principles and First Values that are the context for our diversity.

We can do that. It's that kind of move that da Vinci and his cohorts were doing in a time between worlds and a time between stories, as the medieval world was breaking apart.

That's what we need to be doing now.

289

Kook writes, we need to evolve. We need to participate in the evolution of love.

And the evolution of love is I move from egocentric intimacy to ethnocentric intimacy, to worldcentric intimacy (I am intimate with every human being all over the world), to cosmocentric intimacy (I feel the animals and I feel every human being, and no one's split off and no one's left out of the circle).

And if you're desperate in Honduras, I'm not okay in Amsterdam.

And if you're desperate in the slums of any city in the world—and you have no chance and you have no possibility, and you have no potential, and for you the promise won't be kept, but I'm sitting and living my life by myself in my own self-involved narcissistic world, and I can't hear you and I can't feel you—we've got a global intimacy disorder, which means we are outside the Field of Value.

Now, how do we do it? Let's think carefully.

We want to respect national entities. We want to respect the national identity of every country, because there is a principle of uniqueness in the Field of Value. There are unique countries, and we respect unique countries. Uniqueness—the unique instrument in the Field of Intimacy—is a gorgeous value that's precious and needs to be protected. Of course it does. In the end, uniqueness, intimacy, Eros, evolution, the evolution of love, the evolution of value—those are the very core, my friends, of the Field of Value.

There are no strangers in the Field of Value. We are already allured to each other in the Field of Value. We are already brothers and sisters. This is our code.

We have to find the best motivational architecture that lives across *all* participants in the Field of Value.

We've got to be real careful not to fall into the trap of polarization.

Let's fight for the good.

Let's fight for the Field of Value.

Let's fight for the promise to be kept.

And let's be very, very, very careful to avoid demonization.

For example, in the United States each side is demonized.

Each side has a dimension in its articulation that takes us towards a path of destruction.

When the conservative world looks at the postmodern liberal world, what they basically say is: Those guys are outside of the Field of Value. We have to conserve the Field of Value.

But they don't have a language to do that. They don't have a language for universal grammar of value. They go back to the last language they have, which was a particular Christian language. Or they say, *we stand for America's vision of value*, and that vision of value is going to triumph in the world, and value is good and real, but we don't know how to articulate a universal Field of Value. For us, it just becomes: *it's America*. And then, that can very easily regress to xenophobia. That can regress to gross violations of the Field of Value.

On the other hand, you have strong elements in the liberal world which have abandoned the Field of Value altogether. There are strong opinions, in at least five papers I've read in the last two days, at the very center of liberal world, that don't want to make any real demand on immigrants to adopt a set of universal values that are part of what it means to be a citizen because they themselves don't believe in value anymore (these papers I read were actually European papers, they weren't about the United States). They don't want to protect the identity of individual European countries because they feel ashamed by Europe. They don't think there's anything like European identity, and they don't think that the value that their own liberalism espouses is real. Why would you make anyone swear allegiance to something you feel is not real? Let all the immigrants in and that's fine.

291

And if they come from Islamic fundamentalist places, well, what can we do? Why is that any better or worse than anything that we have?

IN THE FIELD OF VALUE, THE IMMIGRATION ISSUE SOFTENS

What we did today consists of two parts. In the first part, I tried to lay out what are the issues at stake. You can't just talk immigration. We first have to lay out general points for consideration.

Part two was that all of that doesn't actually work if we're not in the Field of Value. If value is not real, then those seven or eight points are almost impossible to resolve. The contradictions—the set of competing interests—become almost impossible to resolve. You can't really deal with the immigration issue unless you deal with the global intimacy disorder. And the global intimacy disorder is based on not participating in a shared Field of Value.

If we resolve that, **if we evolve value theory, if we actually articulate a shared set of First Principles and First Values (which we've done, that's exactly what CosmoErotic Humanism is), then the immigration issue softens.** It begins to almost solve itself. It's not that there are not a lot of important conversations, but the whole thing changes.

Why does it change?

- ◆ It changes because there are no more strangers.
- ◆ It changes because ultimately there are no more immigrants, in some profound sense.
- ◆ It changes because we are all part of the same Field of Value before we are individual nationalities.

There is a world religion as a context for our diversity.

And I am using "world religion" in the same way I would use the words "shared grammar of value." If we share a grammar of value, then the whole thing begins to change.

Once we are in a shared Field of Value, we can have a conversation.

Once we are in a shared Field of Value, then we can trust each other.

Once we are in a shared Field of Value, then the majority of the issues that I raised in my list begin to soften, they begin to be resolvable. We begin to realize: Oh, there is an actual absolute value of bringing people into my country who are in need—but they are not strangers, they are not immigrants, they are brothers and sisters in the Field of Value.

We begin to realize that there is a global intimacy disorder, which we have to overcome because all of existential risks are global. They can only be solved with global cooperation and vision.

When you do immigration the right way, immigrants bring unimaginable gifts to the country they come into. When there is a shared Field of Value, and a country receives people from a different part of the world, and they enter, and they are honored (which is often not the case), and it's done well and beautifully, then the immigrants become the best French and the best Americans.

They just step in all the way. They have a commitment.

It's often true in a religion that converts to the religion become the leaders of the religion, because they don't take it for granted.

They step in. And immigrants actually pour enormous blessings into the countries they come. It's a big deal. It's a big deal.

[Immigrants: "We Get the Job Done"]

BENEATH SURFACE VALUES, THERE IS REAL VALUE

There are no strangers in the Field of Value. In other words, if we're in the Field of Value together, it means that inside of us, literally, is value. Inside of us is goodness, truth, beauty, uniqueness, intimacy. Eros, ErosValue, desire, integrity, loyalty. Those live inside of us. We recognize each other in that Field of Value. We re-cognize, we cognize (as in *cognition*).

Cognition is not just an intellectual process. Francisco Varela, one of the great philosophers of knowing, talked about cognition as a sensual process (these are not his words, mine). **There is a re-cognition, there is a sensuality in our sensemaking.** We recognize each other.

We recognize each other because we realize that underneath the surface value distinctions—the values and norms of my culture—there is real value.

If you were a Buddhist, you'd say underneath relative value, there is absolute value (although Buddhists don't talk in terms of value, which is a problem).

There is value underneath value. There is value that's not the quality of the relative, but the quality of the absolute. Many years ago, I called that *non-dual humanism*, in two volumes called *Radical Kabbalah*, and we had very deep conversations with my dear friend Ken Wilber about this non-dual humanism.

There is surface value, or relative value, or what Kristina Kincaid calls *value that comes from the clench* (borrowing the term from Franklin Jones); *clench value* means you're asserting value, but it's just a social construction; you are trying to proclaim your identity, your status, your place. This is not a horror, that's not a terrible thing to do, that's a natural human thing to do. But we need to get beneath that and see that, underneath, **surface values are pointing to something deeper, and that's depth value.**

We meet in the Field of DepthValue.

When I meet you and I feel your compassion, and I feel your Eros, and I feel your passion, and I feel your integrity, and I feel the poignancy of your heart, and I feel your honesty, and I feel your courage, and I feel your commitment, and I feel your covenant to your children or to your broader community, or I feel your loyalty (a depth loyalty, not a mafia loyalty)—**when I feel that in you, I recognize you**. We have a mutuality of recognition. We are intimate with each other.

When I feel that in you, I am feeling you, and then you feel me feeling you. And then we realize, *oh, we are in a shared Field of Value*. There is a mutuality of value. And now we can have a shared purpose. That's what intimacy is. Intimacy means shared identity. Shared identity means that we're not strangers. We look like we are strangers, but we are not. We have a deep shared identity. That's what it means to recognize each other in the Field of Value.

It is not that the beauty of familiarity with a common topography and a common geography and a common culture is not valuable, it's beautiful. That's a value, but it's a relative value. There is a much deeper common sense, which comes from our common sensuality, that we are together in the Field of Value. There are no strangers in the Field of Value.

There is a conservative columnist, Arthur C. Brooks, who writes about issues of emotion, et cetera. I read one or two of his columns. They're always interesting. I believe that Arthur tells a story (if I remember the details right): he's driving somewhere in South America, sees a woman, calls out to her. Somehow there is some exchange. She doesn't speak English. He doesn't speak her language. They get married. And she is still his wife, but they meet almost beneath the Field of Language. Obviously they managed to communicate, but they didn't have the full cultural expression of language. They found enough words, which are words that represent the Field of Value, to talk to each other in order to court each other.

The point is, there are two dimensions to language—there is a universal ontology of language, and there is a language as a social construction.

295

When Arthur C. Brooks meets his wife, and they meet in some common deeper language, which is the language of the Field of Value, and they create a life. There are no strangers in the Field of Value. It's not about whether I'm Dutch or American or Israeli or Egyptian. **There's a deeper shared language of value in which we are intimate.** We recognize each other. There is a love that surpasses understanding.

In that sense, there is no immigration. Wherever we happen to have been born is overcome by our destiny. **Our point of origination is not the point of our destination.**

The journey of life is to go from origination to destination. And we follow the lure of value.

We are not accidents in an accidental universe who were born in a particular place and therefore we are committed to that place, and everyone is responsible for their own place. No, we can find each other, and help each other, and be together in the Field of Value.

That doesn't mean that we defile the natural organization of the world. We wouldn't say, let's take 20 million people from China and, in a period of two months, resettle them in the middle of the United States. It'd be complicated because it just wouldn't work. The devastation that would emerge from that is unimaginable on all sides, because you have to respect the ecosystem of America and the ecosystem of China.

Even if those 20 million people are hard pressed, we don't immediately transplant them to another part of the world. There's got to be a respect for history, and a respect for yesterday, and a respect for home in its most physical sense, and respect for cultural traditions, which are the surface value. We don't just take 20 million US citizens and put them in the middle of Siberia, because that's a better place to resettle them. We don't. We've got to be careful. Traditions in the world of the relative and the world of our cultural stories matter.

Otherwise, what would naturally happen is that you'd have a set of countries who are not going to work to take care of their citizens—to develop fields of economic prosperity, and social safety networks, and medicine. They'll just say, let those countries that are willing to take people in take them in, and we'll just export them. Each country does need to be, in the best sense that it can be, responsible for its citizens. But sometimes that doesn't work. Sometimes there needs to be a larger picture. There is a larger union.

LOCAL VERSUS GLOBAL: FROM CONTRADICTION TO PARADOX

The states in America were not just independent states. That's what Alexander Hamilton argued for. He was an immigrant himself. The opening song of the movie, *Hamilton* is about him being an immigrant. It's a beautiful song. He had a sense that beyond our individual identity of states, there is a federal government. And he wrote *The Federalist Papers*, which were this major argument for a union in America.

Of course, that didn't go well. It led, in part, to the Civil War. The Civil War had four or five dimensions, but part of it was the sense that we are not part of a union. We are these different groups of states. We are individual states, and we are groups of states; and the southern states are not bound by the union. But Hamilton had a sense that we are bound by a deeper vision of value. That's what the United States was.

What united the United States was the shared vision of value. *The Federalist Papers* were meant to animate the shared Field of Value.

There are also *the global papers*. In some sense, what we are trying to write here at the think tank is the global papers.

What is the shared Field of Value that we are all in?

297

How do we incorporate the intrinsic value of uniqueness, and the unique intimacies of unique countries, and unique ethnic groups, and unique regions, and unique geographies—with them being self-responsible and self-stewarding?

How do we have to be in relationship to tragedy and desperation when individual regions don't go well, and to the need for immigration?

How does that work?

Those are very, very deep questions.

It is not that when we say we are in the Field of Value, we have resolved them all. No, we haven't resolved them all. But now, we can begin to have the conversation. We are one family, and we have multiple values.

- One is uniqueness, irreducible uniqueness of each country, of each quality of intimacy, which is in part real and part contrived. Part of it's a social convention, completely made up.
- And then, there is this unique expression, which has value, and it's a unique expression of beauty and goodness and truth incarnate in the country, which deserves protecting.
- And then there is this larger Field of Value, in which we all participate—one world, one love, one Eros, one family.

We can have this discussion from within the Field of Value. From within the Field of Value, we can begin to articulate a way forward. We need to put all of our energy, and all of our passion, and all of our potency, and all of our heart into the realization that there are individual cantons, and individual localities, and we need to, in some sense, go more and more *local* in the world. There is too much broad global-ness. We need to have local farms, and local communities, and local prosperity, and local potencies, and local poignancies.

That's the paradox.

There is more and more local, which is more and more specific, and more and more unique, and more and more of my unique culture, and the unique quality and unique flavor and unique quality of intimacy. That's my locality.

At the same time, **we need to go more and more global**. We are part of a shared global vision of value. We are part of a shared global federation, a part of, if you will, a world religion—meaning *religare*: we all reconnect to the same source.

How do those work together?

They only begin to work together when you recognize them both as values. Each is a value in the Field of Value. Radical, intimate locality—and radical global intimacy.

The whole immigration issue is rooted in this global intimacy disorder. We are dis-intermediated from intimacy locally, and we are dis-intermediated from intimacy globally.

Locally, we are not even *in* our local places, we are not in our forest, and we are not in our cities, and we are not in our neighborhoods—we are on our phones. We are really not where we are, so we don't create localities. We're dis-intermediated from local intimacy, from the value of local intimacy.

And we don't have a shared Field of Value. We don't have a shared grammar of value, so we are dis-intermediated from global intimacy.

That's the global intimacy disorder.

We respond to it by stepping into the shared Field of Value. It's the Field of Value of unique intimacy locally. It's the Field of Value of the greater global that underlies the whole story.

On the one hand, **there *are* immigrants**, because people come from real places, and they have real histories, and immigration is a real thing.

On the other hand, **there are *no* immigrants** in the sense that we are all immigrants; we are all in motion. We are all unique qualities of value and energy, energy and motion.

We all have to hold each other, and take care of each other, and feel each other's desperation. And we all ultimately have a common fate and a common destiny.

CHAPTER THIRTEEN

US ELECTIONS: WHAT DOES IT MEAN TO PARTNER WITH GOD IN THIS MOMENT?

Episode 422 — November 10, 2024

EVOLUTIONARY LOVE CODE: LET'S MAKE ART

In a time between stories and a time between worlds, the bridge is art.

The philosopher must become the artist, the activist must become the artist.

The great library, the vision of First Principles and First Values, the new Story of Value, the great entry into the Field of Value are all, first and foremost, artistic projects.

In a time between worlds, and a time between stories the age old false split between art and morals must disappear.

Eros and *ethos*, art and morals, are one.

To the artist the moral and the mystery are not in opposition, they're part of the same great dance.

Let's make art. Let's tell the great Story of Value.

A VISION FOR THE FUTURE IS EVERYTHING

It's a big day. It's an important day. It's a wondrous day. It's a day pregnant with peril, and pregnant with potency. It captures this experience of being in a time between worlds and a time between stories.

And this is such an insanely important day in *One Mountain, Many Paths*.

We always have to evoke the field. The field is never just there. We have to step out of our to-do lists, and find the space in between, and evoke the field. And even when we *are* in our to-do lists, doing our thing, we have to do our to-do lists *from within* the field. Our to-do lists live in the field, so we are in the field.

The last week One Mountain was our protest. Kathy Brownback, our Board Chair, who was the Dean of Exeter Academy for many years, just wrote me a text saying how deeply she felt the vision of First Principles and First Values alive as we integrated it last week in great depth with the immigration conversation.

We talked about these seven or eight variables that you need to take into account, but none of them make sense unless we step into the Field of Value. We talked about the implications of stepping into the Field of Value, and how that changes the conversation around immigration. In some sense, it was a very clear protest last week, and the protest stands a week later. It was a protest against Stephen Miller's comment at Madison Square Garden, America's for Americans. We said, yes, depending what you mean, brother Stephen, yes, America's for Americans—if we are protecting a unique identity called America, if we are protecting a unique Field of Value called American values.

But those values have to participate in a larger Field of Value. **They are not xenophobic values, they are not ethnocentric values.** There could be an ethnocentric national character to America, because there is a First Principle and First Value of uniqueness. Because there is a First Principle and First Value of uniqueness, it's legitimate to protect, let's say, France's national character, America's national character, China's national character, Russia's national character. True. But then, we want to step into a larger Field of Value.

What are the values that America stands for, and how do those hold in the larger Field of Value?

We never establish one value (for example, uniqueness against the entire Field), because then we would be transposing that value into an absolute, and then saying that all other values have to serve at the altar of that one value. That never works.

Each value lives in a wider Field of Value. And in the wider Field of Value, we as human beings, we as human beings incarnate *Homo amor*. We incarnate the New Human and the New Humanity, which means we incarnate value.

We participate in the Field of Value, and all the First Principles and First Values live in us.

We are first *Homo amor*. We are first together in the Field of Value. Therefore, we are not strangers to each other. There are no strangers. That which unites us—as we participate in the Field of Value—is much greater than anything which divides us.

On the one hand, there are no immigrants because we are all in the Field of Value already. That's our home before any home. On the other hand, there are immigrants because we each come from a unique identity, a unique character, a unique instrument, a unique intimacy, a unique quality.

We don't want to say to the Irish, "Hey, Irish, why are you doing Ireland? Do Brooklyn." That wouldn't go over well in certain hamlets in Ireland. Walk into an Irish pub and say,

"Forget this Ireland thing, just do Brooklyn,"

and they would say, "No, no, no."

And you would say,

"Well, what's the difference? We're all in the Field of Value."

No, there is a unique beauty. There is unique pleasure to Ireland, to Dublin. There is unique art. There is a unique aesthetic. There is a unique contribution. Dublin is not reducible to Brooklyn, just like Shanghai is not reducible to Moscow. Let's not even talk about Idaho and Montana. And then Marseille.

We protect uniqueness. That's one value. But then, **uniqueness lives in relationship to the larger Field of Value, which we all live inside of together.** From the perspective of uniqueness as a value, there are immigrants, but from the perspective of the Field of Value, which we all incarnate as part of our essential humanity, we are all in the Field of Value.

The Field of Value is our home before any other local home.

It is the ultimate locality that we live in and locate ourselves—what's called *adam kadmon* in the lineage, the Field of holy apples—the Field of Value. We live there before we live anyplace else. Therefore, there are no immigrants. There is no place to go. There are no strangers.

Now, it's a week later. First off, everything we said last week stands. Stephen Miller, the fact that your side won the election doesn't let you off the hook. The protest stands, brother, okay? The protest stands. President-Elect Trump, the protest stands. And Stephen, you actually get this yourself. We are asking you to clarify. Be a leader, clarify. When you say "America for Americans," don't say it in a way that can be interpreted as regressive and violating our shared humanity. I know your teacher in the Hebrew school, Metuka Benjamin, your teacher at Hebrew school. She said you were pretty good in Hebrew school, so go back to those prophetic roots and clarify what you mean.

What you mean is, there are no strangers in the Field of Value.

What you mean is that we all participate in this Field of Value.

What you mean is that that which unites us is far greater than that which divides us.

We honor the unique instrument, and quality of intimacy, but we are all ultimately unique expressions of the same musical score—and our particular note, our particular instrument deepens and adds to that score.

That's a world we can live in.

That's a vision for the future. A vision for the future is everything. It's everything. A prophetic vision is everything. **We have to articulate this vision together.** The world depends on us articulating this vision together.

IT IS A MOMENT OF RECKONING

Today, we are going to engage in an enormously important—new, old, ancient, post-post-modern—enactment called *prayer*. But I want to set a context for the prayer; that's going to be the first part of One Mountain. And then I want to enter with you into the prayer.

The context for the prayer is where we are at this moment in the world.

What's just happened? Because something has just happened, and the whole world is reverberating with what happened.

I want to first speak with the voice of the elemental, the primal, the Field Herself, because we are in this time in-between. We are in a moment of phase transition, a time between worlds and a time between stories.

Phase transition is this place when the temperature and pressure of a system go beyond what the system can withstand, and then matter changes from one state to another. For example, solids become liquids, liquids become gas. The system opens up into new peril and new possibility.

From the moment of chaos, the creative force comes into play, which always moves against entropy and collapse, and towards new possibilities. There would be no world without these transitions, when everything seems to be falling apart, and you think, "Oh my God, did entropy have the last word?" And then we realize, no, it didn't. We realize that there is a new arising. There is a new possibility. There's a new movement towards *wholification*.

Not just in exteriors, but also in interiors, **as old systems of value prove insufficient to meet the new moment, new expressions of value emerge from intrinsic inherent value in Cosmos.** The eternal Tao becomes the evolving Tao. Eternal value becomes emergent new value, and a new life force emerges—the irrepressible creativity of Eros seeking ever deeper contact and ever greater wholeness gives birth to new possibilities.

That's where we are. We are at this moment when the elemental forces are at play. We are in a moment of what James Baldwin described as a reckoning. **It's a moment of reckoning with the immense creative process that is humanity.**

In this reckoning, this time between worlds and this time between stories is filled with competing visions of what just happened. I am not going to spend this One Mountain recapitulating the thousands of articles that have been written around the world in the last four days to explain the events of the American elections. Each article contradicts the next article. They all are mutually exclusive with each other. They all adopt a particular stance. There is truth in all of them, but it's partial.

Let's go deeper. Let's go to the elemental.

THE ARTIST TAKES IT ALL UP IN HER PAINFULLY EXPANDED SOUL

In the space between two world wars, Hermann Hesse wrote a novel, *Steppenwolf.* He writes that every age, every culture, every custom, every tradition has its own character—its own weaknesses, its own strength, its beauties and ugliness, accepts certain sufferings, puts up (and I would add, wrongly) with certain human evils.

Today, for example, for some strange reason, we put up with animal suffering, with cruelty towards animals (which we should not). Why is that? We put up with an immense cruelty to animals. People are having lamb chops all the time. That's somehow acceptable. There is this strange notion of the evolution of value, which doesn't recognize value in an earlier age, and puts up with "acceptable" evils.

But there is a moment when civilizations shift; they move.

For example, a man of the classical age, writes Hesse, who had to live in medieval times would suffocate miserably, just as a prehistoric man would suffer in the middle of civilization. But then there are times— and this is the point of Hesse's that I want to share with you—in which **a generation is caught between two ages, between two modes of life, with the consequence that it loses all power to understand itself** and has no standard, no security, no simple acquiescence.

That's the nature of this moment.

We are in this moment when artificial intelligence is at play.

We are threatened both with the potential death of humanity and the potential death of our humanity.

We are not sure what *truth* means. We know that it means something, but it's bandied about way too lightly.

Value has been deconstructed, and the assumption across the board is that value is not real. There is lip service given to fundamentalism, but **there is an assumption that you don't really need to tell the truth, because that's a subservient value.**

It is, of course, a wrong claim, but there is this feeling across the board— both in the postmodern liberal world and in the conservative world, which is hijacked increasingly by individual powerful figures.

There is a sense that truth is not an ultimate value we need to bow before.

There is a sense that power is what's really at play, and it's all ultimately about power.

There is this sense of collapse.

This is precisely—as Toni Morrison wrote a hundred years after Hesse—**this is precisely where artists have to go to work**. This is precisely where art happens. We are living through this world which is confused and conflicted—this time between stories, this time between values—and there is something new that needs to happen.

That's what Hesse begins to speak about. He says that, in this moment, there is something new that has to happen.

We need to turn to the artist, Hesse says—the artist whose job is to nourish the goodness of the human spirit with such strength and indescribable beauty that the human spirit is, "flung so high and dazzlingly over the wide sea of suffering that the light of it spreading, its radiance, touches others too with its enchantment."

It's a moment for art.

It's a moment to begin to see ourselves as artists, and realize that our great project of enacting a great library in this time between worlds is art.

We are storytellers of the new Story of Value, and also scientists of the new Story of Value, reading chemistry, and molecular biology, and neurochemistry, and neuroscience, and sociology, and anthropology—but at the core, we are artists weaving together different strands, painting a new canvas.

Often the artists perform their art at great personal cost. Hesse considers what it means to be an artist and he writes, it's not easy. You can't just turn to your own personal fulfillment. Sometimes you need to see what's happening in the larger Field, step out of your to-do list and ask yourself, am I actually *Homo amor*?

308

Can I actually embrace the whole?

Can we see the whole and paint a new tapestry?

Hesse writes, "You will instead embark on the longer and wearier and sometimes harder road of life." It's not simple to do. In this harder road, instead of narrowing your world, you'll complicate your complexities still further, because you're going to want to take more in, instead of narrowing your world and simplifying your soul, which we want to do in order to balance the nervous system.

I get that. You've got to do what you need to do that, of course—sleep enough, nourish yourself in all the ways you do. But ultimately, instead of narrowing your world, what the artist does at this time between worlds? Instead of narrowing your world and simplifying your soul, you'll have to absorb more and more of the world. And at last, Hesse writes, take it all up in your painfully expanded soul if you are ever to find peace.

You think, let me turn back to my family.

Yes, of course we take care of our families. Of course, of course, of course. I'm living in Saint Johnsbury because I have a son who needs me to live in Saint Johnsbury.

I believe in taking care of one's family. I just dropped everything to go to New York to spend four hours with my older son. Of course, of course we stand for family.

But family is not where we exhaust our loving. **If I am actually a pillar in the temple, I've got to see the whole thing.**

I've got to be an artist of the whole thing.

You have to be willing to absorb more and more of the world.

And at last, take all of it up in your painfully—and I would add, ecstatically—expanded soul, if you—if all of us—are ever to find peace.

WHEN SOCIETY DISINTEGRATES, WE NEED ART

I want to move on to the English novelist E.M. Forster and his essay *Two Cheers for Democracy*.

He talks about art in the time between worlds, although he doesn't use the word *time*. He writes that **art is the only material object in the universe that may possess internal harmony**.

Just feel that for a second.

Art stands against entropy. Art takes entropy—the dissolution—into account, but there is an interior quality of coherence in art.

All the other dimensions of the world, writes Forster, have been pressed into shape from outside—by forces of power, if you will. When their mold is removed, when the power structure is removed, all other things collapse. The work of art stands up by itself as nothing else does. It achieves something that has often been promised by society, but always delusively.

Ancient Athens, he says, made a mess, but Antigone stands up. The Renaissance Rome made a mess, but the ceiling of the Sistine got painted. James I made a mess, but there was Macbeth. Art is the one, as he calls it, *orderly product*. I wouldn't call it *orderly product*. **It's the one intimate coherence which our muddling race has produced.**

It's the cry of a thousand sentinels. The echo from a thousand labyrinths. It is the lighthouse which cannot be hidden.

Auden writes, the mere making of a work of art is itself a political act. And Iris Murdoch writes, tyrants always fear art because tyrants want to mystify in order to obfuscate, while art tends to clarify.

Back to Forster: If our present society should disintegrate, and who dare prophesy that it won't, what we're going to need is a new figure, and that figure is the figure of the artist, the artist. Society can only represent the final quote, a fragment of the human spirit, but the wider web, the wider vision is held only through art.

OUTRAGEOUS IS OUR TRUST IN YOU

Who are we here?

We are artists, and what does it mean to be an artist?

The word *art* in the original Hebrew is *oman*. It's a beautiful word.

It derives from the word *emunah*, and *emunah* means trust. It is wrongly translated as "faith," but it actually means "trust."

> *Lehagid baboker chasdecha, ve-emunatcha*
>
> *To speak of your love in the morning, to trust you through the night.*

David gives that teaching to Solomon, and we read it in two ways.

First, we speak to the Field of Eternity that's evolving through us, and we say, to speak of your love in the morning, and we trust you through the night.

The artist trusts.

The artist trusts that there is a coherence that's possible.

The artist trusts that out of the fragmentation something fabulous and fantastic can emerge; that there is a new fantasy that can emerge from the fault lines.

Then, in the time between worlds and the space between the cherubs, there is a voice of the Divine that emerges.

The artist is the *oman*, art that has *emunah*, which is trust. The artist knows how I speak of your love in the morning and I trust you through the night.

I trust Reality.

I trust Goodness, Truth and Beauty.

I trust that I can participate, as the evolutionary impulse, in telling a new Story of Value.

But there is a deeper reading.

If you read carefully the hidden nuances of the sacred texts, it's a conversation. It's the Song of Solomon.

The Song of Solomon is not a poetry of love. It's a set of Outrageous Love notes between a lover and a beloved. That's literally what the Song of Solomon is, and it is considered the ultimate canonical document of civilization. When all the books are holy, the Song of Solomon is Holy of Holies. One text says, if all of wisdom didn't exist, all of the world could be governed by the Holy of Holies.

We think love only lives with us, it doesn't live on the other side: *the other side are haters, we're lovers.* No, no, no. Love gets distorted, but **love animates the whole thing.**

Let us feel this deeply—*to speak of your love in the morning, to trust you through the night.* **That's our Outrageous Love note into the evolutionary field**

But then She, the Goddess, She, the Field of ErosValue, She speaks back to us, and She says, to speak of your (= humanity, human being) in the morning, and I trust you through the night.

In the same lineage, another word for the artist is *Rabba*, outrageous. It's a technical word that exists in Hebrew text which is translated as "great", but it doesn't mean great.

If you read and follow the word carefully, there is something called *Ahava Rabba*—not great love, Outrageous Love. *Rabba* is outrageous.

> *Rabba emunatecha*
>
> *Outrageous is my trust in you*

We hear back the echo, where She says to us, outrageous is my trust in you. *Rabba Emuna-Techa* 'Outrageous is my trust in you, God.' But the very same words mean, outrageous is Your trust in me—but not me generally, each one of us personally.

That's trust. She trusts you through the night.

She trusts us not to "get it done," not to check something off on a to-do list.

She trusts us to hold Her hand and be Her.

She trusts us through the night.

That's the artist.

The first word is *oman*. *Oman* is an artist. Art. The same word means trust, this deep trust. *I'm faithful.*

I'm faithful to the memory.

I am not faithful to the dogma. I am faithful to the realization.

I was once on the Inside of the Inside. I said to my beloved, Kristina, my holy partner, about ten-twelve years ago, "She's going to go away. This explosive voice of She that we can feel, She's going to disappear. You have to know that She's going to leave." And KK said, "She's not, She won't." I said, "She will. She will. She'll leave. And then, if you have faith, if you're faithful to the memory, She'll come back."

That's what faith means.

Faith is not blind faith.

We are on the Inside of the Inside.

We are in a moment together.

We are reading science together.

We are all the way inside.

We feel it.

We are faithful to that moment.

She knows. She trusts us.

But what we have to do is to remain faithful to the memory.

We have to find the moment when each of us was so radically inside. We were together on the Inside of the Inside, and we knew it was true. And we've got to remain faithful to that memory of the past. We have to let that memory of the past live in the present, and let that present open up into the future. The greatest commitment to the future is to do with full passion what the present demands.

The greatest commitment to the future is not to bypass the present, but to clarify it. It requires clarification.

THE GREAT LIBRARY IS A POLITICAL PROJECT

In *lehagid baboker* "to tell the story in the morning," what does the word *boker* mean?

It has three meanings.

First, it means 'morning' (*boker tov* 'good morning'). But *boker* also means *bakara* 'discernment, clarification.'

I have to discern the light in the morning. What is the invitation of the morning?

It's so easy to compromise. It's so easy to get off path. It's so easy to get comfortable. Comfort is good, but you also need an optimum place of discomfort—not to be comfortably numb.

'Comfortably numb' has lots of very high versions. **You've got to be willing to be uncomfortable.** When I am uncomfortable, what I can discern (*bakara*), what's mine to do?

What's my gift?

What's my full passion?

The way I do that is a *bikur*—that's the third meaning of *boker* 'visit.'

I have to step out of my bracketed ego self, and I have to visit the Field of Value, and let the Field of Value live and dance in me. That's the experience of waking up. I've got to visit the Field of Value, step out of my narrow separate self, and feel the Goddess speaking and whispering through me.

And then, from that visit to the Field of Value, I go back to my discernment. And then I say, good morning.

The project of the great library is a political project.

I want to be clear about that. And **the greatest political project has to be an artistic project**.

Political projects that are rooted in movements of power don't last. Power ultimately—at least exterior power history—always falls before what I would call *trust history, art history, faith history*. There is a greater history that's at play. **There is a greater story at play.**

There were ten families living in Florence in the Renaissance, and nine of them, we know nothing about. One family, for two or three generations, stepped in and said, we're going to look at the wider field. And the Medicis, and Marcello Ficino, and Pico della Mirandola, and Leonardo da Vinci, infused with the vision of Luria—they painted. The Renaissance was art and a new Story together. It couldn't have been different. Da Vinci was both thinking great thoughts and painting a new world at the same time.

- It was this new vision of embodiment.
- It was this new vision of the feminine.
- It was this new vision of Eros and sexuality.
- It was this new art, and it was this new science.
- It was this new Story of Value.

You can't split them. We are weaving together as one artist—each being a different dimension in the vision—the great political vision of the interior sciences.

We are all part of that same organism—but not as a hive. We are all individuated expressions of this wider symphony of art and spirit. And we each paint a different dimension of this great mural—this great mural of potency, this great mural of possibility.

And we are politicians. We are engaged in the polis. We are engaged in reformulating the vision of what it means to be a human being individually, what it means to be in communion. And if the polis is violated, we protest. If the polis is violated, we rebel. We launch a revolution. That was the French Revolution. That was the American Revolution—the realization that the polis is not an eternal idol that lives forever. Sometimes the Bastille becomes a prison that violates the integrity of society, and the Bastille has to fall.

But right now, we are in a moment which is a time between worlds and a time between stories. Something has happened. Democracy has operated. It has granted a mandate. That's simply what happened. That's just a description of what happened, as *The New York Times* described. And *The New York Times* is obviously a strongly liberal paper that endorsed Kamala Harris. *The New York Times* said, democracy spoke, overwhelmingly. How it happened is not our topic today. Democracy spoke.

We are at a time between worlds and a time between stories. How, in this moment in between worlds, do we respond?

- There are some people who are going to respond through vectors of formal politics, and that's good, and that should be done.
- There are some people who will respond through vectors of international coalitions, and that should be done.
- There are some people who respond through vectors of court-mediated processes, and that's good, and that should be done.

But we have to stay focused on what we desperately know needs to be done, and what we have the capacity to do, unlike any others.

That's an audacious statement. We've been in this for fifteen years. It's just bubbling to the surface in this unimaginably beautiful way.

What's ours to do?

We have to be artists in this time between worlds. We have to understand that the written page, and the audio, and the media—these are canvases of new formulations of words.

There's no chance of moving through this time between worlds, this time between stories, without a shared Story of Value, without evolving First Principles and First Values.

That's what we talked about last week. You cannot discuss immigration without it, and you cannot discuss anything else without it. No conversation is possible.

It doesn't matter what country we live in.

It doesn't matter whether we're on the conservative side or the liberal side.

The abyss that's happened is we are not first in the Field of Value.

And when we are not first in the Field of Value, then we hijack identities from the world of surfaces—not Value, but values to buttress our identity.

And we lie about everything else in various forms, because we're desperately afraid of being consigned to oblivion.

No, no, no.

We are in the Field of Value.

We are all value before we are anything else.

Our valor, our heroism comes from living and being in the Field of Value. That's where we pray from.

BEAUTY MEANS WHOLENESS

Let's be wild artists. Let's be ecstatic artists, but art as a political act.

We will watch carefully, and we will pay attention, because Eros is the placing of attention.

Sex models Eros, and sex is the placing of attention. Sexuality is not about technique. It's not about how many explosions happened. Sexuality is about whether I was able to radically place my attention on the beloved and to feel the radical attention of my lover beloved. In sexuality, we bloom our beloved with the placing of attention.

- You can be involved in the most wondrous sexuality in the world, which seems to be technically proficient and working perfectly, and you feel empty and vacuous.
- Or you can be stumbling your way, but you're placing attention on each other with such beauty, with such poignancy, with such fragility, with such vulnerability that what emerges moves the heavens.

We are erotic artists.

We are erotic artists, and our vision is transfiguration. Transfiguration means that we take opposites, polarities, and we weave them together as new potencies. That's what the artist did.

Whitehead talks about beauty. Art seeks beauty.

Whitehead says the exact same thing as the Solomon lineage does when it describes beauty in the Tree of Life.

In the Tree of Life, beauty is *tiferet*. And it has another synonym, which is *shalom*, wholeness.

> *The more opposites, the more polarities
> I can weave together into a new tiferet
> 'beauty'—into a new shalom 'a new
> whole'—the more beauty I have.*

The value of all values, Whitehead writes in *Process and Reality*, is *tiferet*—the central channel whose center point is ultimate beauty. And beauty means transfiguring the opposites into a wider Field of Value. **No one is outside the Field of Value.**

We have to be artists. The pleasure of the artist is in their irreducibly unique creativity—weaving, painting the stroke of the brush that can only be painted by them.

The artist is mad. That's why we talk about mad love. That's why we don't talk about ordinary love. Ordinary love can't survive the exigent pressures, the cauldron of entropy. Only mad love can do that.

The artist is filled with mad love.

Not mere human sentiment, not a strategy of power, but mad love. The insanity that's the only sanity. It's that mad passion. It's that mad love.

It's that ecstasy, that *ekstasis* in Greek, where I step out of my small self and I feel the currency of Eros moving through me, painting, holding my hand, holding the quill in my hand, holding the computer, weaving.

It doesn't matter whether I am writing a text, or I am writing a marketing piece, or I am engaged in some technical detail. It's all the same. It doesn't matter. It's the same ecstasy. It's the same passion.

We are a Unique Self Symphony. We are politicians. We are committed to the polis. And the polis needs the potency of a new Story of Value without which the center will not hold.

ANYTHING GREAT IS CUMULATIVE OVER DECADES

Let's re-understand ourselves.

We are philosophers, which means we are lovers of knowing. And knowing is carnal knowledge, and **the artist is the one who trusts that there's that which can be painted.** There is beauty to be evoked, and *even when there is ugliness in painting, that itself is redemptive.*

The very act of the artist is an expression of faith.

The first word for art, as we said, is *oman* (and by the way, it's the English word is *amen*). This is all amen.

As we said, the first meaning of *oman* is "art." I'm an artist.

The second meaning is "trust."

The third meaning is "skill" *(emun)*.

This morning I was reading in the Zohar this intense passage in Aramaic about the intense painful skill of loving. There is an expansion of self to develop and master the skill of loving. Love is a great skill. The artist needs the skill. There is an *emun*; there is practice.

Moshe Idel, the greatest scholar of Kabbalah in terms of manuscripts today in the world (he has read more manuscripts than anyone), says, **the only thing that ever accomplishes anything that's great is cumulative over decades**; not ten years—twenty, and thirty, and forty. Anyone who has kids knows that.

To change the source code of culture is a cumulative artistic effort—day after day of practice. It's not a piece on a to-do list. It is a constant ritualized action. It's the textualization of Eros, the creation of a great library in all of Her ways.

I've got to be able to have vision. I've got to see beyond the immediate. I've got to hold the immediate, be fully in what the present demands—and yet, be called into the future.

That's the third meaning of amen: artist, trust, and then this cumulative, daily, radical effort produces greatness

The Story of Value is a great artistic unfolding, the canvas of Reality.

The fourth meaning is so beautiful.

Omen, the nursing mother who holds the child of Reality at her breast.

Moses, the leader, Moses, the artist, Moses, who represents the entire generation (all 600,000 live in Moses; Moses is not the charismatic leader; Moses is Unique Self Symphony himself)—Moses is described in the text as the nursing mother who holds the child at her breast, and the child knows that no matter what, her mother won't drop her. That's what faith means. Faith means, I know my mother is not going to drop me. That's the *omen*. *Omen* is the nursing mother that engenders in the child this knowing: *my mother won't drop me, my father won't drop me*.

We have to be radical here.

We have to say, we have to be the mothers and the fathers, even as we are the sons and the daughters.

It's not enough to be just the sons and the daughters.

It's not enough just to be lovers.

We have to take the responsibility of being the mothers and the fathers— even as we have our own mother traumas, even as we have our own father traumas; even as we feel like we didn't get the blessing of the father, or we got somehow constricted by the mother. We have to loosen the fixities of our early traumas in order to become the mother, to become the father— and to become the *omen*, the artist who practices radically every day, who trusts that there is an internal coherence; there is a possibility of possibility

321

that's yearning to emerge. The *omen* that holds the generation at his breast, at her breast.

And the generation has to know that we're not going to turn away, that we're committed.

Does that sound grandiose?

Well, it is not grandiose. It's actually just grand. *Grand* in the sense of a grand piano trying to make great music. It's an unbearable responsibility. It's also an unbearable joy.

GREAT IS YOUR TRUST IN ME, SHE

Modeh ani lefanecha.

I embrace my I, I am before You.

Leviticus 23 - before means face. *Before* means being on the inside. I'm not just before You, I am on the inside of Your face. It means I am turning towards You. I am turning towards this great artistic work. I embrace my I. I am the inside of Your face. I am turning towards You in this next sacred conversation in the Field of Value.

Modeh ani lefanecha

Melech chai vekayam

It doesn't matter if you are an atheist, or you are a Catholic, or you are a Buddhist, or you are a Taoist, or you are a Native American. We are picking these words as an example, representing in the great world religion, the world, the great art tapestry as a context for our diversity.

Modeh ani lefanecha

Rabba emunatecha

Great is my trust in Thee, She; great is my trust in Thee. Great is my trust in Thee, She. Great is my trust in Thee.

Great is your trust in me, She. Great is your trust in me, She. Great is your trust in me.

Rabba emunatecha

Great is your trust in me, She. Great is your trust in we, She. Great is my trust in Thee, She. Great is my trust in Thee, She.

Rabba emunatecha

INDEX

longing, 148, 221

love, xviii, xxii, xxiv, xxv, xxvi, xxvii, xxviii, xxxix, xl, 9, 10, 11, 12,
15, 17, 28, 44, 53, 54, 62, 63, 64,
72, 73, 74, 79, 85, 94, 96, 104,
107, 112, 113, 119, 129, 136, 137,
140, 146, 159, 160, 166, 178, 179,
180, 184, 202, 211, 212, 215, 219,
243, 244, 249, 251, 255, 263, 264,
267, 268, 270, 272, 281, 286, 288,
289, 290, 296, 298, 301, 311, 312,
319

Love
  desire, xxxiv, xl, 7, 8, 11, 12, 13, 14,
    15, 120, 184, 199, 211, 215,
    268, 270, 280, 294
  story, iii, xviii, xxvi, xxxiii, xxxiv,
    xxxv, xxxvi, xxxviii, xxxix, xl,
    2, 4, 5, 6, 7, 8, 11, 12, 13, 14, 16,
    20, 21, 22, 23, 24, 25, 27, 34,
    73, 78, 79, 80, 81, 82, 100, 114,
    115, 116, 118, 132, 134, 135,
    145, 151, 152, 154, 155, 157,
    158, 169, 171, 177, 181, 182,
    184, 185, 190, 192, 194, 199,
    210, 211, 226, 233, 234, 235,
    237, 240, 246, 249, 250, 253,
    254, 255, 260, 275, 276, 295,
    299, 314, 315

LoveIntelligence, xxvii, 101, 198,
202

M

Mackey, John, 22
Magen David, 60
masculine, 78, 162, 242
master, 60, 65, 320
mathematics, 58, 209, 289
matrix, xxxv, 97

meditation, 30, 64, 65, 66, 72, 134,
142, 144, 208, 213, 214, 223, 240
memory, xxxvii, xxxix, 134, 230,
313, 314
memory of the future, xxxvii, 134
meta-crisis, xv, xvi, xix, xxxiv, xxxix, 131, 135, 141, 142, 167, 169,
170, 171, 172, 175, 177, 183, 208,
212, 214, 227, 253, 254, 271
Metaverse, 68
MeToo, 78
mind, xxxi, 10, 42, 90, 134, 135,
148, 154, 179, 193, 209, 210, 211,
215, 250, 259, 261, 274, 279
miracle, 74
missing tile syndrome, 1
mit, 128
MIT Media Lab, 168, 170, 173, 229
model, 23, 63, 133, 225, 267
modern, xviii, xx, xxviii, xxxvi,
xxxviii, xl, 22, 36, 45, 81, 93, 144,
145, 154, 167, 193, 243, 245, 258,
305
Modernity, xxxiii, xxxiv, 143, 184,
228
monological, 27
Moshe, 92, 264, 320
mother, 9, 29, 39, 88, 90, 140, 241,
242, 321
mundi, 63
Murder of Eros, vii
Murray, Douglas, 34
music, xxii, 12, 65, 66, 69, 72, 73,
177, 178, 322
mystery, xviii, 71, 139, 183, 193,
263, 264, 301

World War II, 31, 139, 141, 151, 162, 272, 275

X

xenophobic, 246, 277, 285, 302

Y

yearning, 322

yoga, 77
Yoma, 124

Z

zemar, 11
Zion, 121, 127, 140, 141, 150, 160
Zohar, 24, 26, 83, 84, 269, 320
Zuboff, Shoshana, 257

Volume 33 — From Polarization to Paradox

LIST OF EPISODES